Best walks in the Lake District

Best walks in the Lake District

Frank Duerden

REVISED BY TOM HOLMAN

PHOTOGRAPHS BY ANDREW MIDGLEY AND TOM HOLMAN

Frances Lincoln

This book is dedicated to those who, over the years, have worked and fought to protect the beauty of the Lake District

Frances Lincoln Ltd
4 Torriano Mews
Torriano Avenue
London NW5 2RZ
www.franceslincoln.com

This revised edition published by [illegible]
First published in Great Britain 1986 by [illegible] and Company Ltd

Revised edition designed by Kevin Brown at park44.com

British Library Cataloguing in Publication data
A catalogue record for this book is available from the British Library.

Printed and bound in Singapore

ISBN 07112 2421 8

9 8 7 6 5 4 3 2 1

frontispiece: Bridge near Styhead Gill

Contents

Acknowledgements

I must acknowledge the very considerable help given to me by a number of people during the preparation of this book. Without their help the book – if ever finished – would certainly have been much the poorer.

In particular, I must thank the staff of the National Park Authority: Michael Taylor (National Park Officer), John Toothill (Chief Administrative Officer), John Nash (Planning Officer) and John Wyatt (Chief Ranger), who gave me the benefit of two long meetings and finally read through the entire manuscript; Mr J. Richards, Deputy Regional Officer of the YHA, who provided me with information about the history of Lakeland hostels; Mr Roger Ward, County Secretary of the National Farmers' Union, who read the section on farming; Mr Voysey and Mr Scott, Forest Managers of the Forestry Commission, who read the sections on Lakeland forests and forestry; Brian Covell, who looked at my notes on Bob Graham; Mr Paul Duff of the North West Water Authority who gave me information about water supplies; and my colleague, Dr Yvonne Williams, who helped me with the sections on geology.

Some information was taken from Landranger and Outdoor Leisure maps by permission of the Ordnance Survey, and the Country Code was included by permission of the Countryside Commission. The maps were based on the 1" map of The Lake District by John Bartholomew & Son Ltd.

Finally, I must thank my daughters, Beverley and Sharon, who in their usual highly efficient manner typed the manuscript for me; and my wife, Audrey, who not only assisted with much of the proofreading but, more importantly, helped me to weather the now familiar physical and psychological pressures of authorship.

F.D.

Introduction to the revised edition

Updating Frank Duerden's book of wonderful walks two decades after they were written, it is clear how much changes in the Lake District—and yet how little. Fences and walls disappear and appear, forests are cut and replanted, paths become ever more worn by walkers. But much else along these routes remains just as it was when this book was first published, and indeed as it was decades and centuries before that. Most of the views you enjoy from these walks will be as pristine and lovely as they were when they were seen by the mountains' first walkers.

The Lake District has some of the best and most varied walking in the country. Other parts of the UK have majestic mountains or serene lakes, and there are great paths, fine views and pretty villages in plenty of regions. But no other area quite has the Lake District's magical combination of all these things in such close and spectacular proximity.

As he intended, Frank Duerden's 40 walks in this book offer something for everyone and every occasion: long horseshoe hikes for those with stamina and a day to spend, to easy strolls for those with limited time or more reluctant walkers in tow. They also showcase all corners of the Lake District, from the busy, easy paths around Buttermere lake to the wide, empty slopes of the Duddon valley or Eskdale.

To get the most out of the walks, choose your days carefully: avoid the popular peaks and honeypot villages at weekends, for instance, and save stiffer treks for the long days of summer. As emphasised elsewhere, take with you proper equipment and get a good weather forecast before you set out. All 40 walks here have been thoroughly checked and updated, but take a map and compass along with this book in any case; you may be glad of it if you take a wrong turn or find yourself in descending mist. Pack also in your rucksack Wainwright's exquisite pictorial guides to the Lakeland fells; also published by Frances Lincoln, they will give extra insight into the mountains you climb.

I would like to thank all those family and friends who joined me at various times in the hugely pleasurable task of updating this book, but in particular my wife Ceri, who walked every step of the way with me. I hope you enjoy these walks as much as we did.

Tom Holman
Cumbria, September 2005

Introduction

My first visit to the Lake District took place in 1949 when, as an enthusiastic but very inexperienced walker and rock-climber of seventeen, I joined two friends on a walking holiday which began at the youth hostel at Damson Dene – now closed – and ended eight days later at the hostel at Ambleside. To say that I fell under the spell of its beauty on my first day there is no exaggeration, nor to say that I am still held by it thirty-five years later. I consider myself privileged to have been able to walk there on so many occasions.

My aim in this book has been to select and describe forty walks which I consider are the best within the Lake District National Park. It would have been useless, of course, to have begun such a task without first drawing up some ground rules by which 'best' could be judged. The ground rules that I used were: (1) the routes should be taken from all areas of the Park so as to reflect its varied landscape; (2) the walks should vary both in length and difficulty, from short easy strolls to long strenuous fell-walks, in order to appeal to as many walkers as possible; (3) they should preferably be circular, returning to their starting point in order to avoid undue reliance upon public transport which may be at best infrequent and at worst non-existent; (4) they should pass through good viewpoints and by features of interest such as old mines, stone circles and waterfalls; (5) the walking should be of good quality (the ascent of long slopes of sliding scree, dreary and seemingly endless grassy plods, or the negotiation of marshy ground may sometimes have to be included if the rest of the route warrants it, but should, I am sure most walkers would agree, be kept to a minimum.)

Even so, with an area so rich in excellent walks the selection of the forty best was not an easy one. I still have occasional twinges of conscience for having omitted one or two. Working according to the ground rules given above, I based the selection upon (a) my own knowledge of the area gained over thirty-five years of walking there, (b) a survey of the many books, particularly walking guides, now available on the Lake District, (c) a careful examination of large-scale maps of the area, and (d) the opinions of friends who know the area well. Finally, all the routes given in the list were walked and surveyed to ensure that maps and descriptions were as accurate as possible.

I make no claims for infallibility. There may indeed be valleys of heart-catching beauty that I have never visited, corners of the hills that give panoramic views my eyes have never seen, and footpaths of superb quality that my boots have never trodden. If these have escaped my notice – and the notice of the many guide-book authors that I have read – then please let me know of them via my publisher. Any comments or suggestions for improving the list will be considered for future editions and they will be very welcome. If nothing else, I hope that this book will initiate a lively debate!

No apology whatsoever is given for including among the walks some old favourites: in most cases they became popular in the first place because of their quality. Nor for including some still relatively quiet and unfrequented routes, because of the danger that increased use of them may take away some of their charm. I do not feel that I have the right to keep to myself anything which has given me so much pleasure. I ask only that you treat the countryside kindly and with consideration for others, so that the beauty which you have enjoyed is never lost.

A good friend of mine, on returning from his first long look at the Lake District, wrote that it confirmed his feeling that it was in some way special, belonging not so much to England as to itself. I cannot put it better. The magic which I first felt so many years ago is still there, as strong and as captivating as ever. I hope that this book will help you to find it.

Frank Duerden, 1985

The Lake District National Park

The National Parks and Access to the Countryside Act of 1949 gave authority for the establishment of a National Parks Commission which would be responsible for the creation of National Parks; ten were created by the Commission in England and Wales between 1950 and 1957.

In 1968 the National Parks Commission was replaced by the Countryside Commission which thereby took over responsibility for the Parks. A further change came under the Local Government Act of 1972; a separate Authority was set up for each National Park, and the Lake District National Park Authority was created by further legislation in 1997.

The National Park Authorities had two main aims: to preserve and enhance the natural beauty of the areas designated as National Parks, and to encourage the provision or improvement of facilities for the enjoyment of open-air recreation and the study of nature within the National Parks. In their work they were to have regard for the social and economic needs of the people living within these areas.

There is a widespread misconception that somehow the land of a National Park was 'acquired' by the nation. This is very far from being the case. In the Lake District National Park, for example, only a very small amount has been purchased or leased by the Park Authority, and the vast bulk is still in private hands or owned by bodies such as the National Trust and the Forestry Commission.

The Lake District National Park Authority is the local planning authority for the area, with the same planning powers as are divided between county councils and district councils elsewhere. It considers all applications for planning permission with powers to

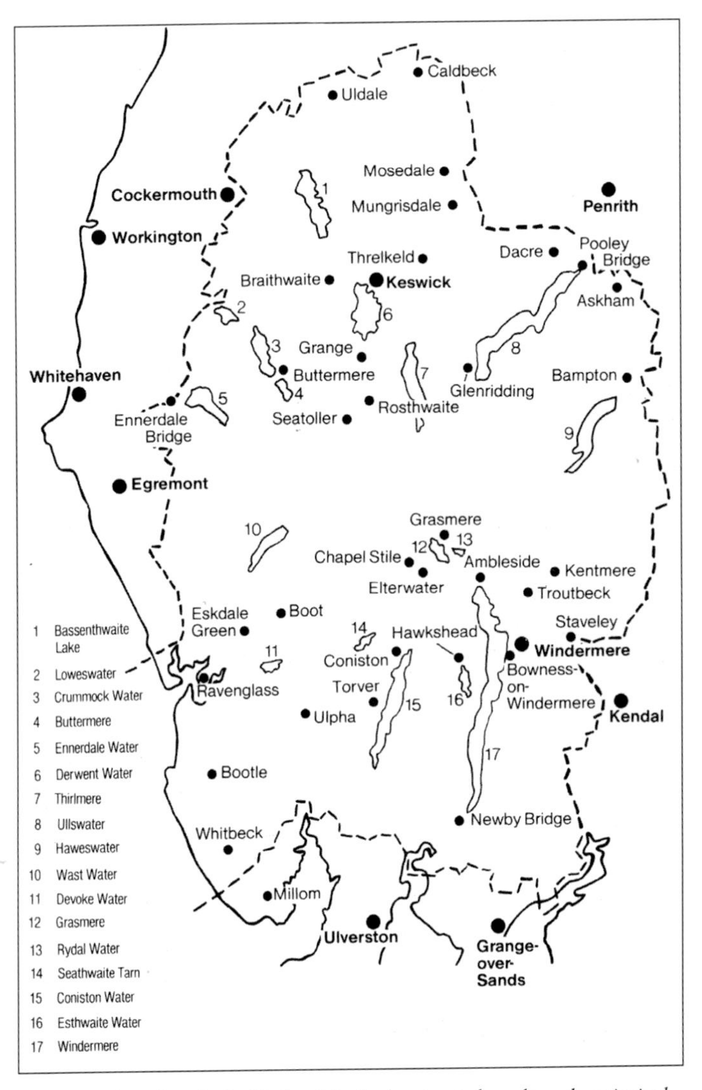

Figure 1 The Lake District National Park, showing its boundary, the principal lakes, and the main towns and villages in and around the park.

Looking across Derwent Water

ensure that its decisions are observed. In addition to this planning function, it has the power to promote certain schemes for the benefit of visitors: for example, the provision of car-parks, toilets, information centres and accommodation. Other functions, however, such as education, housing and highways, still remain the responsibility of Cumbria County Council and the district councils within the Park.

Members serving on the Lake District National Park Authority are appointed by councils and other public bodies. In addition, the Board runs a National Park Visitor Centre at Brockhole between Windermere and Ambleside, information centres at Windermere, Coniston, Ullswater, Grasmere, Hawkshead, Keswick, Pooley Bridge, Borrowdale and Waterhead, and the Coniston Boating Centre. Rangers are the Authority's representatives in the field and valuable help is provided by voluntary wardens and work parties. Voluntary wardens are involved in holding instructional courses on map-reading or drystone walling, for organizing work parties, for leading parties and patrolling areas. More details about all aspects of the work of the Lake District National Park Authority can be found online at www.lake-district.gov.uk. The site also has a very useful daily weather forecast for the Park.

Information Centres are situated at:

Borrowdale: 01768 777294
Bowness and Windermere: 01539 442895
Coniston: 01539 441533
Grasmere: 01539 435245
Glenridding: 01768 482414
Hawkshead: 01539 436525
Keswick: 01768 772645
Pooley Bridge: 01768 486530
Waterhead: 01539 432729

SOME FACTS AND FIGURES ABOUT THE NATIONAL PARK

Designated: 13 August 1951. The Park was the second to be designated, the Peak District National Park being the first.
Area: 880 sq miles (227,919 hectares). It is the largest of the National Parks, the second largest being Snowdonia which occupies 838 sq miles (217,100 hectares).
Emblem: A view of the head of Wast Water with Great Gable beyond – one of the finest views in Lakeland.
County: Originally it fell within the three counties of Cumberland, Westmorland and Lancashire; it now takes in one third of the county of Cumbria.
Population: A little over 40,000 people live in the National Park, a figure that has remained fairly constant for around 50 years.

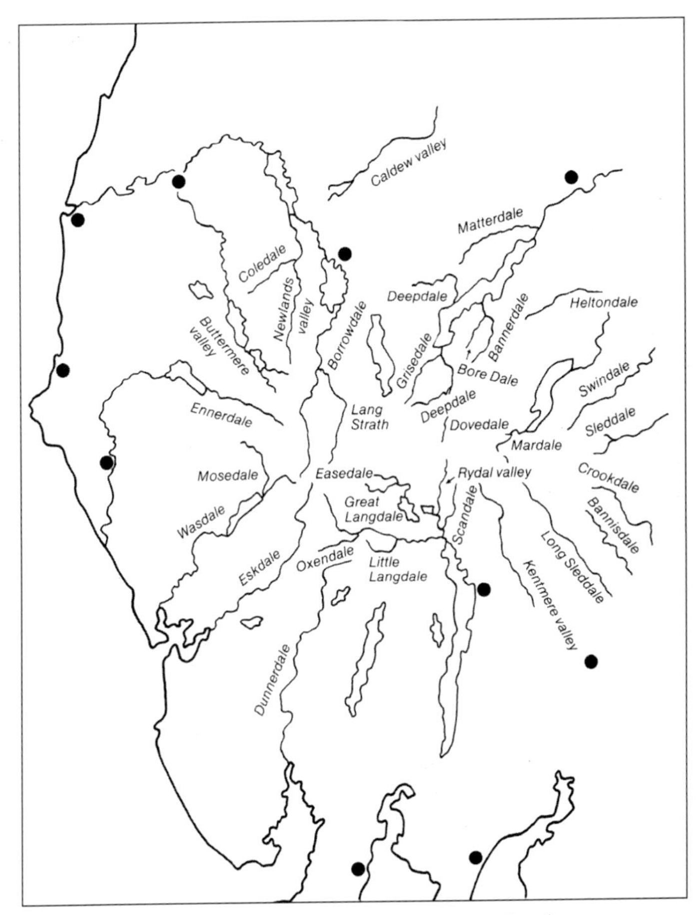

Figure 2 The principal dales of the Lake District National Park

Houses: Of the total number of 'household spaces' in the Park capable of permanent occupation, around a fifth are holiday or second homes. In some areas, such as Grasmere, the proportion is nearer half.

Land ownership: Of the total area of the Park, 58.7% is still privately owned. The rest is owned by:

National Trust	24.8%
United Utilities	6.8%
Forestry Commission	5.6%
National Park Authority	3.8%
Ministry of Defence	0.2%

Visitor numbers: About 12 million people visit the Park each year, of whom around 2 million stay for at least one night.
Where visitors come from: 90% of the day visitors and 50% of overnight visitors come from northern England (i.e. Cheshire to Humberside northwards), with a particular concentration from the North-West.
Walkers and climbers: About 10% of visitors do some fell-walking and 0.5% some rock-climbing. The proportion of visitors doing shorter walks in lowland areas is much greater.

PUBLIC TRANSPORT INTO AND WITHIN THE LAKE DISTRICT

Railways

Four lines serve the area of the park. Consult www.thetrainline.com for the most up-to-date information on services.

(1) The Inter-City line from Preston to Carlisle, which runs outside the eastern boundary of the Park, with stations at Oxenholme and Penrith.
(2) The Inter-City line from Lancaster to Barrow-in-Furness which runs largely outside the southern boundary of the Park, with stations at Silverdale, Arnside, Grange-over-Sands, Kents Bank, Ulverston, Dalton and Roose.
(3) A short branch-line from Oxenholme (where it links with the Inter-City service) to Windermere, with stations at

Farm in Little Langdale

Kendal, Burneside and Staveley.

(4) The west coastal line from Barrow-in-Furness to Carlisle (linking at each end with Inter-City lines), with many intermediate stations.

Tourist Information Centres are situated at:

Barrow-in-Furness: 01229 812871
Carlisle: 01228 625600
Lancaster: 01524 32878

In addition there are three privately operated railways which may be useful (note that services may be restricted or stop altogether during the winter):

(1) The Ravenglass and Eskdale Railway (7 miles, 11km). Trains drawn by steam or diesel locomotives stop at Muncaster Mill, Irton Road, The Green, Beckfoot and Eskdale (Dalegarth) (see page 65). Information from The Ravenglass and Eskdale Railway, Ravenglass, Cumbria CA18 1SW. Telephone: 01229 717171, www.ravenglass-railway.co.uk.

(2) The Lakeside and Haverthwaite Railway (3½ miles, 5.5km). This operates steam locomotives from Haverthwaite (on the A590) to Lakeside at the southern end of Windermere, stopping at Newby Bridge. There are connections with steamers at Lakeside for Bowness-on-Windermere and Ambleside. Information from Lakeside and Haverthwaite Railway, Haverthwaite Station, near Ulverston, Cumbria. LA12 8AL. Telephone: 01539 531594, www.lakesiderailway.co.uk

(3) South Tynedale Railway, Alston, runs trains hauled by preserved steam and diesel locomotives along the scenic South Tyne valley from Alston to Kirkhaugh from Easter to October, with specials at Christmas. Telephone: 01434 382828 (talking timetable), www.strps.org.uk.

Buses

National Express coaches (Telephone: 08705 808080, www.national-express.com) run to the main towns in and around the National Park from London, Birmingham, Glasgow, Manchester and other centres; buses from other parts may be used to connect with these. Public service buses run from all the main towns around the Park area, including Barrow-in-Furness, Ulverston, Grange-over-Sands, Kendal, Windermere and Ambleside to the south; Cockermouth, Keswick and Penrith to the north; and Whitehaven and Workington along the coastal strip. The operator is Stagecoach: for further information telephone Traveline (08706 082608) or visit www.stagecoachbus.com.

In addition, a number of mini-buses are used for regular service routes over some of the narrower and steeper roads of the Park area. These are operated by:

Mountain Goat Bus Company, Victoria Street, Windermere LA23 1AD. Telephone: 01539 445161. www.mountain-goat.com.

Lakes Supertours. Telephone: 01539 442751, www.lakes-supertours.co.uk.

Boats

Regular boat services are available on a number of the larger lakes, which may be useful for transport purposes. In some cases they link up with train and bus services. Information may be obtained from the following:

Coniston Water: The SY *Gondola*, first launched in 1859 and completely renovated by the National Trust, is now operated between Coniston and Brantwood. Service information from Coniston: 01539 441288.

Derwent Water: A regular motor launch service is run from Keswick, in both clockwise and anti-clockwise directions around the lake, stopping at Hawes End, Low and High Brandelhow, Lodore and Ashness Gate. Keswick-on-Derwentwater Launch Co Ltd, 29 Manor Park, Keswick, Cumbria CA12 4AB. Telephone: 01768 772263.

Ullswater: MY *Raven* and *Lady of the Lake* are operated on a regular

The fells around Buttermere

service, Easter to October, usually between Pooley Bridge, Howtown and Glenridding. Ullswater Steamers, Glenridding Pier, Glenridding, Cumbria CA11 0US. Telephone: 01768 482229.

Windermere: A regular service for car and foot passengers runs from Ferry Nab, Bowness, to Ferry House, Far Sawrey, except on Christmas Day and Boxing Day. The General Manager, Windermere Iron Steamboat Co Ltd, Ulverston, Cumbria LA12 8AS. Telephone: 01539 531188.

ACCOMMODATION

The Blencathra Centre

Blencathra Centre, Threlkeld, Keswick, Cumbria, telephone 01768 779601, www.field-studies-council.org/blencathra, is run by the Lake District National Park Authority and Field Studies

Council, and is situated on the slopes of Blencathra about 6 miles (10km) to the north-east of Keswick. It offers self-contained hostels for group booking and holiday cottages, giving accommodation throughout the year. Visitors can plan their own programmes, but many courses are provided there, from winter walking to landscape photography. Information, reference and teaching facilities are available to youth and school parties.

Camp-sites

There are thousands of permanent tent pitches on licensed or exempted sites within the National Park. In addition, there are many other sites which operate under the so-called '28-day rule' – this allows land to be used for tents for a total of 28 days in any one year. The larger licensed sites are marked on the Ordnance Survey's Explore and Landranger maps. The Lake District National Park website, www.lake-district.gov.uk, has detailed information on camping within the Park area.

Caravans

A large number of licensed caravan sites within the area of the National Park provide caravans for hire, temporary sites for touring vans, and permanent sites for static vans, but not residential sites. A licence allows a site to remain open from 1 March to 31 October (or in some cases 14 November) only.

HF Holidays Guest Houses

HF Holidays, Imperial House, Edgware Road, London NW9 5AL, telephone 020 8905 9556, www.hfholidays.co.uk, has two guest houses within the Park. They are:

Monk Coniston, Coniston
Derwent Bank, near Keswick

Holiday Fellowship guest houses are open to all and provide comfortable accommodation: single or shared bedrooms, full meals and evening entertainment. Normally walking excursions are available, but these are optional and the Centres may be used simply for accommodation.

Hotels and private guest houses

As this region is one of the main holiday areas in the British Isles, there is an abundance of private accommodation in the villages and in farmhouses and cottages in the country. These will be heavily booked in the main tourist months of July and August and at those times advance booking is advised; there should be no problem at other times. National Park accommodation bureaux are available at all the Information Centres listed on page 16, with the addition of:

Ambleside: 01539 431576
Windermere: 01539 446499

The *Ramblers Yearbook and Accommodation Guide*, published by the Ramblers' Association, lists hundreds of addresses throughout the United Kingdom and is published annually.

National Trust holiday cottages, campsites and basecamps

Book online at www.nationaltrustcottages.co.uk or telephone 08704 584422, fax 08704 584400. Cottages and campsites are situated on Trust land throughout the Park. Basecamps and bothies, available for groups, of the same sex, offer simple self-catering accommodation. More information about the accommodation options can be found online at www. nationaltrust.org.uk.

Ramblers Holidays

Ramblers Holidays operates a guest house on the shores of Buttermere: Dalegarth Guest House, Hassness Estate, Buttermere, Cockermouth, Cumbria CA13 9XA; telephone 01768 770233; email dalegarth-buttermere@supanet.com. Accommodation is in twin or three-bedded rooms. With the exception of one or two weeks, a programme of guided walks is offered, although guests may follow their own itinerary if they wish.

Youth hostels

There is a higher density of youth hostels in the Lake District National Park than in any other area of the British Isles: 22 are situated within the Park itself and there are two others just outside, which are also useful. Further information can be obtained from the YHA Handbook, published annually, or online at www.yha.org.uk

Useful websites

Many websites give details of accommodation within and around the Lake District National Park. Here is a selection:

www.cumbria-the-lake-district.co.uk
www.golakes.co.uk
www.lake-district.gov.uk
www.lakelandgateway.info
www.twglakedistrict.com

The face of Lakeland

DRYSTONE WALLS

Although it is likely that the art of building drystone walls is an ancient one, the earliest extant record of a wall in the Lake District dates from the thirteenth century when the Cistercian monks of Furness Abbey were granted the right to enclose an area of their land in upper Eskdale 'with a dyke, wall or paling as the abbot and monks should think most convenient to them ...' During the following centuries the building of walls around farms and villages must have been commonplace, although by the end of the eighteenth century the proportion of land enclosed by them would still have been comparatively small. The rest was common land over which local inhabitants had certain rights.

The enclosure movement, mainly concentrated in the sixty years between 1760 and 1820, and relying upon Act of Parliament to enforce enclosures and extinguish rights over this common land, has been described as one of the most notable developments in English agriculture. Enclosure Bills, sponsored by the principal landowners of the area to be enclosed, were prepared and presented to Parliament. After royal assent, Commissioners were appointed and they did the actual work of drawing up the award by allocating the land to the landowners concerned, who in turn undertook to enclose the land, usually in a specified manner and by a certain date. Between 1760 and 1844 there were more than 2,500 such Acts which dealt with over four million acres (about 1,619,000 hectares). It is scarcely surprising therefore that the procedure for enclosure was simplified and standardized by a series

Bridge in Little Langdale

of General Enclosure Acts, of which the most important were in 1801 and 1845.

Enclosure in the Lake District took place mainly after the General Enclosure Act of 1801. The long straight walls of the fells, easily distinguished from the irregular boundaries of the valley fields, were the product of this movement. In the main, the pattern of walls in the Lake District was established by about the middle of the nineteenth century.

The life of the waller in the cold, wet and windy conditions of the fells could not have been an easy one. To provide secure foundations, the line of the wall would be marked by a shallow trench in which two parallel rows of large and usually square stones – 'footings' – were set. Further courses would be placed on to these so that, in effect, two walls were being built, bound together by occasional rows of 'through' stones which were often left projecting on each side of the wall. The gap in the centre was filled by a rubble of small stones – the 'hearting' – and the top was completed by a single row of flat stones placed on edge. As the building progressed, each course of stones would be carefully placed so that it was slightly inset relative to the one below; the width of the wall thus gradually decreased, this 'batter' adding considerably to its stability. At the junction of two walls to be maintained by different owners, a 'wall head' was formed for identification, and occasionally a square 'hogg hole' was constructed at the base to allow sheep to move from one side of the wall to the other.

No mortar whatsoever was used in the construction of a drystone wall – hence its name. The product was essentially a balanced structure depending entirely for its durability upon the craft of the men who built it.

The stone for the wall was collected on the fellside around the site or, if necessary, from a local quarry. The walls of Lakeland therefore show differences in the type of stone used as well as in the individual style of the wallers themselves.

FARMING

The pattern of farming within the Lake District is determined by the physical characteristics of the land and the climatic conditions. Mountain and moorland areas with their great elevation, their steep, often precipitous slopes and their acidic soils, subject to a harsh combination of heavy rainfall, high winds and excessive cloud cover, are not suitable for growing crops (apart from softwood trees). Farming over those areas of the Lake District, therefore, is largely confined to breeding sheep and, to a much smaller extent, raising beef herds. Within the dales, however, flat fields with a richer soil-cover and much milder weather conditions permit the rearing of dairy herds and the growing of a very few crops, mainly for the purpose of livestock feeding.

A typical hill farm is made up of four areas: the open fell; the 'intake' or rough grazing land which is enclosed by long straight walls built during the enclosure period; the 'inbye land' or improved pasture; and finally meadows around the farmstead. Sheep spend most of their lives on the open fell where each has its own 'heaf' from which it rarely wanders; they are brought down only for shearing, dipping, lambing and eventually for sale. The concentration of sheep upon the fell is low, one ewe and her lamb to each area being typical. The inbye land is used for mating, for lambing, and for the grazing of hill cattle; while the meadows produce a valuable crop of hay and silage used for feeding during the winter.

Around the end of November the rams (tups) run with the ewes, normally one for every 50–60 in the flock. Colouring rams on the breast when they are turned out is a common practice to ensure that all ewes have been served; by changing the colour after a period of 18 days, the progress of mating can be followed.

About twenty-one weeks later, from mid-April to mid-May, the lambs are born. By the end of May the ewe and her lamb have

Herdwick sheep

been returned to her heaf, to stay there until shearing or dipping begins in July. Only the ewes are shorn, the lambs being left until their second summer: a typical yield from a Herdwick is about 3½–4½ lbs (1½–2kg). Dipping to control disease and external parasites is an essential practice in good husbandry and is covered by regulations. Dips given around the end of August, and again in October, control parasites such as maggot fly, ticks, lice and keds, and diseases such as scab.

As winter approaches, the female lambs, now well grown, may be brought down into the intake or in some cases sent away until the spring to lowland farms where the conditions are milder. Lambing starts in the ewes' third summer, i.e. when they are two years old. After three crops of lambs it is customary to sell them off to lower farms, where they are kept for two more years. During this period they are mated with Bluefaced Leicester or Teeswater tups to produce crossbred types. Male lambs usually have a worse fate in store for them, as the majority, not being required for breeding purposes, are castrated and sold away for fattening before slaughter.

Mountain and moorland sheep are pure-bred types, of which in Lakeland the Herdwick was long regarded as predominant, although nowadays it only accounts for about 10 % of the total stock. Its early history is obscure, although there is an old tradition that they came originally from a ship wrecked on the Cumbrian coast. Their endurance in bad weather and their ability to survive on the poorest grazing are unsurpassed, but their most remarkable characteristic is their 'hefting' instinct which keeps a sheep for its entire life on the hillside where it was raised. For this reason a farm is sold along with its flock, to provide continuity. Lambs are born with dark, almost black, wool which becomes lighter as they grow older. The face of the adult sheep is white, and broad with an arched nose, only the rams having horns.

The most abundant sheep in Lakeland is the Swaledale. In this breed both rams and ewes are horned, and can be recognized by their black faces and grey muzzles. Other common varieties found in Lakeland are the Rough Fell. Finally, there are smaller numbers of Dalesbred and some crossbred sheep.

Many of the hill farms carry small herds of cows – usually crossbred – intended for beef production. These remain on the inbye land during the summer but are taken into shippons during the winter months where they are fed on hay or silage.

In lowland areas where the pastures are better, dairy herds are maintained. Each cow is normally calved each year, ensuring milk production for about ten months. The most common variety is the Friesian, exceeding in numbers all the other dairy breeds put together. They are large animals, with well-defined black and white patches, and produce a higher milk-yield than any other breed. An increasing number of Canadian Holstein are also now appearing.

THE WORK OF THE FORESTRY COMMISSION

It is not generally realized that Great Britain imports about 80 % of its wood and wood products – higher than most other countries in the world. This will not seem surprising, however, when it is known that a mere 12 % of the total land area is now given over to woodland (compared, for example, to 64 % in Sweden and 27 % in France), the end production of an extensive and continuous clearance of forest which has been going on since about 3,000 BC. Although many small woods were established by private owners from the sixteenth century onwards, the severe demands of the First World War were only met by extensive felling, a loss which had not been made good when the Second World War began. It was against this background that the Forestry Commission was established in 1919, its main aim being to reduce this country's dependence on imported timber.

The Forestry Commission has wider powers and responsibilities than might be thought. It is responsible for promoting knowledge of forestry, for developing efficient uses of wood products, for research into the practice of forestry, for combating diseases, for assisting private forestry by advice and financial help, and for the efficient production of wood by the development of forest areas. It recognizes that it must also show concern for land environment and agriculture, and provide facilities for recreation.

The land for the national forests of the Commission is acquired either by purchase or by long-term lease. In the main it is marginal agricultural land of poor quality, suitable only for sheep grazing. As the upper limit of economic afforestation is about 1,800 feet (550m) this has led to most planting being in valleys, on low hills or on the lower slopes of mountains. Before planting the ground is often ploughed, furrows being about 6–7 ft (1.8–2.1m) apart. Conifers are planted into these at intervals of 6 ft (1.8m). A forest worker can plant between 500 and 1,500 trees in a single day. These young trees are raised in the Commission's own nurseries and transplanted into their final quarters as 2–3 year old plants. Access roads and fire-breaks are essential features which must be provided throughout the forest areas. Later cultivation is comparatively light: some weeding may be carried out and in some cases the lower side-shoots are removed from young trees, but otherwise they are left to grow naturally. Thinning starts 20–25 years after planting and provides a valuable interim crop, usually equal in total volume to the final yield.

It is the present practice of the Commission and of private owners to confine their plantations largely to coniferous trees. This reflects current demand in this country, which is mainly for softwood; the much quicker rate of growth of conifers compared to broadleaved trees; and finally the nature of the land available for afforestation, which mostly is not suitable for growing trees other than conifers to a marketable size.

Scots pine is the only native conifer now planted; it is still in favour in the eastern half of the country, but in the west its slow rate of growth is a disadvantage and other species are usually preferred. Altogether about twenty different types are grown on a commercial basis, the most common ones being the Corsican and Lodgepole pines, Norway and Sitka spruces, Japanese and Hybrid larches and the Douglas fir.

Plantings by the Commission began on the Thornthwaite Estate to the north-west of Keswick in 1919. There are now four major forests: Thornthwaite, Ennerdale, Blengdale and Grizedale, with smaller areas elsewhere. Some opposition to planting – particularly of 'foreign' species – had existed long before the activities of the Forestry Commission, but this mounted considerably in 1933 with the acquisition of land in upper Eskdale and the Duddon valley. Following lengthy discussions between the Commission and the Council for the Preservation of Rural England (CPRE), an agreement was finally reached in 1936 by which the Commission agreed not to acquire land for afforestation within a boundary which enclosed the central 300 sq miles (777 sq km) of the Lake District. This agreement (subject only to some modification in 1955) has been maintained and forms the policy of the Lake District National Park Authority, although considerable planting has taken place outside the specified area. The Forestry Commission has also made positive efforts to harmonize its plantations with the landscape, although such moves inevitably take many years to become effective.

Extensive areas of the Park's forests have been opened to public access along the forest roads; car-parks and picnic sites have been established, and nature and long-distance trails created. Two major Visitor Centres have been built, the first at the Whinlatter Pass, 2 miles (3.2km) north-west of Braithwaite on the B5292, and the second on the Hawkshead-Satterthwaite road at Grizedale, between Windermere and Coniston Water.

THE GEOLOGY OF THE LAKE DISTRICT

The rocks of the Lake District form part of a highly eroded dome whose centre lies in the region of Carrock Fell to the north of Skiddaw. The National Park area, therefore, covers the southern

High Hows Wood in winter

reach of this dome. Within this area there are three principal rock types, which lie in broad and roughly parallel bands, trending SW-NE across the Park.

To the north, a large but irregular area from west of Ennerdale across the Buttermere valley, Bassenthwaite Lake and Derwent Water to east of Keswick, is made up of Skiddaw Slates. These were formed 440–500 million years ago out of muds deposited in the warm, shallow seas of the Ordovician period, by a compaction process caused by pressure. As the rocks are relatively easily eroded by weathering, the hills of this region are smooth and rounded; where crags do exist they are well broken and loose, and for this reason are generally not used by rock-climbers.

A large, roughly rectangular area stretching from the western end of Wast Water to the eastern ends of Ullswater and Haweswater is covered by rocks of the Borrowdale Volcanic Series. These arose – as the name implies – from violent volcanic activity towards the middle of the Ordovician period, which produced vast lava flows and ash-fall over a wide area to a depth of 2–3 miles (3–5km). Although varied in nature, rocks of the Borrowdale Volcanic Series are very hard-wearing, producing the dramatic scenery and the large climbing-cliffs of central Lakeland.

The third of the main areas covers the south of the Park across Coniston Water and Windermere to beyond Kendal. The rocks of this region were laid down in the Silurian period, which followed the Ordovician, 400–440 million years ago, when Cumbria was still covered by warm shallow seas. Although some of these rocks, more resistant to erosion than others, have produced prominent rocky knolls, the landscape generally is lower and more gentle than that further north.

Several other types of rock come to the surface within the area of the National Park, although over much smaller areas. Granite occurs in four main locations: a large area from south of Eskdale to the lower end of Wast Water, a smaller area across the upper end of Ennerdale, and two smaller areas near Threlkeld and on

Carrock Fell. This has been worked at several quarries. A thin belt of limestone runs along the junction of the Borrowdale Volcanic Series and the Silurian rocks in a SW-NE direction, and there are other more substantial areas in the extreme south and east. Finally, there is a belt of red sandstone along the west coast line.

THE ICE AGE IN LAKELAND

It is usually stated that the Ice Age began about two million years ago and ended about 10,000 years ago, a period referred to as the Quaternary era. This statement however requires some qualification. In the first place, while this may well be a reasonable picture for the middle latitudes of Europe – in which Britain lies – there is evidence to indicate that other parts of the world were affected by glaciers and ice-sheets at a much earlier date and over a longer period; indeed, some are still affected to this day. Furthermore we know that the Ice Age even in Britain was not continuous, but was broken by periods in which the weather was relatively warm – perhaps similar to our climate today. There is no evidence at the moment to tell us if we in Britain have seen the last of the Ice Age, or whether we are merely living in still another interglacial period.

At their greatest extent, ice-sheets covered most of the North American continent as far south as Kentucky, a considerably greater area than the Antarctic ice-sheets of the present day. In Europe an enormous sheet of about four million sq miles covered most of Scandinavia and Siberia. In the west this joined with the British ice-sheet, which had developed separately, to form a coherent whole. Ireland, Scotland and Wales were covered entirely, and the ice extended southwards over England to the general line of the Thames and Severn estuaries. This huge sheet was fed by glaciers rising in the hill and mountain areas of the Scottish Highlands, the Southern Uplands, the Lake District, part of the Pennines, the Welsh mountains and the mountain groups of Ireland. It is not

The view from Castle Crag

known for sure why the Ice Age occurred, although the way in which glaciers and ice-sheets form is well understood.

Most glaciers originate in mountain areas because conditions there are suitable for snow to accumulate and survive permanently. Generally, snow deposited in the winter months when temperatures are low will disappear due to melting in the summer months when temperatures are high. If the deposition exceeds the loss, then snow will accumulate over the years. This will most likely take place in hollows where there is some shelter and where additions of snow can also occur due to drifting and avalanches. Gradually, under the increasing pressure provided by further falls, the soft snow in the base layer compacts, firstly into hard snow (called firn or névé) and then into ice. Although ice may appear solid, it can in fact flow. Downhill movement therefore takes place, probably along the easier lines offered by the valleys of mountain streams. There will, of course, be some melting and evaporation from the ice surface, and this will increase as the glacier flows down into lower, warmer regions. Eventually, the flow rate will no longer be sufficient to meet this loss and the glacier will end.

In the Ice Age conditions were so abnormal that glaciers from the mountain regions were able to reach lowland areas, where they spread out, joining up with adjacent flows to form a single ice-sheet. Boulders, carried down on glaciers originating in the Lake District, have been found throughout Lancashire and Cheshire, over the North York moors and as far south as Nottingham and Derby.

Erosion by ice flow can be spectacular. In the mountains the grinding action produces deep hollows whose back walls are plucked by the ice into steep cliffs. Winding valleys, the product of stream action, are straightened by the ice which shears away any side ridges in its path. The large amount of debris, boulders and ground-up material removed by this process is carried down on the ice flow, and eventually dumped at the end as a heap (called a terminal moraine). At the end of the Ice Age, as the glaciers retreated for the last time, the landscape was revealed in its eroded state. The main valleys were straight with characteristic U-shaped cross-sections and sheared-off side ridges ending in steep cliffs. Side valleys, produced by smaller and less abrasive glaciers, were left high up on the surrounding walls, producing spectacular waterfalls and cascades. In the hills huge hollows were left (called cirques or combes), which rapidly filled with water to form tarns. Terminal moraines, isolated boulders (erratics), thick clay deposits and smooth ice-scored rock beds were much in evidence.

With the passage of time, of course, this landscape was slowly modified by the action of rain, sun, wind and frost. Ten thousand years, however, is very short in geological terms and the Lake

District landscape of today is still therefore much as the Ice Age left it.

LAKELAND WEATHER

As might be expected, the central mountain area around the Scafells has the highest rainfall in the Lake District, with an annual average of more than 150 inches (3,810mm). The wettest place of all is probably Esk Hause at the base of Great End, where the average is of the order of 185 inches (4,700mm). Moisture-rich air, coming in mainly from the south-west, is forced to rise as it encounters the high mountain mass. As it rises it begins to cool and the moisture within it condenses to form fine droplets – which appear as cloud – and ultimately larger drops, which fall as rain. The convergence of the main valleys towards the central mountains undoubtedly adds to this effect. As would be expected from this, the coastal area to the west and south-west and the Eden valley to the north-east between Penrith and Carlisle enjoy much drier conditions; in neither area does the annual rainfall exceed 40 inches (1,016mm). Keswick, at the mouth of Borrowdale, has only one-third to one-half the rain that falls at Seathwaite at the head of the dale and a mere 8 miles (13km) away.

The rainfall will vary, of course, during the year, the wettest months being November, December and January and the driest April, May and June, with a small secondary 'peak' of rainfall in August being fairly common. The incidence of cloud and sunshine is related to the rainfall figures. The western coastal area and the Eden Valley enjoy long periods of sunshine, while on the mountains of the central area the cloud-cover may be almost continuous during the winter months.

Snowfall is less than might be expected, being relatively light around the fringes of the Lake District and well up into the dales. With increasing altitude, however, the picture changes rapidly;

falls become heavier and the snow lies longer. This is particularly true in the north-eastern region, which receives the brunt of the easterly winds bringing snow. The Helvellyn range is popular for skiing, and the last lingering remnants of the winter snow will usually be found there or on the neighbouring High Street group.

THE PLACE-NAMES OF CUMBRIA

Cumbria, like other parts of the British Isles, has been subjected to repeated invasion and settlement over the past 2,000 years. The place-names of the area reflect this, as each new wave of immigrants naturally used words from their own language to describe local features or changed those already existing by their usage of them. A careful study of place-names can therefore give some indication of the distribution and the customs of the region's earlier inhabitants.

The earliest place-names probably date from the Celtic races who occupied the Lakeland area from about 1,000 BC to the coming of the Anglo-Saxons in the fourth and fifth centuries AD – and in the more remote areas till a much later date. The word 'combe', similar to the Welsh 'cwm' and meaning 'a deep valley or hollow', as well as the county names of Cumberland and Cumbria (the land of the Cymru), derive from the Celts. So also do the strange-sounding names of Glenderamackin (a stream to the east of Blencathra) and Penruddock (a village just north of the present Keswick-Penrith road).

Anglo-Saxon settlement in Cumbria took place mainly along the west coast and up some of the richer valleys. The words 'mere' and 'water', now in common usage, are derived from the Old English of these people. Thus Buttermere, literally translated as 'Butter Lake', was a tribute by them to the richness of the pastures surrounding it.

Most influential of all, however, were the Vikings who invaded around the tenth century, coming in from Norway via the western sea-board of Scotland and the Isle of Man. The Vikings were essentially settlers who brought their culture with them, as the abundance of place-names derived from Old Norse bear testimony. So also do the words 'fell', 'beck', 'gill', 'tarn', 'force' and 'dale', which are in common use throughout Lakeland.

Even in comparatively recent years names have occasionally been added, and are still being added. Adelaide Hill near Windermere was so named after a visit by Queen Adelaide in 1840, and Doctor's Bridge in Eskdale because it was widened in 1734 on the orders of a Dr Edward Tyson, so that he could drive his carriage over it.

THE EARLY DEVELOPMENT OF ROCK-CLIMBING IN THE LAKE DISTRICT

The sport of climbing mountains for enjoyment is a relatively recent development. For most of recorded history mountains were regarded as at best being useless and dangerous, and therefore to be ignored; or at worst being dreadful and dangerous, and therefore to be avoided. Even in the early eighteenth century it was still considered necessary for bishops to exorcize glaciers, and proper for a Fellow of the Royal Society to attempt a classification of Alpine dragons.

Not until well into that century did these attitudes change, and then only for scientific purposes. The exploration of the Alps – largely completed by the 1850s – was accomplished by the botanist in pursuit of rare plants and by the natural scientist armed with thermometer and barometer. As with most things, the transition was slow and the point of change difficult to determine. On the first ascent of Mont Blanc in 1786 scientific instruments were carried and temperature and pressure dutifully recorded; by the

Crinkle Crags guarded by Lakeland drystone walls

1850s these had been discarded even as a mask for eccentricity. In what is usually referred to as the 'Golden Age' – between 1850 and the ascent of the Meije in 1877 – every major peak in the Alps was climbed, largely by members of the British middle class accompanied by professional guides and motivated by a love of mountains and of mountaineering.

It was around that time – at the end of the 'Golden Age' – that British rock-climbing began. The rocks of Sca Fell, Great Gable and Pillar were developed initially over long weekends and short Easter and Christmas breaks by young men seeking to improve their mountain skills for the more serious Alpine seasons of the summer. It became the custom for small groups to gather at the Wastwater Hotel at Wasdale Head. Readings of Aristotle and Plato in the morning were followed by hard fell-walking and the exploration of gullies in the afternoon. Although modest by today's standards, rock-climbs were accomplished and, with the passage of time, they began to acquire an importance of their own.

Of all the climbs done in this period, the ascent of the Napes Needle in 1886 by W.P. Haskett Smith is considered the most important. Partly, this was due to the unusually open and exposed nature of the climbing at a time when it was more customary for men to hide themselves away in the seemingly secure depths of gullies and chimneys, but far more important was the highly sensational and extremely photogenic appearance of the pinnacle itself. Nothing stimulated public imagination more than the appearance of photographs and postcards of the Needle, usually with the small figures of intrepid conquerors on its minute summit.

In the next few years the 'gully epoch' was to end as climbers began to venture on to ridges and arêtes, and then on to open slabs and walls. With this came a great rise in the standard of climbing. The ascent of Eagle's Nest Ridge Direct by the team of G. Solly, W.C. Slingsby, G.P. Baker and W. A. Briggs in 1892; Fred Botterill's superb lead in 1903 on a slab on Sca Fell which now bears his name; and finally the conquest of Central Buttress on the same cliff by Siegfried Herford and George Sansom in 1914, were the outstanding landmarks in this development.

Following the 1903 accident, however (see page 218), and the First World War in which several leading climbers (in particular Herford) lost their lives, the pace of development in Lakeland slowed considerably. It revived for a while in the 1920s, kindled no doubt by the publication of a series of guide-books by the Fell and Rock Climbing Club and under the leadership of a new generation of climbers: H.M. Kelly, G.S. Bower, C.D. Frankland and others. The first ascent of Great Central Route on Dow Crag by J.I. Roper in 1919 is regarded as marking its beginning. But by 1930 this revival was already in decline, and the main development of British rock-climbing passed to Snowdonia, where – in the hands of Kirkus, Menlove Edwards, Harding, Brown and Whillans – it was to stay for some thirty years.

Safety

In the last few years Rescue Search Teams in the Lake District have been called out on average around 300 times each year; 2004 was the worst year for a decade with 366 calls. In this year 437 walkers and climbers had to be rescued, of whom 211 were injured and 41 were killed. In most of these cases death followed a collapse, which may or may not have been the result of a heart attack, rather than a fall.

The routes described in this guide vary considerably in length and difficulty. Some of the easy walks should, with reasonable care, be safe at any time of the year and under almost any weather conditions; some of the more difficult walks, however, cross very wild country and are only suitable, even on good summer days, for fit walkers who have the correct clothing and equipment and know what they are doing.

It must be strongly emphasized that conditions can change very quickly in mountain areas, not only during the day but from one part of a mountain to another or as you climb to higher ground. You must bear this in mind when choosing your clothing and equipment before a walk. The challenge of a walk will also generally be greater (perhaps very much greater) in the winter, when snow and ice are lying on the mountains, than in the summer months.

So, please, for your own safety in mountain and moorland areas (and so that I won't have your fate on my conscience):

DO: Carry suitable clothing and equipment, which should be in good condition.

Carry sufficient food for the day, plus more for emergencies.

Carry a map and compass and make sure that you know how to use them.

Plan your route carefully before you start.

Leave a note of your planned route with a responsible person (and stick to it unless changed circumstances make it dangerous to do so).

Report your return as soon as possible.

If it appears that you are going to be seriously delayed then inform your base, or the police, as soon as possible.

Keep warm (but not too hot) at all times.

Eat nourishing foods and rest at regular intervals.

Avoid becoming over-tired.

Know some First Aid and the correct procedure in case of accidents or illness.

If you are leading a party always go at the pace of the slowest member, and never separate (except possibly in the event of a serious accident in order to obtain help).

Obtain a weather forecast before you start and take this into consideration at the planning stage. Take weather changes into account as you proceed. A written report/forecast is put up daily at each Information Centre within the Park area. A recorded local forecast with fell conditions may be obtained by telephone 0870 0550575 or online, where it is updated twice daily at www.lake-district.gov.uk/weatherline.

DO NOT: Go on to the fells by yourself unless you are very experienced; three is a good number.

Explore old mine workings or caves, or climb cliffs.

Attempt routes which are beyond your skill and experience.

HOW TO GIVE A GRID REFERENCE

A grid reference is a very useful method of pin-pointing a position on an Ordnance Survey map. The grid lines on OS 1: 25 000 and 1: 50 000 maps are the thin blue lines going vertically and horizontally across the map, covering it with a network of small squares.

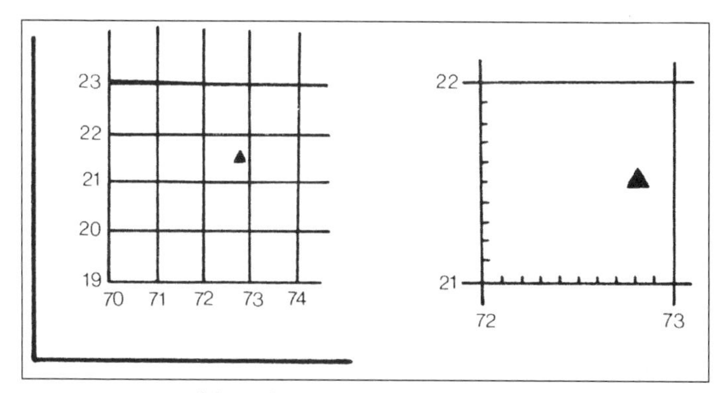

Figure 3 A section of the Ordnance Survey Landranger map (1: 50 000) with the position of a youth hostel marked.

The method of determining a grid reference is as follows:

Step 1: Write down the number of the 'vertical' grid line to the left (or west) of the hostel. This is 72.

Step 2: Now imagine that the space between this grid line and the next one to its right is divided into tenths. Estimate the number of tenths that the hostel lies to the right of the frist grid line. This is eight. Add this to the number in Step 1, making 728.

Step 3: Add on the number of the grid line below the hostel (i.e. to the south). This is 21; so the number becomes 72821.

Step 4: Now repeat step 2 for the space between the grid lines below and above the hostel. The hostel is five tenths above the bottom line. Add this to the number, making 728215.

This is called a six-figure grid reference. Coupled with the number of the appropriate Landranger or Explorer sheet, it will enable any point to be identified.

Step 5: The numbers of the grid lines repeat after 100. There will therefore be many other places in the United Kingdom with exactly the same six-figure grid reference. To overcome this problem, each large square (with sides made up of 100 small squares) is designated by two letters; on the Landranger sheets these are given on the small diagram which shows the adjoining sheets. In the example above, if the large square is designated by SP, then the full grid reference is SP 728215. There is only one place in the United Kingdom with this grid number.

THE COUNTRY CODE

The original Code was prepared by the Countryside Commission many years ago with the advice, help and co-operation of many organizations concerned with the countryside. It was written to help you get all the pleasure you can from the countryside while contributing to its care. It remains a sensible set of 'rules' for the walker. The Code was:

Enjoy the countryside and respect its life and work. It is a living countryside; part of our heritage which gives life to both resident and visitor.
Guard against all risk of fires. Plantations, woodlands and heaths are highly inflammable; every year acres burn because of casually dropped matches, cigarette ends or pipe ash.
Fasten all gates. Even if you found them open. Animals can't be told to stay where they're put. A gate left open invites them to wander, a danger to themselves, to crops and to traffic.
Keep your dogs under close control. A dog which chases cattle or sheep can do a great deal of harm. Keep your dog on a lead wherever there is livestock about, and also on country roads.
Keep to public paths across farmland. Crops can be ruined by people's feet. Remember that grass is a valuable crop too, sometimes the only one on the farm. Flattened, it is very difficult to cut.
Use gates and stiles to cross fences, hedges and walls. A damaged field boundary may allow livestock to stray and will necessitate costly repairs. Keep to the recognized routes, using gates and stiles.
Leave livestock, crops and machinery alone. Crops and machinery are

best left alone, and farm animals are best viewed from a distance so as not to disturb them.

Take your ltter home. All litter is unsightly and spoils the countryside for others, and some is dangerous as well. Bring litter back from walks for proper disposal; in the country it costs a lot to collect it.

Help to keep all water clean. Do this for the sake of all living things.

Protect wildlife, plants and trees. Wildlife is best observed, not collected. To pick or uproot flowers, carve on trees and rocks, or disturb wild animals and birds, destroys other people's pleasure as well.

Take special care on country roads. Country roads have special dangers; blind corners, high banks and hedges, slow-moving tractors or animals. Motorists should reduce their speed and take extra care; walkers should keep to the right, facing oncoming traffic.

Make no unnecessary noise. To see the countryside at its best you have to try to be part of it, to disturb it as little as possible, and take nothing from it except happy memories.

However, in recent times the publishing organisation has become the Countryside Agency and following the enactment of 'right to roam' legislation the Code has become the Countryside Code, with sections applicable to both the public and land managers:

For the Public

Be safe – plan ahead and follow any signs.
Leave gates and property as you found them.
Protect plants and animals, and take your litter home.
Keep dogs under close control.
Consider other people.

For Land Managers

Know your rights, responsibilities and liabilities.
Make it easy for visitors to act responsibly.
Identify possible threats to visitors' safety.

Notes on the route descriptions and maps

Difficulty

The routes have been selected to give a wide range both of length and of difficulty to make the book attractive and useful to as many kinds of walker as possible. It does make it essential, however, for the sake of both interest and safety to give a clear indication of the difficulty of each.

A number of factors play a part in determining the time necessary to complete a walk. The most important of these factors are distance and the amount of climbing involved, and the effect of these can be assessed by Naismith's Rule (see below). Roughness of terrain or difficulties of route-finding can also, of course, play a part, but usually these are restricted in their effects to a small proportion of the total distance.

The method used in this book involved three stages: (1) a calculation of the total time required for each route on the basis of Naismith's Rule; (2) listing the routes, in order from shortest time needed to longest; and (3) a review of the list after surveying each route. The difficulty of each route can be assessed by the reader in three ways. (1) The total distance and the amount of climbing involved, which are given at the head of each route description. Difficulties of a special nature, e.g. Sharp Edge on Route 11, are pointed out in the introduction to the route. (2) Its position in the list – Route No 1 is the easiest, No 40 the hardest. And (3) its grading. The walks have been divided into categories – easy, moderate, and more strenuous.

As a guide, a 'typical' walk within each category would be:

Easy. A short walk (say, up to 5 miles, 8km) over good paths, with no problems of route-finding. Some climbing may be

Haweswater from High Street

involved, but mostly over fairly gradual slopes with only short sections of difficult ground.

Moderate. A longer walk (up to 10 miles, 16km) mostly over good paths but with some more indefinite sections where routefinding will be difficult. Mountain summits may be reached, necessitating climbing over steeper and rougher ground.

More strenuous. A fairly long walk (10–20 miles, 16–32km) with prolonged spells of climbing. Some rough ground calling for good route-finding ability, perhaps with prolonged stretches of scrambling.

Distance

These are 'map miles', which take no account of the amount of climbing involved. They are given in miles and kilometres.

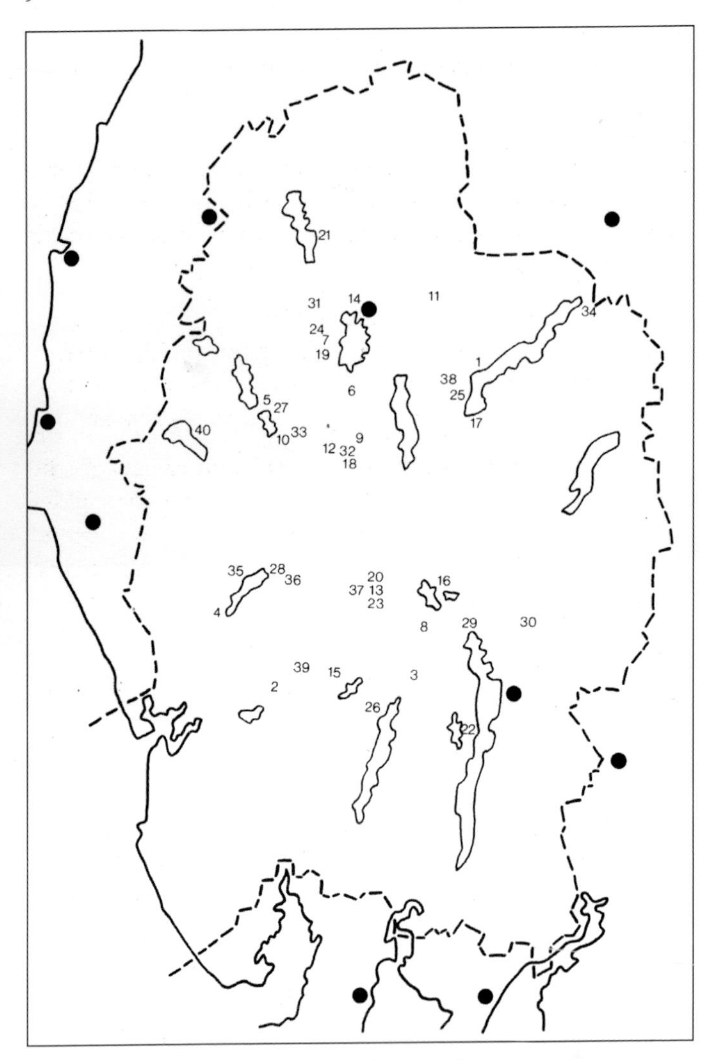

Figure 4 This sketch map shows the starting points for Routes 1 to 40, in relation to the principal lakes and towns of the National Park (see diagram on page 13).

Ascent

These figures are also given in both feet and metres.

Naismith's rule

An estimate of the time required to complete each route is not given in the book, as this will vary so much from one walker to another. But the usual method of estimating time is by Naismith's Rule, which is:

'For ordinary walking allow one hour for every 3 miles (5km) and add one hour for every 2,000 ft (600m) of ascent; for back-packing with a heavy load allow one hour for every 2½ miles (4km) and add one hour for every 1,500 ft (450m) of ascent.'

For most walkers this tends to *under-estimate* the amount of time required, and each walker should try to form an assessment of his own performance over one or two walks. The Rule also makes no allowance for rest or food stops, for the roughness of the ground, or for the influence of weather conditions.

Car-parks

Almost all walks start at a car-park or parking place. This is indicated on the first map of each route and in the information given on the starting point.

Route descriptions

The letters 'L' and 'R' indicate left and right respectively, and for changes of direction imply a turn of about 90° when facing in the direction of the walk. 'Half L' and 'half R' indicate a turn of approximately 45°, while 'back half L' and 'back half R' indicate turns of about 135°. All bearings given are magnetic bearings. It should be assumed that all stiles and gates mentioned in the description are crossed, unless there is a statement to the contrary. PFS stands for 'Public Footpath Sign', PBS for 'Public Bridleway Sign', and OS for 'Ordnance Survey'.

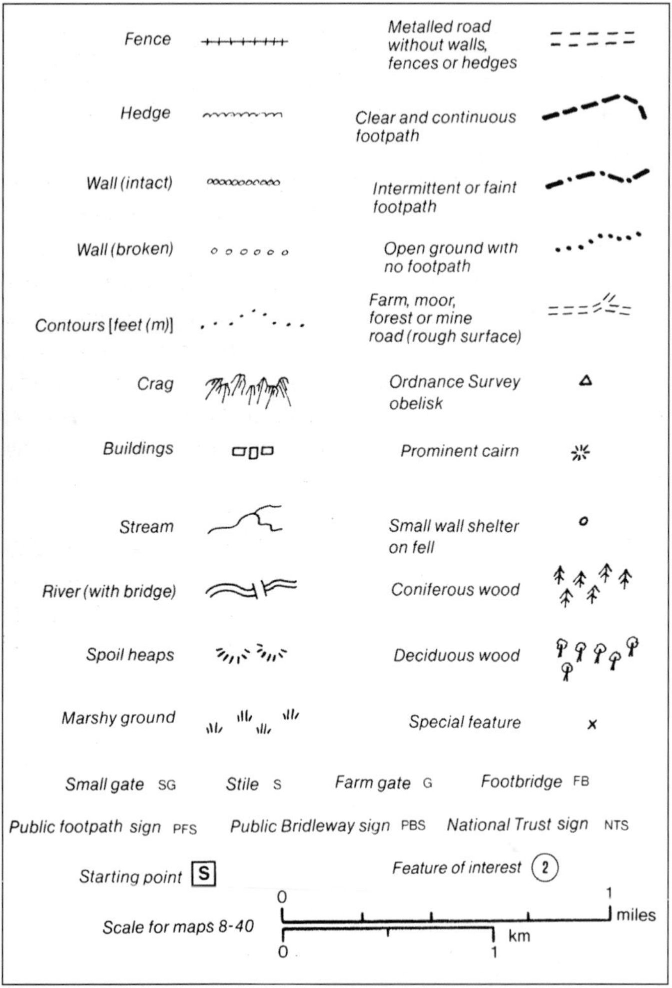

Fence
Metalled road without walls, fences or hedges
Hedge
Clear and continuous footpath
Wall (intact)
Intermittent or faint footpath
Wall (broken)
Open ground with no footpath
Contours [feet (m)]
Farm, moor, forest or mine road (rough surface)
Crag
Ordnance Survey obelisk
Buildings
Prominent cairn
Stream
Small wall shelter on fell
River (with bridge)
Coniferous wood
Spoil heaps
Deciduous wood
Marshy ground
Special feature
Small gate SG
Stile S
Farm gate G
Footbridge FB
Public footpath sign PFS
Public Bridleway sign PBS
National Trust sign NTS
Starting point S
Feature of interest 2
Scale for maps 8-40
0 1 miles
0 1 km

Figure 5 Key to signs used on the route maps.

The maps

The maps take the same numbers as the routes; where there is more than one map for a route they are given the suffixes A, B, C, etc. Thus, Route No 34 has four maps: 34A, 34B, 34C, and 34D to be used in that order.

The maps for Routes 8–40 are drawn at a scale of 2 inches to one mile (1: 31 680). The maps for Routes 1–7, which are relatively shorter, are drawn to a scale of 4 inches to one mile (1: 15 840). Place-names were mainly taken from the Bartholomew's 1" to 1 mile map of the Lake District, and are generally the same as on Ordnance Survey maps. The maps have been drawn, with one or two exceptions, so that the route goes from the bottom to the top of a page. This will enable the walker to 'line-up' the map, i.e. hold it in the same direction as his route, while still holding the book in the normal reading position.

The arrow on each map points to grid north.

For mountain and moorland areas it is strongly recommended that, in addition to this guide, Ordnance Survey Explorer or Landranger maps are carried; these should be used where difficulty of route-finding arises, if the route is lost, or where bearings have to be estimated.

Features of interest

Some information on features of interest along the way is given with each route description. The best position for seeing these features is indicated both in the route description and on the accompanying map.

The location of each feature of interest is indicated by the number of the appropriate Landranger (1: 50 000) sheet with a six-figure grid reference. Thus: (89–176170) is the location of the church in Buttermere which is at grid reference 176170 on Sheet No 89.

Access

The routes described have, as far as is known, been walked for a long time without objection either by legal right or by tradition, and it is not expected, therefore, that any difficulties will be encountered.

Easy Routes

ROUTE 1 | Aira Force and High Force

A short but beautiful walk up the west bank of the Aira Beck to the magnificent waterfall of Aira Force which is 65 ft (20m) high. The return can be made from there by crossing the stream and following the path back along the opposite bank, but it is better to continue further on the same side and make the crossing by the second waterfall, High Force. The paths are very clear throughout. There are small bridges at the top and bottom of Aira Force giving superb view-points.

Length: 2 miles (3km) | Ascent: 325 ft (100m) | Starting and finishing point: The large National Trust car-park near Aira Point on the north side of Ullswater, about 3 miles (5km) along the A592 from Patterdale (90–400201) and about 150 yds (140m) from the junction with the Dockray road (A5091) | Maps: Landranger 90; Explorer OL5

ROUTE DESCRIPTION (MAP 1)

Before starting, walk a few hundred yards along the road left from the car-park for a view of an unusual tower – see ① Lyulph's Tower. Then walk back through the car-park to a gap in the wall at the far end (National Trust sign). From there continue in the same direction along a clear path, soon going through a small gate and then another in a wall. A few yards further along, the path bends L past a seat – do not take the path to the right here. Follow the clear path to the L of the river, soon passing Aira Force. Do not cross at the bridges here (except to shorten the walk) but continue on the same side of the stream to a further bridge

High Force

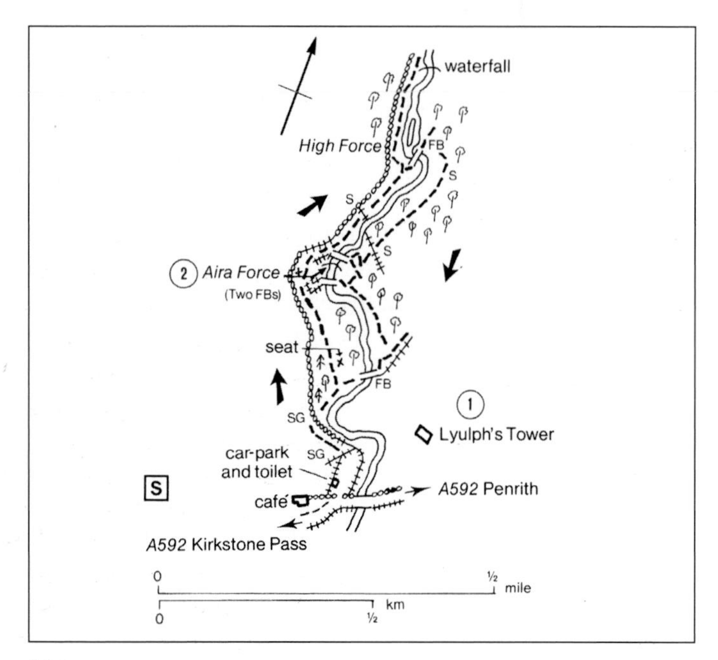

Map 1

and beyond, past High Force, finally reaching the top (third) fall. The National Trust property and the path end just beyond here.

Return to the last bridge just below High Force and cross. Follow the path up the short slope beyond and then R to go downstream. Continue on the clear path past Aira Force (descend to both bridges for superb view-points and see ② Bridge at Aira Force). Eventually, about 350 yds (320m) below Aira Force, at fence go down R to bridge. Cross stream and go ahead to join path used earlier. Follow back to car-park. (Most people, particularly on hot, dry and dusty summer days, will immediately leave it again, for there is a very welcome tea-room just outside the entrance, to the right.)

① *Lyulph's Tower (90–404202)*

Lyulph's Tower, a short distance away from the car-park at the start of this route, was mentioned in Wordsworth's The Somnambulist: *'List, ye who pass by Lyulph's Tower'. Despite its appearance it is comparatively recent, built by an eccentric, Charles Howard of Greystoke, later eleventh Duke of Norfolk, around 1780 as a shooting-lodge on a site occupied by the remains of an earlier tower. There is some doubt about the origin of the name. One possibility is that it was derived from L'Ulf or Ulfr (or similar) – an Old Norse personal name – after which Ullswater itself is named, i.e. Ullfr's Lake. The tower is still owned by the Howard family and is not open to the public, but can be seen from the road.*

② *Bridge at Aira Force (90–400206)*

The upper stone bridge directly above the large fall '... was built by friends in memory of Stephen Edward Spring Rice, C.B. 1856–1902'. There is a memorial tablet on one parapet. The falls were purchased by the National Trust in 1906. (The National Trust owns more land in Cumbria than in any other county. All visitors to the Lake District should be glad of this, as the Trust is one of the greatest forces for conservation in Britain.)

ROUTE 2 | Stanley Ghyll

Formed since the end of the Ice Age by water action cutting into the Eskdale granite, the Ghyll is a magnificent ravine with a waterfall 60 ft (18m) high. The interest of its rock formations and rich plant life was the reason for its being taken under the care of the National Park Authority in 1964 by agreement with the Stanley family of the nearby Dalegarth Hall – and after whom the Ghyll is named. This walk follows a nature trail, but returns by a different route. Care should be taken beyond the top footbridge where the going is rougher.

Length: 2½ miles (4km) | Ascent: 325 ft (100m) | Starting and finishing point: Car-park by Dalegarth Station in Eskdale (89–172007) | Maps: Landranger 89 and 96; Explorer OL6

ROUTE DESCRIPTION (MAP 2)

By far the best way to reach the starting point is by using 'La'al Ratty', the Ravenglass and Eskdale Railway, from lower in Eskdale – see ① below. Also of great interest – but more particularly at the end – is the tea-room at the station.

Leave the car-park into the road and turn R. After 250 yds (230m) turn L down a lane opposite the old school (signs for Dalegarth Falls, Stanley Ghyll and Trough House Bridge). The road soon bends R and goes over a bridge. After a car–park the surface becomes rough, and shortly afterwards bends L at the entrance to a drive. Go through a gate and continue down lane, ignoring path to R and gate to L. Go through the small gate ahead in a wall where the lane turns R (signed 'Waterfalls').

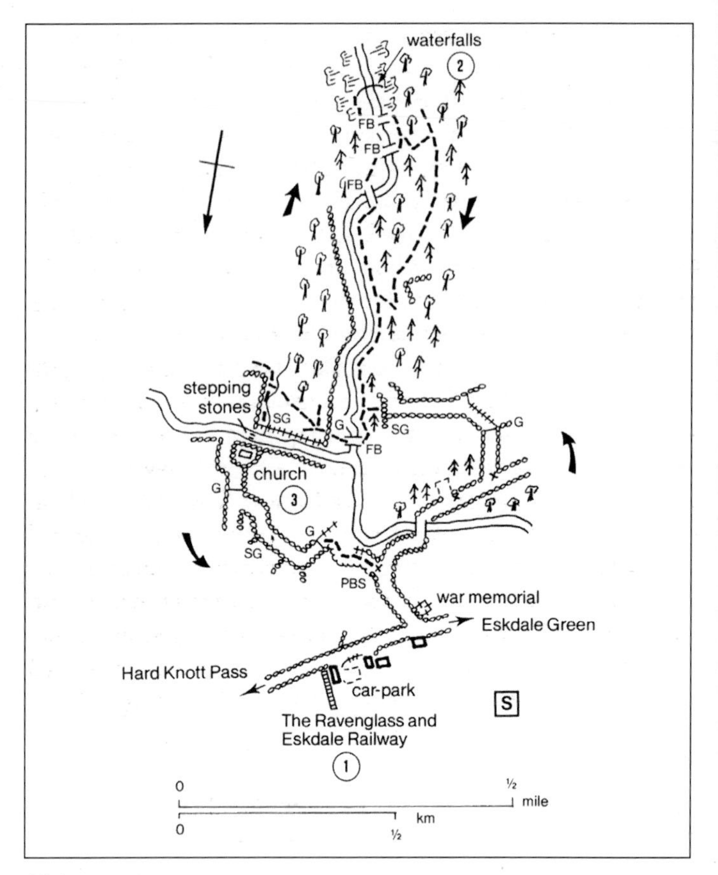

Map 2

Go through the small coniferous wood to the stream and turn R. Follow the stream on its R bank, crossing a footbridge after 575 yds (525m). Re-cross at a second footbridge 100 yds (90m) further along, and 50 yds (45m) further still at a third footbridge, return to the opposite bank. Above this last footbridge the path continues to the L of the stream by the waterfalls for a short distance, but it is steep and rough in places. Stanley Ghyll is one of the most interesting places within the Park, making this an excellent point to enjoy some chocolate and a rest before starting back – see ② Stanley Ghyll. Return to the top bridge and cross.

Follow the stream down towards the second bridge. Do not cross but fork L up a path ahead of the bridge. After a few yards, bend L. Higher up, by a small slab bridge, turn back half R. Follow the path through woods, dropping down to the path by the stream followed earlier. Turn L. Lower down, do not turn L on your approach path but keep by the stream to a footbridge.

Go over the bridge and through gate ahead and follow the path half R across the field to a wall corner; then follow path half L across another field and turn L to stepping-stones. Cross and go down lane to R of church. If the river is high do not attempt to cross, but return along the paths used earlier. (One golden rule is: never, never pass by a church without looking inside; there will always be something to interest you. But remember that someone loves it and keeps it clean, so don't, please, take your mud in with you. See ③ St Catherine's Church, Eskdale.) After a gate turn L into a bridleway. After a small gate and a gate, this joins the road used earlier; here turn R and soon R again back to the starting point.

① *'La'al Ratty' – The Ravenglass and Eskdale Railway*

With a track gauge of only 15 ins (38cm) – compared to 4 ft 8⅜ ins (143.2cm) on all national lines – and with scaled-down locomotives, the Ravenglass and Eskdale is classified as a miniature railway. Within the British Isles only one other miniature railway exceeds it in length: the Romney, Hythe and Dymchurch Light Railway, which, running for 14 miles (23km), is exactly twice as long.

Laid originally at a gauge of 3 ft (91cm), the line was opened for goods in 1875 and passengers a year later, its main support coming from Whitehaven Iron Mines Ltd who used it for transporting iron ore from its mine near Boot. Almost from the start of operations the railway company experienced financial difficulties, and after struggling to survive for many years it was forced to close down in 1913.

Two years later, however, the railway was leased by a new company, Narrow Gauge Railways Ltd, who gradually reopened the line on the present gauge with new locomotives and rolling stock. The opening of the Beckfoot granite quarry near Dalegarth in 1922 provided very welcome extra income for the line – the granite was taken away to a crushing plant at Murthwaite, 2½ miles (4km) away, and then on to the main line at Ravenglass. This association was later sealed by an amalgamation of the two companies concerned.

In 1960, following closure of the quarry some years earlier, the railway was put up for sale as a going concern at auction, the winning bid being made by the Ravenglass and Eskdale Railway Preservation Society, formed earlier that year with funds provided by individual donations – in particular from Mr Colin Gilbert, a Birmingham stockbroker and miniature-railway enthusiast, and Sir Wavell Wakefield (later Lord Wakefield). A Ravenglass and Eskdale Railway Company, which is still in being, was formed to own and operate the railway.

It is the aim of the Company to preserve the railway in its present form by operating it as a viable commercial concern. It operates miniature steam-locomotives with both open and closed carriages, except during the winter months when a very limited service is maintained with diesel. It is run by a small permanent staff, supported by temporary summer workers and volunteers from the Preservation Society. The origin of the name 'Ratty', by which the railway is popularly known, is now obscure. One theory is that it derived from Ratcliffe, the name of the contractor who built the original line in 1875. More details and a timetable can be found at www.ravenglass-railway.co.uk

② Stanley Ghyll

The word 'Ghyll' is an eighteenth or nineteenth-century corruption of 'Gill' an Old Norse word meaning 'a ravine'; Stanley is the name of the family which inhabited – and which still inhabits – Dalegarth Hall, passed earlier on the route. The physical characteristics of the area which produced the waterfalls were formed in the Ice Age. Eskdale contained a huge glacier which ground away the side ridges to produce a fairly straight valley of characteristic U-section. Higher up the Ghyll, a minor glacier also cut into the bedrock, but to a lesser extent. When the glaciers retreated, a 'hanging valley' was formed, with waterfalls where the drop into the main valley occurs. Since that time considerable river-erosion has also occurred, producing the deep ravine.

③ *St Catherine's Church, Eskdale*

The early history of this lovely dale chapel, situated by the stepping-stones over the Esk, is now obscure, but it is possible that it was founded in the twelfth century. The present building is largely the result of a major restoration in 1881. It is a simple building with a small bellcote at one end and combined nave and chancel. Inside there is a font which was restored in 1876 after spending sixty years in a local farmyard, where it was used (as one authority states intriguingly, but without giving details) 'for vile purposes'. There is also a pitch pipe, bought more than 150 years ago, which was used to give the note for hymn singing, and an old treble bell which may have been cast in the fifteenth century. The church and churchyard were used for burials from Wasdale in addition to those from Eskdale until 1901, the corpse road by Burnmoor Tarn being used for the conveyance of the coffins either on horseback or on light carts. (Walkers who intend to use the Burnmoor track into Wasdale may be interested to learn that, according to local legend, at least one body was lost en route.)

ROUTE 3 | Tarn Hows

Although somewhat artificial in character, Tarn Hows nevertheless has considerable charm and beauty. Because of this it attracts vast numbers of visitors each summer. It is better to do this walk, therefore, out of season on suitable days, when the tarn is by contrast a place of great peace and tranquillity. The route can be limited to a simple circuit of the lake, but it is much better to include a short diversion down to Glen Mary Bridge and back via the waterfalls, which adds a mere mile (1.6km) to the walk.

Length: 2¾ miles (4.5km) | Ascent: 600 ft (180m) | Starting and finishing point: National Trust car-park on minor road to the south of the tarn (96/97–326995) | Maps: Landranger 96/97 and 90; Explorer OL7

ROUTE DESCRIPTION (MAP 3)

Leave car-park by entrance nearest to lake and turn R along road. Almost immediately leave road L on track which soon curves L. After about 15 yds (14m), fork L onto grassy path. Follow path over the top of the ridge and down on the far side to meet a wall on R. The path continues to descend, curving L and then R along a beautiful grassy ledge. Go through gate, and then at wall corner bend L, and then lower down L again. At ruined barn turn back half R, and after a few paces back half L (do not go through gap in wall ahead). Follow wide track to gate. In lane turn R and continue down path to the road at Glen Mary Bridge.

Sunset, Tarn Hows

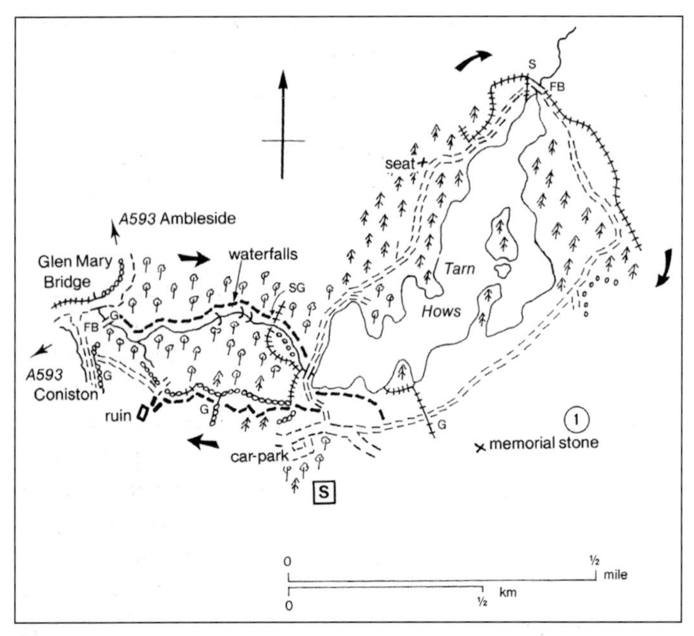

Map 3

Cross footbridge over stream to R and turn R through small gate, following path to L of stream. Continue with stream as it bends L and then R past magnificent waterfalls (signs for 'Tom Gill Waterfall'). Above the top fall go through a small gate in a fence and continue up path by the stream to reach the tarn at the stream outflow.

Turn L along a broad path. This path goes completely around the lake, eventually returning to the stream outflow. Keep on it throughout, except towards the end where, after passing through a gate and by a wood on your R, you leave the main path to the R along a clear but narrower path which drops down towards the tarn shore. If you want to make a detour for a fine viewpoint, about 50 yds past the gate turn L onto a path, following it L across the hillside, over a stile and then on to a memorial stone – see ① Tarn Hows. From here you get full view of the storm damage which felled thousands of trees in the area in January 2005. The total distance around the tarn is 1¾ miles (2.8km).

Arrive back at the stream outflow. Turn L along a broad track which immediately bends L. Follow track up hill, bending R to car-park.

① *Tarn Hows (96 and 90–330000)*

A small stone on the hillside to the south-east of Tarn Hows is inscribed: 'NATIONAL TRUST THE TARNS are given in memory of SIR JAMES SCOTT of YEWS and of ANNE LADY SCOTT, 1930'. The view from here, over the tarn, is superb and one of the finest in Lakeland. Appreciation of this should not be lessened by the knowledge that it is to some extent artificial: the water level was raised by a dam and weir constructed at the south-west tip – which produced a single large tarn – and trees alien to the area were planted. It is an example of what can be achieved by sensible and careful development. The name 'The Tarns' refers to its earlier form before the raising of the water level, when there were several stretches of water.

ROUTE 4 | Wast Water Foot

The view up Wast Water towards Great Gable is acknowledged to be one of the finest in the Lake District; it was appropriate therefore that it was chosen as the emblem of the National Park. It can be seen to perfection from the permissive path around Low Wood at the foot of the lake. This route, which starts by the lake, is circular and includes the permissive path. It also forms part of an official nature trail.

Length: 4¼ miles (6km) | Ascent: 150 ft (50m) | Starting and finishing point: Use one of the small parking places on the shore of Wast Water, where the road from Nether Wasdale meets the lake (89–149049) | Maps: Landranger 89; Explorer OL6

ROUTE DESCRIPTION (MAP 4)

From your parking place walk along the road with the lake to the L. Follow the road as it swings R away from the lake, and then a few yards further along goes L over a cattle-grid. After 250 yds (230m) turn R along a farm road through a wood (a small gate to Wast Water youth hostel is on the opposite side, just before the turn). After a few yards the way bends between walls. At the end cross a ladder stile by a gate and bend L. Follow the track, which soon bends R and drops down the field to a lower cross track. Turn L (PFS). Follow to a gate and stile. Keep on the clear track in the same direction. Do not go L at a fence corner but continue to a gate and stile straight ahead. After the gate, turn R with fence to R (PBS 'Buckbarrow') and

Boathouse, Wast Water

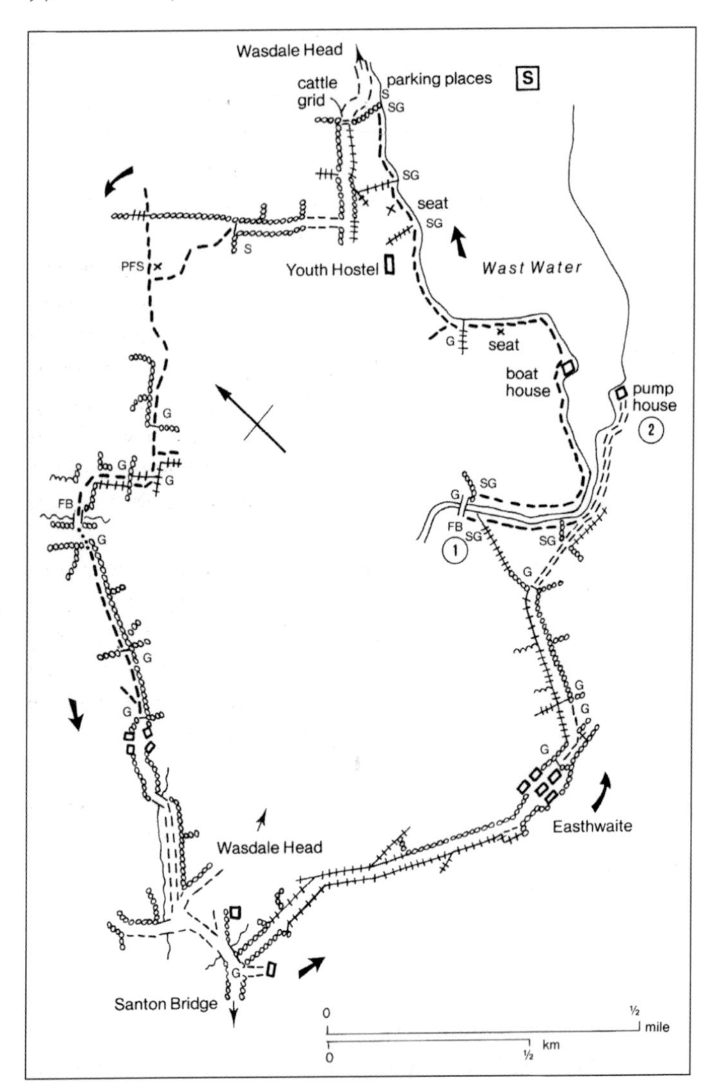
Wasdale Head
cattle grid
parking places
S
SG
S
SG
seat
SG
S
Youth Hostel
Wast Water
PFS
G
seat
boat house
pump house
2
G
G
G
FB
G
SG
G
FB
SG
1
SG
G
G
G
G
G
G
Easthwaite
Wasdale Head
G
Santon Bridge
0
½
mile
km
0
½

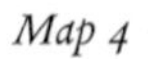
Map 4

go through a further gate. Soon bend L to a small bridge (do not take the path on the R).

Cross the field to a gate opposite and follow the path in the same direction with a wall to the L (PBS 'Strands'). At a farm go through the farmyard and over a bridge at the far end. Continue down the farm road (with a stream to R) to meet a metalled road near a bridge.

Go down the road straight ahead (sign 'Santon Bridge and Drigg'). After 100 yds (90m) go over a bridge and turn L immediately afterwards (PFS 'Wast Water'). Go down farm road to reach Easthwaite Farm. Cross the farmyard between buildings to leave by a gate at the far end. Go down the farm road, passing through three more gates. Soon go through a small wood and reach the river bank. Turn back half L along a path to the L of the river. Pass through two small gates and continue to a bridge (see ① Lund Bridge). Cross.

On the far side, turn R through a small gate and follow a path through a wood on the L bank of the stream. Keep on this path with the stream then the lake to the R, for just over 1 mile (1.6km) to road. On the way you will pass a boathouse, a pump house on the opposite bank, and finally a large mansion – see ③ Wasdale Hall. Go down the road to your parking place. Water is taken from a number of lakes in the Park, and one or two schemes have been highly controversial, but few people would, I think, quarrel seriously with the lovely little pump house at Wast Water – see ② Pump house.

① *Lund Bridge (89–142039)*

This lovely little bridge was originally a pack-horse bridge. There is another fine example by the hotel at Wasdale Head.

② *Pump house (89–146039)*

The pump house on the far shore of the lake extracts water for use at the Sellafield site on the west Cumbrian coast. Extraction was originally

Looking north, up Wast Water

limited to a maximum of 7 million gallons (32Ml) per day, but has since been increased. One million gallons may sound like a lot of water, but it is only equivalent to about ¼ in (6mm) of depth over the whole of Wast Water! Wast Water is the lake nearest to Sellafield, but it was chosen primarily because of the high purity of its water. This is essential to prevent corrosion of the stainless steel used both in the reactors of the nuclear power station and in the nuclear fuel reprocessing plant.

③ *Wasdale Hall (89–145045)*

Wasdale Hall was built between 1829 and 1843 for a Yorkshire wool merchant, Stansfeld Rawson, on a

site previously occupied by a farm. It was sold by auction in 1864 to John Musgrave, a solicitor in Whitehaven, and again in 1920 to H.W. Walker, a tanner from the same town. It was bought with an estate of 53.5 acres (22 hectares) in 1959 by the National Trust out of various Lake District funds, and is now let to the YHA. Built of stone, it occupies a superb position at the foot of Wast Water looking out towards The Screes. (Every YHA member has his list of favourite hostels. Wasdale Hall is very high on mine, to be visited if possible in the spring when all is still quiet, and daffodils add colour to the lawns.)

ROUTE 5 | Around Buttermere

The lake of Buttermere, framed on three sides by high fells, is considered by many to be the most beautiful in the Lake District. This lovely walk – almost entirely on footpaths – starts at Buttermere village and goes around the lake, keeping close to the shore for most of its distance. Go to Buttermere when you are tired and overburdened by life's problems, and come away refreshed – but try to avoid weekends and school holidays when the area becomes very busy!

Length: 4¾ miles (7.5km) | Ascent: 50 ft (15m) | Starting and finishing point: Car-park in Buttermere village by Fish Hotel (89–195150). This quickly becomes full at peak times; there is further parking on the road down into Buttermere | Maps: Landranger 89; Explorer OL4

ROUTE DESCRIPTION (MAP 5)

Walk down the rough farm road to the L of the Fish Hotel. The flat plain that you are now crossing is a reminder that Buttermere is slowly disappearing because material is being washed into it from the neighbouring fellsides – as are all lakes in the Lake District. But don't hurry, it is likely to be around for some time yet – see ① Buttermere. The road soon bends L and through a gate. After 150 yds (140m), go through gate ahead and follow clear path half R towards lake (Do not go through the gate to the R which leads to Scale Force). Go through further gate at the lakeside (National Trust sign), and turn R towards stream (Sour Milk Gill) coming down the mountainside, soon crossing small footbridge. Turn L, cross second footbridge, and go through small gate into wood. Keep along the

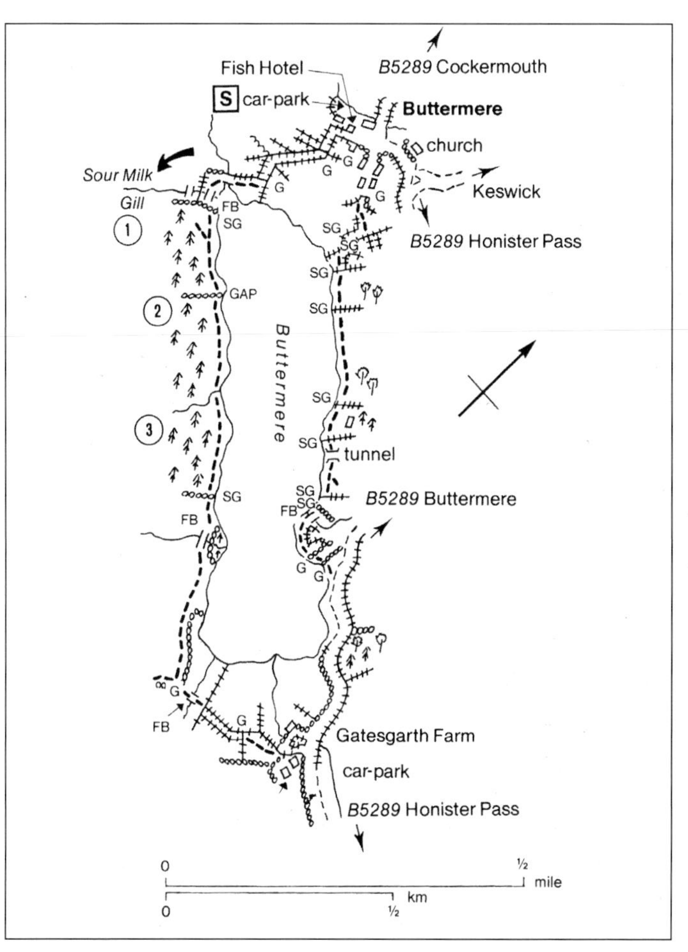

Map 5

very clear path by the water's edge. (The best time to come here is after heavy rain when the appearance of the gill will give a clue to the origin of its name – see ② Sour Milk Gill.)

Later, the path splits; keep along the route by the edge of the water. After about ¾ mile (1.2km) pass through a small gate and continue in the same direction on a clear path which later runs by a wall and crosses a footbridge. At wall corner (beyond end of lake) turn L through gate, go over footbridge, and along path between fences. At farm go through small gate and turn R alongside stream to road. Here turn L over a bridge.

After a short distance the road runs by the lakeside; where it bends away, leave half L along path. (This and other large areas of the Lake District are owned by the National Trust. Of these, the Buttermere valley could perhaps be considered the finest – see ③ the National Trust, for more information about this.) Continue along the path by the lake shore for 1 mile (1.6km), passing through a tunnel under the rock, to far end of lake. Here, where lake shore swings L, go through a small gate and keep by fence in same direction, soon bending R, then L, through a small gate. Go R up rough rocks to small gate and follow very obvious path between fences. Turn L at next small gate and continue back to the village, entering through farmyard. Buttermere church is only a few yards away and is well worth a short visit before your search for refreshments – see ④ the parish church of St James, Buttermere.

① *Buttermere*

A product of the Ice Age and its aftermath, Buttermere was once joined to Crummock Water to form one large lake. Debris coming into the valley, particularly from Mill Beck, produced the flat plain south and west of the village which now separates them.

② *Sour Milk Gill (89–172162)*

The stream coming down the steep slopes of Red Pike to the foot of the lake near the village almost certainly owes its name to its whitish appearance after heavy rain. There are a number of others with this name in the Lake District. A very noticeable feature as one crosses the lower part

of the Gill where it enters the lake is the reddish colour of the rock debris. This is granophyre, an igneous rock similar to granite, which outcrops here and up the length of the gill as one ascends. It is from this rock that Red Pike gets its name.

③ *The National Trust*

The entire lake of Buttermere, Burtness Wood and Horse Close to the south, and Kirk Close to the north, are all owned by the National Trust. Further along the valley, Crummock Water and Loweswater with some neighbouring properties are also Trust possessions. These were obtained partly by gifts from private individuals and partly by purchases both before and after the Second World War. In addition, vast areas around the valley are also covered by restrictive covenants owned by the Trust.

④ *The Parish Church of St James, Buttermere (89–176170)*

There is a local legend that a chantry chapel was built to the east of Rannerdale Farm (by Crummock Water) to celebrate the victory of a Saxon Earl, Boethar, over Norman invaders. More firmly established, however, is the date of the chapel-of-ease with adjoining schoolroom, which was being used in the middle of the eighteenth century.

The present small church was built in 1840 with stone taken from Sour Milk Gill on the opposite side of the valley. A sanctuary at the eastern end and a vestry on the north side were added in 1884. The church's interior was completely refurbished between 1929 and 1935 and electric light installed in 1957. The two stone pillars at the entrance to the church enclosure, and the font bowl, are from the earlier chapel. There is no burial ground at Buttermere and burials are conducted at Lorton about 5 miles (8km) away.

The small building below the church was constructed in 1871 and served as a schoolroom until 1950. It is now a village hall.

ROUTE 6 | King's How

Scenically the most interesting part of Borrowdale – and one of the best in all Lakeland – lies immediately to the south of Grange where the dale narrows dramatically into a ravine nearly ¾ mile (1.2km) long. Called appropriately the Jaws of Borrowdale, it offers two superb viewpoints: Castle Crag and King's How. Neither attains any great height, but both are hills of considerable character well worth climbing for their own sake. Route 9 includes the former and this route the latter.

Length: 3½ miles (5.5km) | Ascent: 1,100 ft (340m) | Starting and finishing point: Bowder Stone car-park on B5289, 5 miles (8km) from Keswick towards Rosthwaite (90–253169) i.e. ½ mile (800m) south of Grange Bridge | Maps: Landranger 90; Explorer OL4

ROUTE DESCRIPTION (MAP 6)

Leave the car-park and turn R along the road (footpath for pedestrians). After about ¼ mile (400m) turn R and follow path, narrow at first through bracken. Go R at junction. A further path joins from R (see ① Greatend Crag). Continue to small gate in wall. Beyond, cross the stream (do not pass through small gate to L) and rise steeply in wood on a clear path. At the top the path swings R alongside a fence. Do not cross fence at stile but continue on R of fence. Path leaves fence to R at small plain, and then climbs, swinging L. Just above broken wall, path turns L and continues to climb to reach small cairn at junction. Turn R for a few yards to memorial stone and summit of King's How. (The Lake District has probably a greater concentration of memorial stones than any

The Bowder Stone

other hill area of Britain – see ② King's How.) The views out across surrounding fells and Derwent Water are magnificent.

Return to cairn and turn R, soon descending steeply to stile in fence. Cross, and after 350 yds (320m), cross wall at ladder stile and continue along clear path. After ¼ mile (400m), by small wind-bent hawthorn tree, path turns half R downhill, leading towards Rosthwaite in valley below. After a long descent, reach edge of coniferous forest. Continue around the edge of the wood to a ladder stile in wall. Cross and follow the clear path down through the wood to the road, where turn R. Ignore the first PFS turn to the R, and after 600 yds (550m) turn R up path (PBS 'Bowder Stone'). The path leads past the Bowder Stone and on to car-park. First-time visitors have two treats in store for them at the Bowder Stone: a ladder to get them to the top, and a hole cut

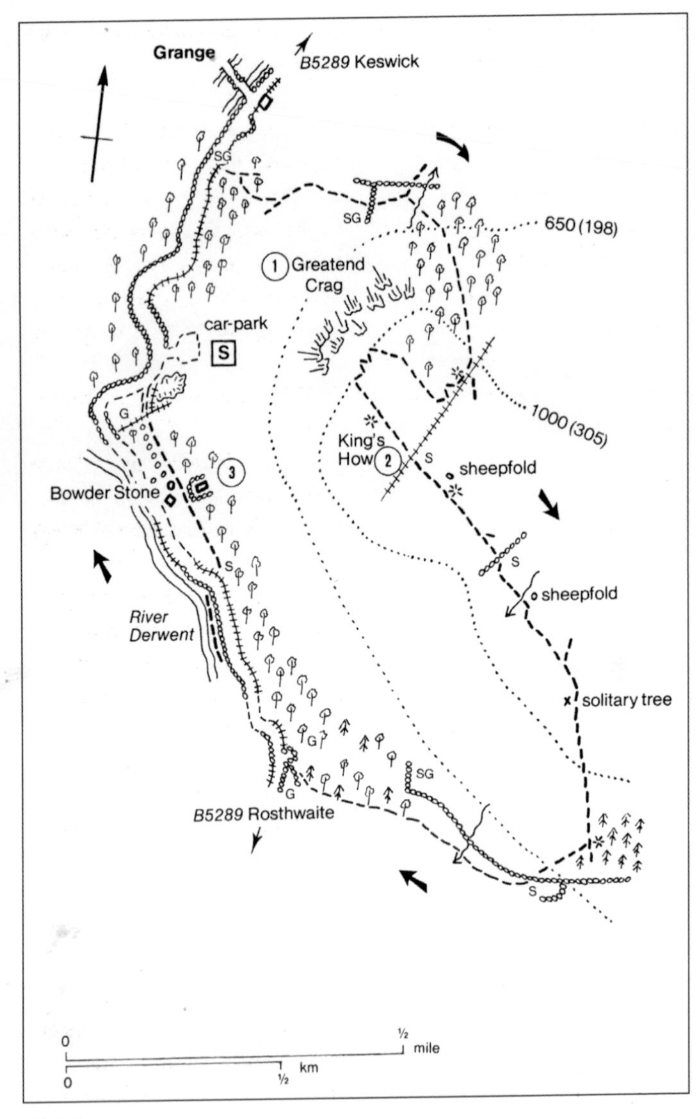
Grange
B5289 Keswick
SG
650 (198)
1 Greatend Crag
car-park
S
G
1000 (305)
King's How 2
S
sheepfold
3
Bowder Stone
S
S
sheepfold
River Derwent
solitary tree
G
SG
G
B5289 Rosthwaite
S
0
½
mile
km
0
½

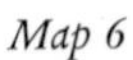
Map 6

through the base by which – if dry – they can shake hands with their companions. See ③ the Bowder Stone.

① *Greatend Crag (90–259170)*

The large and steep cliff over to the right below the summit of King's How on the rise through Cummacatta Wood is Greatend Crag. Although a number of hard routes have been made there, the crag is damp and well covered with vegetation and not therefore as popular as others locally.

② *King's How*

A few feet below the summit of King's How is a slab of rock bearing the following inscription:

IN LOVING MEMORY OF
KING EDWARD VII
GRANGE FELL IS DEDICATED BY
HIS SISTER
LOUISE
AS A SANCTUARY OF REST AND
PEACE
HERE MAY ALL BEINGS GATHER
STRENGTH AND
FIND IN SCENES OF BEAUTIFUL
NATURE A CAUSE
FOR GRATITUDE AND LOVE TO
GOD GIVING THEM
COURAGE AND VIGOUR TO
CARRY ON HIS WILL

King's How, Borrowdale Birches and the Bowder Stone – a total of 311 acres (126 hectares) – were purchased for the National Trust by subscription in 1910, the year of the King's death. Louise was Duchess of Argyll, who died in 1939 at the age of ninety-one.

③ *The Bowder Stone (90–254164)*

The massive boulder – reputed to be about 2,000 tonnes in weight – lying on the western slopes of King's How in the Jaws of Borrowdale is the famous Bowder Stone. It may have fallen from the cliffs above, but an alternative explanation is that it is an erratic carried down by a glacier and left there when the ice retreated at the end of the last Ice Age. The name is derived from the middle English word 'bulder-stan' or large boulder. The small cottage nearby was built by Joseph Pocklington (see page 136) as a home for a guide, towards the end of the eighteenth century. He was also responsible for the hole cut through the base of the boulder, which enabled visitors to shake hands with their guide from opposite sides!

ROUTE 7 | Cat Bells

The ascent of Cat Bells – with the possible exception of the ascent of Skiddaw – must be the most popular walk in the Keswick area. The hardest part occurs at the beginning, with a steep but safe climb up to the small summit. Beyond, the way is much easier: a short ridge walk, followed by a descent down the eastern face, to a good path which skirts along the flanks back to the starting point. There are breathtaking views to both sides of the ridge – over Derwent Water to the east and the Newlands valley to the west – and back over Keswick to Skiddaw and Saddleback. Walkers with young children or long memories will be interested to learn that Cat Bells was the home of Mrs Tiggy-Winkle (see page 199).

Length: 4 miles (6.5km) | Ascent: 1,400 ft (420m) | Starting and finishing point: For walkers without cars the best starting point is Hawes End landing stage, reached by ferry from Keswick (90–251213). Car-owners can use one of the car-parks at 90–247213. Take the Swinside road from Portinscale, going L at each of two junctions. The first car-park is ½ mile (800m) beyond the second junction near a cattle-grid, where the road bends sharply; the second a short distance beyond along the Skelgill road | Maps: Landranger 90; Explorer OL4

ROUTE DESCRIPTION (MAP 7)

From Hawse End landing stage take the path directly ahead through wood to reach road after 110 yds (100m). Turn R, and after 50 yds (45m) take path L (PFS 'Cat Bells') by wall to further road. Go ahead along road and through small gate on L by cattle-grid. (Car-owners join here.) Cut corner by turning L to rejoin road, where turn L. Almost immediately leave road R up

Looking toward Keswick from Cat Bells

wide track (signed 'Bridleway'), and after 50 yds (45m) go back half R. The path climbs very steeply through zig-zags (a memorial tablet to a man whose name should never be forgotten will be passed on the way – see ① Thomas Arthur Leonard) and eventually reaches the first summit. Beyond, follow path along undulating ridge to final climb to summit of Cat Bells. The origin of the name 'Cat Bells' is a sad little story – see ② Cat Bells.

Continue beyond summit, descending to col to meet crossing track at cairn. Here turn L and descend steeply on path through zig-zags (short sections of fence). Lower down path bends R and descends gradually to meet wide lower path. Take next path leading L. Path runs along lower slopes of Cat Bells with superb views

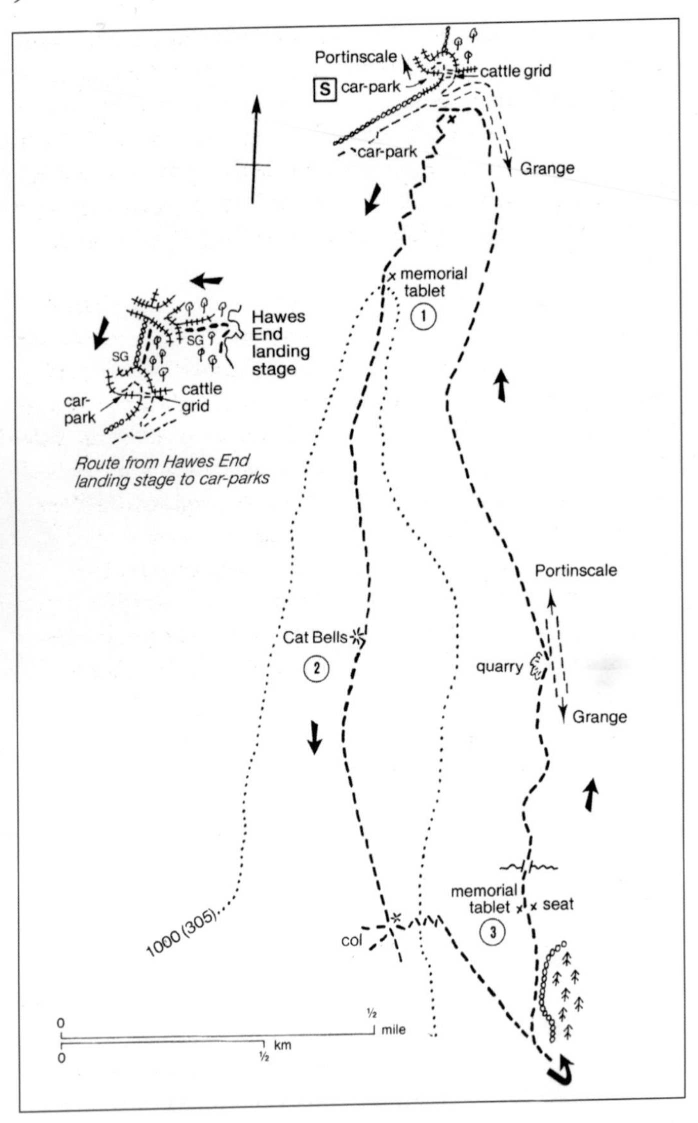
Portinscale
S car-park
cattle grid
car-park
Grange
memorial tablet
1
Hawes End landing stage
SG
SG
cattle grid
car-park
Route from Hawes End landing stage to car-parks
Cat Bells
2
Portinscale
quarry
Grange
memorial tablet
seat
3
col
1000 (305)
0
½
mile
km
0
½

Map 7

R over lake. The beauty of the Lake District has inspired the work of many writers, poets and artists, and a seat placed on the lower path in a particularly beautiful position is a memorial to one of them – see ③ Sir Hugh Walpole. After ¾ mile (1.2km), path reaches road by quarry, but leaves again immediately to resume original direction. Eventually it reaches road again; cross road as it bends to the L and take footpath on R leading to cattle-grid.

① *Thomas Arthur Leonard*

On a small rock outcrop during the steep rise towards the summit of Cat Bells the climber will find a stone tablet to the memory of: Thomas Arthur Leonard. Founder of Co-operative and Communal Holidays and 'Father' of the open-air movement in this country. Born London March 12th 1864. Died Conway July 19th 1948. Believing that 'The best things any mortal hath are those which every mortal shares' he endeavoured to promote 'Joy in widest commonality spread'.

T.A. Leonard was the Minister of a Congregational Chapel in Colne, Lancashire who began in 1891 to organize holidays for local mill people. This led to the formation in 1892 of the Co-operative Holidays Association which set out 'to provide recreative and educational holidays by purchasing or renting and furnishing houses and rooms in selected centres, by catering in such houses for parties of members and guests, and by securing helpers who will promote the intellectual and social interests of the party with which they are associated'. The first property, the Abbey House at Whitby, was leased in 1896.

The Co-operative Holidays Association later became the Countrywide Holidays Association (CHA). In 1913 the Holiday Fellowship was formed, also at the instigation of Arthur Leonard who wished to extend the work of the Co-operative Holidays Association of which he was then General Secretary. This was intended as a companion organization to the CHA, and goodwill between the two organizations continues to this day (see page 23). Many of those connected with the foundation and early years of the CHA have also been closely involved with the setting up of other well-known organizations connected with rambling and the countryside.

A detailed description of some of this early work was given in a book Adventures in Holiday Making *written by Arthur Leonard and published by the Holiday Fellowship in 1934, but now unfortunately long out of print.*

② *Cat Bells*

The Forest of Inglewood, lying to the north-east of the Lake District from Penrith to Carlisle, was described by an early scribe as 'a goodly great forest, full of … all manner of wild beasts'. One of these 'beasts' was undoubtedly the wild cat, for this animal was common in most English forests up to the eighteenth century. It had, in the wild, no enemy of any significance and its eventual extermination in England must be laid firmly at man's door. The destruction of its habitat, and persistent hunting – of which there are records from at least the eleventh century – caused a decline in its numbers, and the last wild cat in England is said to have been killed in Northumberland in 1853. Any 'wild cats' seen since then were almost certainly feral domestic cats. In Scotland the wild cat was reduced to low numbers in the Scottish Highlands and parts of the Hebrides, though it is now more commonly found. Afforestation by the Forestry Commission and some relaxation from persecution may account for this.

In the Lake District wild cats were killed in considerable numbers up to and including the eighteenth century, particularly in the north-east. The name Cat Bells is derived from the Old English word 'Catt' and the Middle English word 'belde' and means 'the den of the wild cat'. Catstye Cam – the name of a small peak to the east of Helvellyn climbed on Route 25 – may also mean 'the ridge with a steep wild cats' path'.

③ *Sir Hugh Walpole (90–249192)*

A tablet placed on a rock face by the path around the base of Cat Bells reads: 'To the Memory of Sir Hugh Walpole, C.B.E. of Brackenburn. This seat is erected by his friend Harold Cheevers, September 1941.'

Hugh Walpole was born in Auckland, New Zealand in March 1884. His father, an Anglican clergyman, had an incumbency there, but came back to England with his family on his appointment as Principal of Bede College, Durham. Walpole was educated in England, at King's School, Canterbury and Cambridge University, afterwards becoming a teacher at a boys' preparatory school. He soon gave this up, however, and became a full-time writer and journalist. His first novel The Wooden Horse *was published in 1909. During his life-time he became a very popular writer, producing forty novels and volumes of short stories and some non-fiction works. His saga 'The Herries Chronicle'* – Rogue Herries (1930), Judith Paris (1931), The Fortress (1932), Vanessa (1933), The Bright Pavilions (1940) *and* Katherine Christian (1943) – *was set in and around Borrowdale and did much to popularize the area.*

In 1923 Walpole bought the house 'Brackenburn', directly down the slope from the seat, where he stayed intermittently until his death there on 1 June 1941. He is buried in the south-west corner of the church-yard of St John's Church in Keswick, a beautiful view-point for the north-western fells.

Moderate Routes

ROUTE 8 | Little Langdale

Little Langdale lacks both the length and the grandeur of its great brother to the north, but it is a delightful place which captures the hearts of all who visit it. The walk described here is, justifiably, one of the most popular in the Lake District. Two waterfalls, Skelwith Force and Colwith Force, are on the way, as is Slaters Bridge, one of the most enchanting footbridges to be found anywhere. Take your time over this walk; it is far too good to be hurried over.

Length: 6 miles (9.5km) | Ascent: 450 ft (140m) | Starting and finishing point: Elterwater village (90–328048). There is a car-park by the bridge | Maps: Landranger 90; Explorer OL7

ROUTE DESCRIPTION (MAP 8)

From the centre of the village walk down to the bridge. Fifty years or so ago the first stretch of this walk would not have been as peaceful or as safe as it is now – see ① the Gunpowder Mill at Elterwater. Immediately before the bridge turn L into the car-park and go through the smaller gate to the R. Follow the clear path by the river. Leave the wood at a small gate and cross open fields to the L of Elter Water (for the origin of this name see ② Elter Water). Pass through a gate and rejoin the river bank on the opposite side, following the lower path to Skelwith Force. At the end, beyond the Force, go between the buildings of a stoneworks to the road, passing a shop and restaurant. Turn R over Skelwith Bridge. Go along the road bending R and up the hill.

Near Elterwater

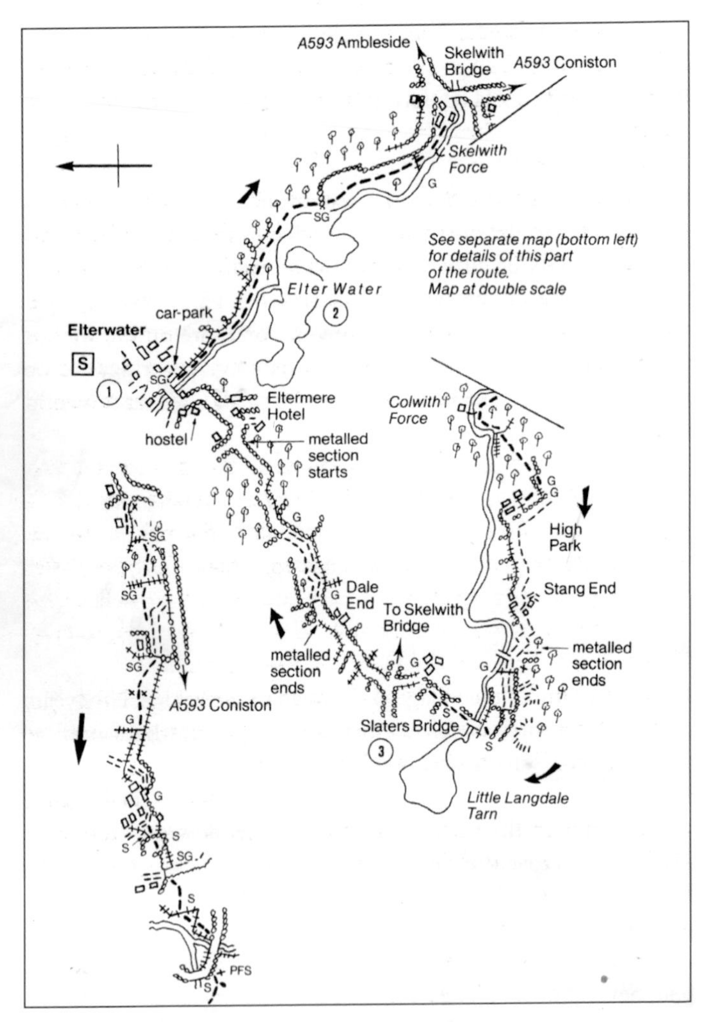
A593 Ambleside
Skelwith Bridge
A593 Coniston
Skelwith Force
G
SG
See separate map (bottom left) for details of this part of the route. Map at double scale
Elter Water
2
car-park
Elterwater
S
SG
1
Eltermere Hotel
hostel
metalled section starts
G
Dale End
G
metalled section ends
To Skelwith Bridge
G
G
S
Slaters Bridge
3
Colwith Force
G
G
High Park
Stang End
metalled section ends
G
S
Little Langdale Tarn
SG
SG
SG
A593 Coniston
G
G
S
S
SG
S
PFS
S

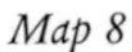
Map 8

Turn R on a footpath immediately after the last cottage on the R (PFS 'Colwith Bridge'), through a small gate into Bridge How Coppice. Enter a wood through a small gate and leave by one at the opposite side. Cross the field to a farm road and go along it to the L of the farm through a gate. Here go through two small gates and cross the field ahead on an obvious path to a gate. Continue ahead between fences to the farm (PFS 'Elterwater and Coniston'). Go through the farmyard, leaving at the far end between two small buildings. Cross a drive and continue on the footpath to a stile in a wall, then cross a field to a further stile. Go on to road. Immediately leave the road through a small gate ahead. The path bends half L downhill to a stile. Descend steeply to river and on to a road.

Turn R along the road. Just before the bridge, go L over a wall and stile (PFS 'High Park ½m'). Take the footpath to the R (signed 'Colwith Force'). Follow footpath through a wood, branching L next to fencing and passing above Colwith Force, later going through a gate out of the wood. Keep by a wall, crossing a gate after 75 yds (70m), and head towards the farm, turning R through the farmyard then L to the road. Turn R.

Continue down this delightfully peaceful road past Stang End Farm. After a small bridge the surface becomes rough. Later the farm road reaches a stream at a bridge. Do not cross but keep on the same side, with Atkinson Coppice on the L and going through two gates. After the second gate go R over a stile to a small footbridge (see ③ Slaters Bridge). From the bridge go up the hill with a wall on the R. At the farm enter a farm road and go to metalled road.

Go L, then immediately R up a narrow road (sign 'Unsuitable for Motor Vehicles'). Keep along this for 1¼ miles (2km) to a T-junction by the Eltermere Hotel. The metalled section ends at a farm, Dale End, and resumes a short distance before the hotel. Turn L back to Elterwater village.

① *The Gunpowder Mill at Elterwater (90–327049)*

The partly wooded area to the north-west of Elterwater – now used as a timeshare enterprise – was the site of a gunpowder mill which operated for about 100 years from 1824, when first licensed, into the period between the two World Wars. It was owned by the Lowwood Gunpowder Company of Kendal, which also worked mills elsewhere. Along with several other mills in the Lakeland area, it supplied blasting powder to quarries and mines throughout the United Kingdom and in many countries overseas.

Gunpowder (Black Powder) is a granular mixture of three materials: carbon, saltpetre (potassium nitrate) and sulphur, a typical mixture having these in the proportion of 15:75:10. On coming into contact with a flame or spark this will readily ignite to produce large quantities of gases, which give enormous pressure when released in a confined space. It is this, of course, which gives gunpowder its great value as a blasting medium. Its use declined from about 1875 with the development of safer and more powerful explosives. Two of the materials used had to be imported: the saltpetre and sulphur, but charcoal was obtained – in the early years at least – from the local burning of wood.

The field by the car-park in Elterwater was used as a firing range, to test the efficiency of samples of powder.

② *Elter Water*

Despite numerous stories to the contrary, the name of this lake at the entrance to Great Langdale was derived from the Old Norse 'Elptarvatn' or 'the lake of the swans'. This probably refers to whooper swans which still visit it, and many other lakes, during the winter.

③ *Slaters Bridge (90–312030)*

This footbridge over the River Brathay in Little Langdale is believed to have been constructed by quarrymen as a more convenient route to the quarries on the Tilberthwaite Fells. It is one of the most interesting and beautiful footbridges in the Lake District.

ROUTE 9 | Castle Crag

Castle Crag is the small peak situated in the Jaws of Borrowdale about one mile (1.6km) to the south of Grange. Despite its low elevation – a mere 950 ft (290m) – it is an imposing height with sides of impressive steepness: factors which were no doubt taken into consideration in its selection as a site for a hill-fort 2,000 years or so ago.

Length: 5¼ miles (8.5km) | Ascent: 1,300 ft (390m) | Starting and finishing point: Car-park down a lane opposite the post office in Rosthwaite, Borrowdale (90–258148) | Maps: Landranger 90; Explorer OL4

ROUTE DESCRIPTION (MAP 9)

Leave the car-park into the road and turn R. Keep straight down the road (PFS 'Grange'), through a farmyard (Nook Farm) and down a lane to the river. Cross at the stepping-stones and turn R through a small gate, following a path by the river. (Alternatively, if the river is high, go down on the R side and cross a bridge.) After the bridge, go through two gates and return to river. By a prominent knoll the path bends to the L and then R. (Do not go through the gate and up the hill.) Soon go through gate into wood.

The path is very clear, keeping within the woods a little way in from the stream. At a fork keep L (PFS 'Grange') and L again further along. Follow cairns through a disused quarry and then a wall gap. Shortly after at a junction go R (PFS 'Grange'). Descending, soon reach a wall gap; beyond continue down to a

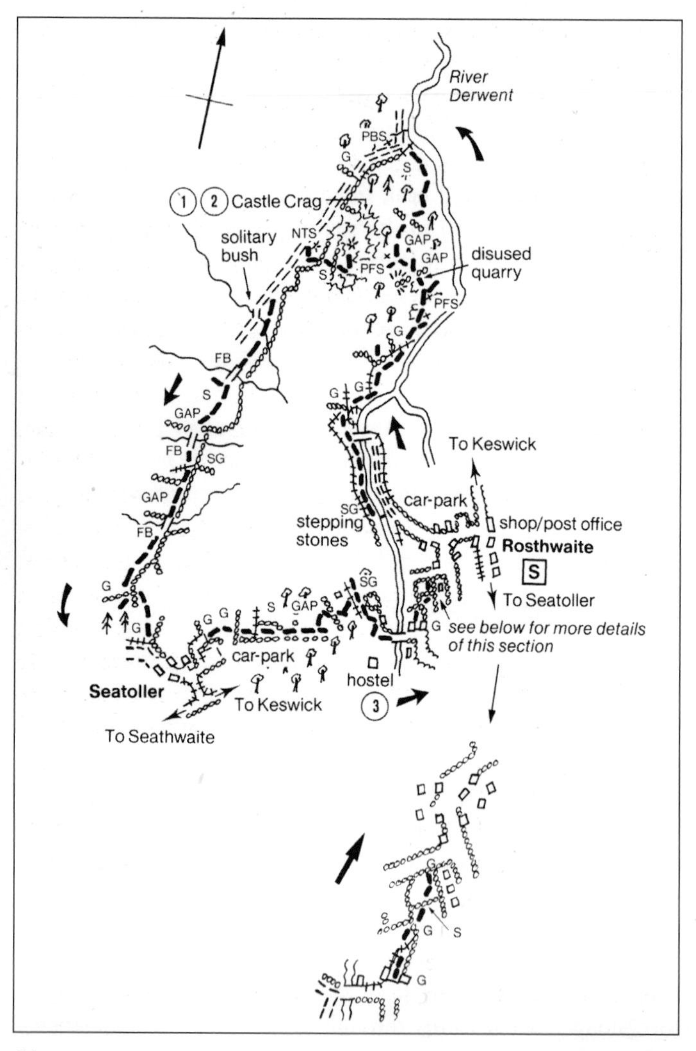
River Derwent
PBS
G
S
1 2 Castle Crag
solitary bush
NTS
GAP
GAP
disused quarry
PFS
S
PFS
G
FB
S
GAP
G
G
FB
SG
To Keswick
GAP
car-park
SG
stepping stones
shop/post office
FB
Rosthwaite
S
SG
G
To Seatoller
G G
S
GAP
G
G
see below for more details of this section
car-park
hostel
Seatoller
To Keswick
3
To Seathwaite
G
S
G

Map 9

wide grassy path. Follow this to the river. Continue by the river on a lovely path to a stile by a gate.

Immediately after the stile go L at a junction (PBS 'Seatoller, Honister'). Go up a wide path, leaving the forest at a gate. Continue up the valley and along a little stream until a large cairn. Castle Crag is now on your L. At the cairn, take a faint track half L which soon bends back half L past a seat (one of the numerous Lakeland memorials – see ① Memorial Seat) to a stile. Go up to a second stile. Turn R for 50 yds (45m), then L steeply up zig-zags. At the top, carefully avoid quarry workings and rise to the summit of Castle Crag, a magnificent viewpoint over the Jaws of Borrowdale and a place steeped in history, which on a fine and clear day is an ideal place for quiet reflection – see ② Castle Crag. Descend by the same path.

At the large cairn back in the valley, turn L, i.e. resume your original direction. Continue for about ¼ mile (400m), then leave the main track half L on a side path at a cairn, following an arrow. (If you miss this, you will pass a hawthorn bush by a stream a short distance further along.) Follow path to a footbridge. Beyond, turn L, over a stile and then on with a wall on your L (do not go through the gate). Eventually reach a corner where three walls meet with two gates, about ¾ mile (1.2km) from the footbridge. Go through the L-hand gate and follow the footpath downhill to a road (PFS 'Seatoller'). Turn L into Seatoller.

Walk through the village and turn L into the car-park. Immediately after the small bus shelter turn L, passing toilets. At the top turn R to a gate. A few yards further go L at a junction and leave the wall, climbing into woods. Go through a further gate in wall and later over a stile by a gate in a fence. Follow the clear path through the woods (Johnny Wood), passing through a gap between walls. Some 150 yds (140m) further along meet another wall coming down on the L. Shortly after, the path swings L and then R and descends to a gap in a wall. From there descend steeply to a small gate in a fence. Beyond, turn R and ahead of the hostel (see ③ Longthwaite (Borrowdale) Youth Hostel) turn L to a bridge (PFS 'Stonethwaite, Rosthwaite').

Go up the road, and where this bends R go L through a gate between cottages. Go through a gate and continue on the R side of the field to a gate in a field corner. Go half L across the next field to a stile. Continue past several houses to a gate and lane. Turn R, then L, and continue back to the car-park.

① *Memorial Seat (90–249159)*

By the seat low down on Castle Crag is a memorial plaque: 'The land surrounding the summit of Castle Crag was given to the Nation in memory of Sir William Hamer, M.A., M.D., F.R.C.P., by his wife Agnes, whom this seat commemorates. 1939'.

② *Castle Crag (90–249159)*

Castle Crag was given to the National Trust in 1920 by Sir William Hamer and his family in memory of his son John Hamer, 2nd Lieut. 6th KSLI (born 8 July 1897, killed in action 22 March 1918) and of ten other men of Borrowdale who were killed in the First World War. The crag was the site of a small hill-fort of uncertain date, although Roman pottery has been found there. There are still some traces of this fort around the summit, which was situated at a strategic point in the Borrowdale valley, a very narrow stretch between areas of wide flat land known as the Jaws of Borrowdale. Its precipitous slopes would have made it a formidable position to assault. The name of Borrowdale, in which Castle Crag resides, was derived from the Old Norse 'Borgardalr' or 'Borgarárdalr', meaning the 'valley with a fort'.

Extensive quarrying has taken place around the hill. The valley between Castle Crag and the eastern slopes of High Spy is thought to have been formed during the Ice Age when water draining down from the fell was forced to run parallel to the edge of a glacier which filled the main valley of Borrowdale. Accelerated erosion took place along a fault line.

Castle Crag from King's How

③ Longthwaite (Borrowdale) Youth Hostel (90–255142)

This is a purpose-built hostel which opened in 1939. An extension was added thirty years later but not, unfortunately, in the Canadian red cedar of the original building. Above the fireplace in the Communal room there is a mural of Pillar and the head of Ennerdale by the well-known local artist, W. Heaton Cooper.

ROUTE 10 | The Ascent of Hay Stacks

Frank Smythe, a famous Everest climber of the 1930s, is usually credited with the observation that altitude is not the only – or indeed the most important – factor in assessing the 'worth' of a mountain. Nowhere is this better illustrated than in the case of Hay Stacks. Although failing to reach the generally accepted figure of 2,000 ft (610m), which would qualify it as a mountain, it has nevertheless more character than many hills of much greater height. Walker and writer Alfred Wainwright called it "the best fell-top of all," and his ashes were scattered here in 1991. Most people who climb Hay Stacks fall in love with it.

Length: 4½ miles (7.5km) | Ascent: 1,700 ft (520m) | Starting and finishing point: Car-park by Gatesgarth Farm at eastern end of Buttermere (89–195150) | Maps: Landranger 89; Explorer OL4

ROUTE DESCRIPTION (MAP 10)

Leave the car-park and turn R along the road. Do not cross bridge but turn L between fences (PFS 'Buttermere, Ennerdale'). Go through small gate and then another to the L, crossing field to pick up path along fence and then between fences. In the next field go over bridge and through a gate at wall corner. Do not follow path to R, but continue up steep path ahead. This soon bends L, crossing wall, and climbs obliquely up the hillside with a broken wall on the L, soon passing through a small gate. Higher still the path crosses a further wall at a gap and continues to a col (Scarth Gap).

Just past the large cairn on the col, turn L and follow the path which bends R. After a few yards turn L up a steep path. The

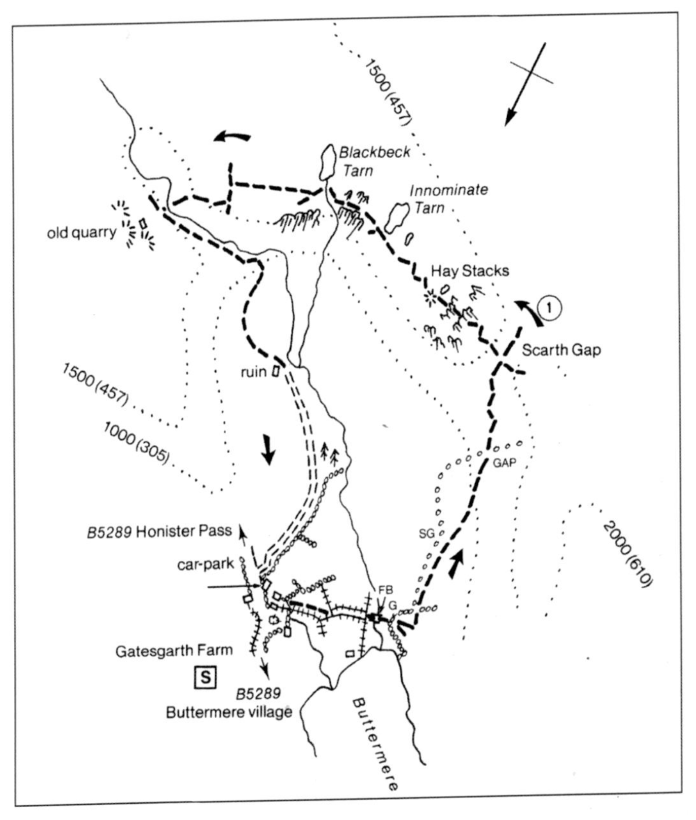

Map 10

ascent to the summit is steep and rough with stretches of broken rock, but with one or two wonderful grassy ledges on which to sit and rest. The summit is a cairn situated to the L of a small tarn. The rise from Scarth Gap to the summit of Hay Stacks offers exciting glimpses of Ennerdale over to the right, to be explored more fully in Routes 33, 35 and 40. But, in the meantime, see ① Ennerdale Forest.

On the way up Hay Stacks

A path continues beyond the summit, past another cairn and descending slowly to pass a further tarn on your R (Innominate Tarn). Just after tarn, on a very clear path with cairns, descend and traverse ledge with deep gully on L and cliff on R. At end bend R and cross stream coming from a second tarn (Blackbeck). Rise from stream and continue on obvious cairned path, bending R after a few yards. After 500 yds (460m) where path comes from R, turn L, and 125 yds (115m) further along go R at junction; the path is marked by a cairn. Follow the path towards spoil heaps on hillside, soon crossing stream and rising to cross-track. Turn L.

Follow this lovely path downhill as it goes in a wide arc across the hillside, rocky at first but smoother down in the valley. After 1½ miles (2.4km) reach the road by car-park and Gatesgarth Farm.

① *Ennerdale Forest*

The first purchase of land in Ennerdale by the Forestry Commission was made in 1925; some of their holdings were leased in 1927 to the National Trust, with whom it now works to manage the area. Planting of Ennerdale Forest began in 1926 and was largely completed by 1950. The principal tree species used are Norway spruce, Sitka spruce, European larch and Japanese larch. The main body forms a compact block from the north-east shore of Ennerdale Water up the valley on both sides of the River Liza to just beyond Hay Stacks. There are, in addition, several smaller areas to the west and south-west of the lake. With a third partner, United Utilities, the woodlands are now being felled and restocked progressively, and the opportunity is being taken to improve the appearance of the forest, working to detailed landscapeprescriptions. The area is now known as 'Wild Ennerdale'; more information on the work being done there can be found at www.wildennerdale.co.uk.

Under Commission byelaws visitors' cars are not allowed to enter the forest area, but may be left at the free car-parks provided at Bowness Knott, Bleech Green and Broadmoor. In addition to paths with public right-of-way, about 16 miles (26km) of forest road have been opened to the public, together with two long-distance trails, the Nine Becks Walk and Smithy Beck Trail (see page 318).

ROUTE 11 | The Traverse of Blencathra (Saddleback)

Compared to its close neighbour Skiddaw, Blencathra is a neglected mountain, yet it is superior in almost every way. Although fairly short, the route described here, which uses Sharp Edge for the ascent and Hall's Fell Ridge for the descent, is one of the finest mountain expeditions in the Lake District. Walkers of a nervous disposition should note however – preferably before starting – that Sharp Edge is a narrow rock arête with fair exposure. Nor is that all, for the exit up Foule Crag at the end of the arête will probably be thought harder. Hall's Fell Ridge is a difficult descent in places, and this is not a walk for the beginner, or on a cold day when the icy ridges can be dangerous. This is a short walk but a challenging one!

Length: 4½ miles (7.5km) | Ascent: 2,100 ft (640m) | Starting point: Scales on A66, 6 miles (9.5km) from Keswick towards Penrith (90–343269). Cars may be parked in the lay-by or in the village. Finishing point: Threlkeld just off A66, 4 miles (6.5km) from Keswick towards Penrith (90–320254) | Maps: Landranger 90; Explorer OL5

ROUTE DESCRIPTION (MAP 11)

From Scales, walk along A66 towards Keswick for about 200 yds (185m). Turn R up footpath between two cottages (PFS). Go through small gate in wall and turn R, taking path which slowly climbs up hillside away from wall. After about 600 yds (550m) the path swings L. After a further 225 yds (210m), climb steeply up L and through short zig-zags to go around the top of a small crag. At the top the path contours along hillside to a broad col.

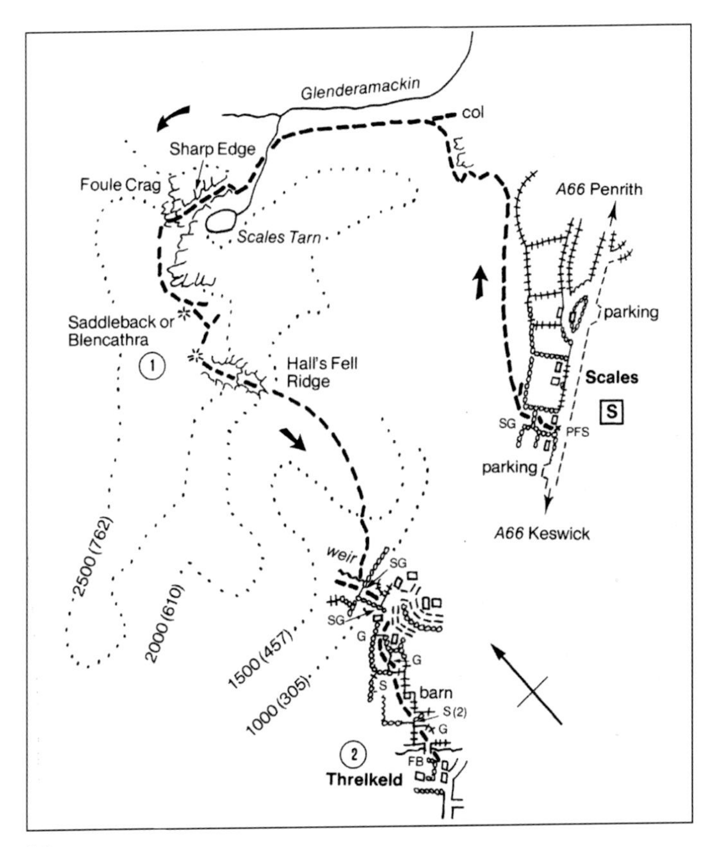

Map 11

Continue over to meet second path coming in from R. Go L along this, through valley to L of stream. Eventually by two cairns at stream junction the path swings L, crosses subsidiary stream, and rises on R bank to tarn (Scales Tarn).

Sharp Edge is the prominent arête to the R of the tarn. Climb path to its R edge and continue along arête. At end continue directly ahead up the rocks (Foule Crag) to reach the grassy top

Sharp Edge on Blencathra (Saddleback)

of the ridge. At the top follow path along the edge to the L, to reach the summit (cairn). An alternative and easier way up, avoiding Sharp Edge, can be taken by forking L by the tarn and following the clear path across the hillside. The origin of the name of this mountain is not at all obvious when you are standing by the sum-

mit cairn, but it is from a point about 4 miles to the east of it – see ① Blencathra (Saddleback).

At the summit go L from your approach route to the top of Hall's Fell Ridge (165° magnetic). The ridge is narrow and the way down will be obvious after an initial scramble down an indistinct rocky path. Where the ridge broadens much lower down towards the fell wall, the path swings to the R to cross a stream above a small weir. After crossing, turn L and go through a small gate in wall corner (by sheepfold) and down path by wall to second small gate. Continue ahead to PFS, where turn R to gate to R of farmhouse. Keep to R of wall, then hedge, to gate. In next field cross corner to ladder stile, and in further field keep to R of barn to ladder stile. Cross stile a few yards away and go across field to gate and footbridge. Pass cottages to enter Threlkeld. This is not, perhaps, the loveliest of Lakeland villages, but there is more to it than is obvious at first sight – see ② Threlkeld.

① *Blencathra (Saddleback)*

The mountain is unusual in having two names in common usage. Blencathra is the more ancient and is probably of Celtic origin; Saddleback appeared about 200 years ago. It is likely that both relate to the characteristic shape of the mountain, which resembles a chair or saddle when viewed, for example, from the A66 around Penruddock as one approaches from the direction of Penrith.

② *Threlkeld (90–320253)*

Although there are remains of an earlier settlement on the rising slopes to the south of the Glenderamackin river, the first records of the present village are from early in the thirteenth century. Although originally probably largely concerned with agriculture, the opening of the lead mines nearby at Gategill in the seventeenth century and the granite quarry to the south towards the end of the nineteenth have given Threlkeld a semi-industrial atmosphere. Nowadays, it is to a large extent a dormitory village for Keswick, with a fair proportion of holiday cottages.

The present church was built in 1777 on the site of an earlier one. The two bells and three tablets which now hang in the church, and an old chalice, are relics of the former building. A major restoration of the interior took place in 1910–11.

The school at Threlkeld was built in 1849 to replace an earlier one. Under the will of the Reverend Christopher Cockbain, who had retired to Threlkeld where he was born, a sum of money was set aside so that each child could receive a copy of the New Testament on leaving the school at eleven years of age.

ROUTE 12

The Ascent of Great Gable (via Windy Gap)

Although Great Gable is far from being the highest peak in the Lake District – there are seven others of greater altitude – there is no other which is as popular or as well-loved. It was highly appropriate, therefore, that the view from Wast Water, which includes Great Gable as its central feature, should have been chosen as the National Park emblem. Its bold and imposing shape, its magnificent rock scenery, its situation within the main walking and climbing area of Lakeland, and finally its assured place in the early history of British rock-climbing are all significant factors in its popularity. To climb Great Gable by any route is a highly rewarding experience.

Length: 6 miles (9.5km) | Ascent: 2,450 ft (750m) | Starting and finishing point: National Trust car-park at the top of Honister Pass (Honister Hause) on the B5289 road from Borrowdale towards Buttermere (89–225135). (All YHA members will be pleased to discover that there is a very convenient youth hostel only a few yards away – see ① Honister Hause Youth Hostel.) | Maps: Landranger 89; Explorer OL4

ROUTE DESCRIPTION (MAP 12)

(No visitor to Honister Hause can fail to notice the ravaged hillsides on both sides of the pass nor the sight and sound of quarrying activity. This is the famous Honister Quarry where greenstone has been worked for at least 300 years – see ② the Honister Quarry.) Leave the car-park at Honister Hause and pass the quarry

On the way up Great Gable

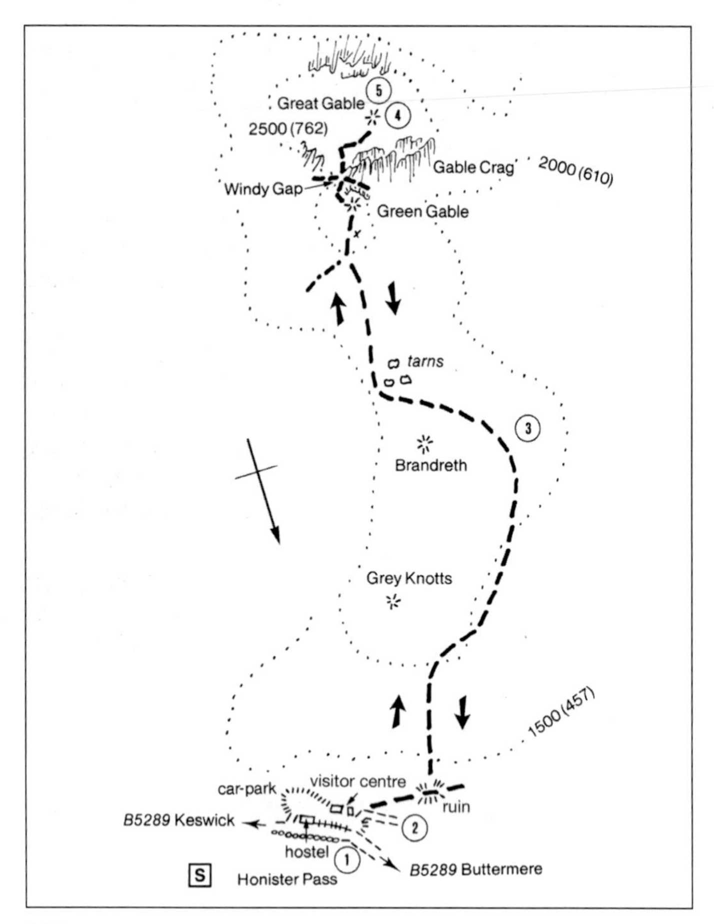

Map 12

buildings and shop going up the quarry road ahead. After a few yards leave the quarry road to the L up a rough path. Almost at the top, at the ruin of the old drum house, turn L on an obvious path – there is a good view of Great Gable to the R of this path.

The path is clear and well-cairned. Walkers using this guide are following along this section the general line taken in the old days by pack-horse trains and illicit whisky smugglers, for a well-known path, Moses' Trod, crosses the fellside hereabouts – see ③ Moses' Trod. Follow the path as it goes across the flanks of Grey Knotts and Brandreth, crossing a stile in a fence and using the cairns to plot your way over the rocky ground. Pass to the L of three small tarns on the col beyond. From there rise up to the summit of Green Gable. Descend steeply on a path which goes half L beyond the summit to reach a large cairn on Windy Gap. Climb up the obvious steep path ahead to reach the summit of Great Gable, which is not only the highest point of an extremely fine mountain but also the site of a memorial to members of the Fell and Rock Climbing Club killed in the First World War. Surely no finer or worthier place could have been found for it. See ④ the War Memorial Area.

Cross the summit half L to reach a prominent cairn on the top of a cliff (see ⑤ Westmorland Cairn) for a superb view into Wasdale before returning to Honister Pass by the same path.

① *Honister Hause Youth Hostel (89–225135)*

The low building by the roadside on the Borrowdale side of the quarry visitor centre at Honister Hause is a youth hostel. The hostel opened originally in 1942 using the old quarrymen's barracks; this was replaced in 1961–2, however, by the present building, which is of almost identical appearance and uses the same site.

② *The Honister Quarry (89–225135)*

It is likely that some working of the greenstone at Honister Quarry took place during the middle of the seventeenth century, although on a fairly small scale. Production increased considerably late in the following century, when a growing population and a movement away from the countryside resulted in the rapid growth of many towns and cities, bringing with it an increased demand for building materials.

Unlike most other quarries in the Lake District, those at Honister were 'Closehead' quarries – enormous caverns reached by levels driven into the hillside – situated on both sides of the Honister Pass. After removal from the quarry face, the rock was 'sledded' down the steep hillside, a quarter-ton per journey, to the dressing-shops. Sledding was carried out using a barrow with two inclined shafts; a workman running between the shafts, and going downhill ahead of the barrow with its load, had the task of controlling both its rate and its direction of descent. A more dangerous and unenviable job can scarcely be imagined! It is hardly surprising that visitors to the quarry commented on the worn appearance of workers there. Few could have been sorry when this horrific method of transport was replaced by tramways using gravity around 1880.

The large blocks of stone were reduced to smaller blocks, called 'clogs', before removal from the quarry. On the dressing-floor these clogs were 'riven' into slates about ¼ in (6mm) thick and then 'dressed' to the required shape.

Working still continues at Honister, where a rough road leads up to open quarries on the flanks of Fleetwith Pike. Most of the hard work has now been taken out by improved mining techniques, the use of lorries, and the introduction of diamond-tipped saws, although riving and dressing are still done by hand in the traditional manner.

③ *Moses' Trod*

This well-known path – 'trod' is an old dialect word for 'path' – runs from Honister Pass to Wasdale Head. Using the contours cunningly to keep climbing to a minimum, it skirts the flanks of Grey Knotts, Brandreth and the two Gables before dropping down into Wasdale. It was used as a pack-horse route until the middle of the nineteenth century for the transport of slate from the Honister quarries to the Esk estuary, a total distance of about 15 miles (24km), but fell into disuse when the road into Buttermere was improved. The identity of Moses is somewhat doubtful, but he is reputed to have been a smuggler who used this route to transport illicitly distilled whisky and wad to Ravenglass *(see page 260)**.*

④ *The War Memorial area*

In 1923 the Fell and Rock Climbing Club of the English Lake District (founded in 1907, and the premier climbing club of Lakeland) purchased an area of 1,184 acres (480ha) above 1,500 ft (457m) to the north and south of Sty Head Pass as a memorial to members who had fallen in the Great War of 1914–18. This area, which included the summits of Kirk Fell and Great Gable to the north and Lingmell, Broad Crag and Great End to the south, was presented to the National Trust for safekeeping.

A memorial tablet on the summit of Great Gable – made of bronze, showing in relief a map of the memorial area with the names of the twenty members of the Club who had fallen in the War – was unveiled on Whit Sunday, 8 June 1924. About 500 people were present at the ceremony. Each year a short and simple service is held around the memorial, nowadays on Remembrance Sunday. At 11 a.m. – the official time of the end of the War in 1918 – a two-minute silence is observed, after which poppies and wreaths are placed at the foot of the tablet.

⑤ *Westmorland Cairn (89–211102)*

The large cairn at the top of the crag on the southern edge of the summit area of Great Gable is called Westmorland Cairn. It was built in the 1870s by the two Westmorland brothers, Thomas and Edward, to mark what they considered to be the finest view-point in the Lake District. It certainly takes some beating.

ROUTE 13 | The Ascent of Pike o' Blisco

Pike o' Blisco suffers by being in the land of plenty, for visitors to Great Langdale are more likely to be attracted by the Langdale Pikes on the opposite side of the valley, Crinkle Crags to the west, or by the Scafells further afield. Yet it is a fine peak with magnificent views from the summit and an intriguing name – whose derivation is as yet unknown – which should not be missed. The Wrynose Pass and Blea Tarn are included in this route. Apart from a very short and easy scramble towards the top of the Pike, nowhere is there any real difficulty.

Length: 7½ miles (10.5km) | Ascent: 2,200 ft (640m) | Starting and finishing point: National Trust car-park by New Dungeon Ghyll Hotel in Great Langdale (90–295064) | Maps: Landranger 90; Explorer OL6

ROUTE DESCRIPTION (MAP 13)

Walk through the car-park away from the hotel towards the entrance. Just before turning L to the road, go R over a stile and up a path through a small plantation (slate sign 'Path to Dungeon Ghyll, Mickleden'). The path climbs the hillside to the R of a wall to a small gate (ignore the gap in the wall earlier); go through this and then immediately turn L to another small gate. Great Langdale is one of the most interesting valleys in Lakeland, historically and geologically – see ① Great Langdale, the long valley.

Follow the path on the L along the wall, soon crossing a footbridge and eventually emerging at a small gate. Turn half L and follow path to another small gate. Follow the path down to a footbridge and a small gate. Do not turn L over bridge, but go through the gate on the opposite side of the road and cross the second bridge just ahead. From bridge go straight ahead along road. Follow road past a campsite to barn. Beyond, continue along road, now with stream on R which soon curves away to the R. After the second bend L in the road, leave it on path to R.

The path runs across the hillside to the L of the stream, passing a small conifer forest on the opposite side. Where the stream branches, keep to the L of the L-hand branch, soon crossing it by a small holly tree. The clear path, well-marked with cairns, now rises steadily, keeping near to the L-hand stream.

No difficulty should now be found in following the path, which is clear and marked throughout with cairns, to the summit ridge, although near to the top two short and easy scrambles have to be negotiated. At the top turn L along the ridge to reach the main summit cairn and enjoy the wonderful views on all sides.

For the return route, retrace your steps for a few yards to a crossing path, where turn R. Follow this path down the mountain side for about 500 yds (460m) to reach an obvious crossing track at a large cairn; Red Tarn is just to the L. Turn L to pass the tarn on its L shore. Continue along this path which descends steadily for approximately ¾ mile (1.2km), over two stiles, to reach the road (see ② the Three Shire Stone) near to the summit of Wrynose Pass. Although not obvious at this point – or anywhere else for that matter, if not sought out – the Wrynose Pass marks the route taken by an important Roman road which ran from Ambleside to Ravenglass – a tortuous path, contrary to the generally held belief that Roman roads always ran in dead-straight lines. (See ③ the Roman Road.)

Turn L and descend with road for just over 1 mile (1.6km) until a wall meets the road on the R. At the public footpath sign leave half L across a flat grassy area (no path at first) to pick up a path through bracken. Follow this very clear path for ⅔ mile (1.1km), passing a ruin and a wall to the R, towards a prominent rocky peak. Just before the peak the path bends to the L by a stream to pass it on its L side. Reach small gate into wood. Enter wood,

View across Red Tarn

immediately turning R then L (do not cross footbridge). (Some idea of the scale of the Ice Age in the Lake District can be obtained by reading ④ Blea Tarn.) Walk along path between bushes to a small gate at the far end of the wood. Continue along the footpath by a wall which later bends R. Continue in the same

direction to gap in wall; here the path bends half R by fence to road via a gate near cattle-grid. Turn L.

Where the road bends L, cross fence on R at stile in corner and resume the original line with wall on L soon descending steeply. Pass through small gate into a wood and continue to descend to

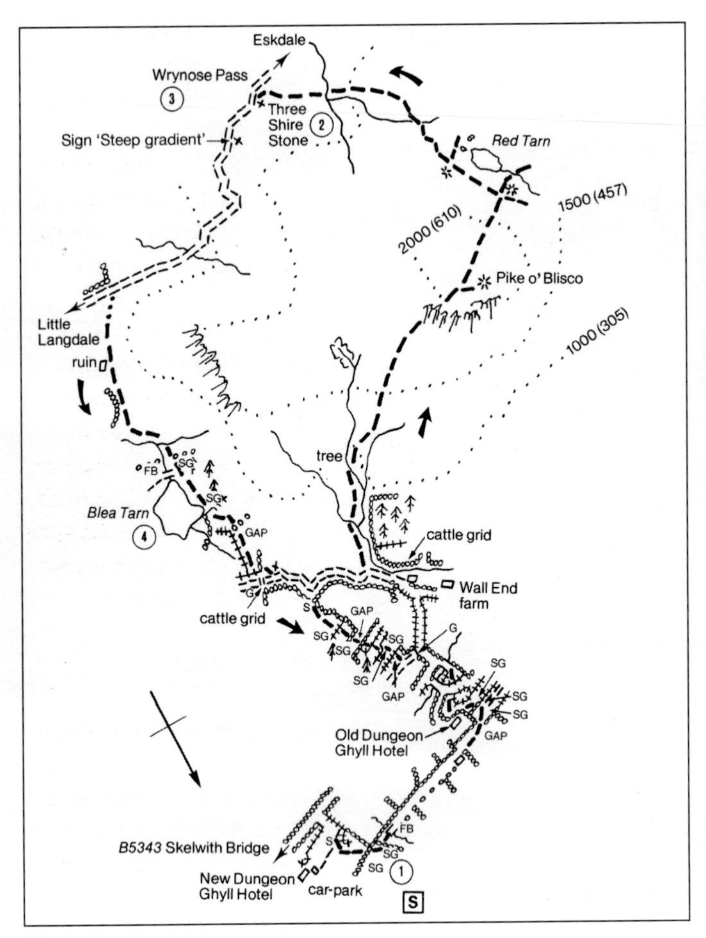

Map 13

further small gate. Beyond, cross narrow field to gap in wall and down through second wood, passing through two more small gates. Finally cross field half R, passing through gap to camp-site road. Here turn L along it to reach road, where through a gate turn R. Follow for ⅔ mile (1.1km) back to car-park.

① *Great Langdale – the long valley*

Great Langdale shows considerable evidence of glacial action and it is likely that the valley was occupied by a glacier on at least three occasions. The last remnant of glacier, which disappeared about 8,200 BC, was probably around the head of Mickleden where there are small moraines. Overdeepening by glacial action led to the formation of a lake below Elterwater village which still exists, and one around Chapel Stile, which has now disappeared due to natural infilling.

The farms and villages of the valley are mainly located on the north side, where they receive greater periods of sun and generally higher temperatures. The name Langdale means 'the long valley'.

② *The Three Shire Stone (90–277027)*

Before the boundary changes of 1974 the area of the National Park was divided between three counties: Cumberland, Westmorland and Lancashire. The tall monolith by the summit of Wrynose Pass was erected to mark the meeting point of these three counties. Westmorland – a delightful county, beloved by many – was eliminated altogether by the 1974 changes, and the boundaries of Lancashire were altered considerably in order to create a new county, Cumbria, within which the entire area of the National Park now lies. The name Cumbria has, admittedly, a good ring about it, but not as good, I think, as those that it replaced. The word 'Lancashire' *is on the west side of the stone, and* 'W.F. *1816*' *on the other. On the hillside across the road from the Three Shire Stone is a superb example of a glacial erratic – a large boulder carried down by a glacier during the Ice Age and left behind on its final retreat.*

③ *The Roman Road*

The line of the modern road from Little Langdale to Eskdale over the Wrynose and Hard Knott Passes marks the approximate course of a Roman road probably constructed in AD 79–80 by army engineers during the campaign of Agricola against the northern tribes. It is likely, therefore, that – both in its inception and in its later use – it was primarily a military road used for the passage of armed patrols and supply trains rather than by commercial and civilian traffic. It ran from the Roman fort of Galava, slightly south of Ambleside – where it probably linked up with the road going north-east over High Street (see page 276) and another heading southwards to Lancaster – to a harbour at Ravenglass. It was considered sufficiently important to be included in the Antonine Itinerary, an official list of Roman roads compiled during the third century. Although in general most Roman roads follow a very straight alignment, there are exceptions to this, particularly in mountain areas where the Roman engineers deliberately planned their routes for the convenience of future users. Nowhere is this clearer than over the Wrynose and Hard Knott Passes, where the road followed a tortuous path in its bid to provide easy gradients. Going via Skelwith Bridge and Little Langdale, it began to climb at about Fell Foot Bridge, remaining on the north side of the line of the present road to the Three Shire Stone. It returned again to the north at the beginning of Wrynose Bottom and remained there until it crossed the River Duddon at approximately the same place as the present bridge. From there it went via Black Hall to the fort at Hard Knott Pass (see page 145) and then down into Eskdale.

④ *Blea Tarn (90–293044)*

During the Ice Age, when the main valley of Great Langdale was occupied by a glacier, it is likely that for some periods a subsidiary flow developed over the col which separated it from Little Langdale, i.e. to the north of the present site of Blea Tarn. As a result the col itself was lowered considerably by ice erosion, which also produced the characteristic shape of the valley in which on the main valley floor, the ice over it would still have been several hundred feet thick.

The tarn and a considerable area around it were acquired by the National Trust in 1971. Its name is derived from the Old Norse word 'blá' for 'dark' – hence 'the dark tarn'.

ROUTE 14 | Around Derwent Water

The circuit of Derwent Water is one of the classic walks of the Lake District. There is a short stretch of road through Portinscale early in the walk and another past the Lodore Falls Hotel, but otherwise the way is along excellent paths, much of it through magnificent woodlands. The views across the lake and to the surrounding fells are superb at almost every point, but that from Friars Crag late in the walk is probably the best. The going throughout is very easy with virtually no climbing and it is only the length which brings this walk into the moderate category. The lake launches – which run a regular service clockwise and anti-clockwise – can be used to break the journey at several points.

Length: 10 miles (16km) | Ascent: 150 ft (50m) | Starting and finishing point: Moot Hall, Market Square, Keswick (89–266234) Maps: Landranger 89 or 90; Explorer OL4

ROUTE DESCRIPTION (MAP 14)

Leave the Moot Hall (but not before reading ① the Moot Hall, Keswick) from the north-western end (i.e. the opposite end to the main entrance of the Information Centre) and cross Market Place. Continue along Main Street to the bridge over the Greta (about 550yds, 500m). Immediately after the bridge turn L (PFS 'Portinscale ½ mile'). After 60 yds (55m), turn R through a small gate and follow the clear path across two fields, separated by a small gate, to a road, where turn L. Cross the suspension bridge and continue down the road to a T-junction and take the L fork. (It is worth making a short detour at the T-junction, up the road to the right – see ② Wells in Portinscale.) After about 700 yds

(640m) the road turns sharp L, then later R. At the right bend turn L down a lane (signed 'Nichol End Marina and Launches') to lake.

Just before the lake, turn R and go up to R of Nichol End Marina. By house cross to wide path opposite and follow through woods to gates of Lingholm Gardens. Go through small gate to R of entrance (PFS 'Catbells') and follow path between fences. At end, cross field with Cat Bells ahead of you to small gate and footbridge on far side and continue again between fences to road.

Turn L, pass drive, and take path (signed 'Launch Jetty') on L to Hawse End landing stage. At lake turn R and follow the path by the shore. Cross stile and follow fence to path which bends L through wood. At end go half R across field to Low Brandelhow landing stage and gate. Go through gate and follow path by shore through wood for ⅝ mile (1km) to High Brandelhow landing stage.

Immediately afterwards follow path as it swings R, and go up banking (steps). At the top go ahead to small gate. Beyond, turn L to shore and on towards boathouse. Pass between huts and house to gate. Continue along drive, turning L on path opposite 'The Warren' cottage. Reach shore and follow path along it, eventually reaching small gate in stone wall. Cross, and follow path beyond over clear ground. After 75 yds (70m), go L at junction. Path is indefinite but passes to R of prominent clump of trees to reach board walks leading towards bridge over river and across the field to road. Some very fine crags will be seen ahead and to the right during the next mile or so – see ③ Rock-climbing around Derwent Water.

Turn L and walk along road for ¾ mile (1.2km), passing the Lodore Falls Hotel. For much of the distance until the Kettlewell car-park, a path just to the right of the road can be followed to avoid the traffic. 225 yds (210m) after the car-park turn L through small gate to shore and follow path around headland, returning to road by Ashness landing stage. A large house will be visible

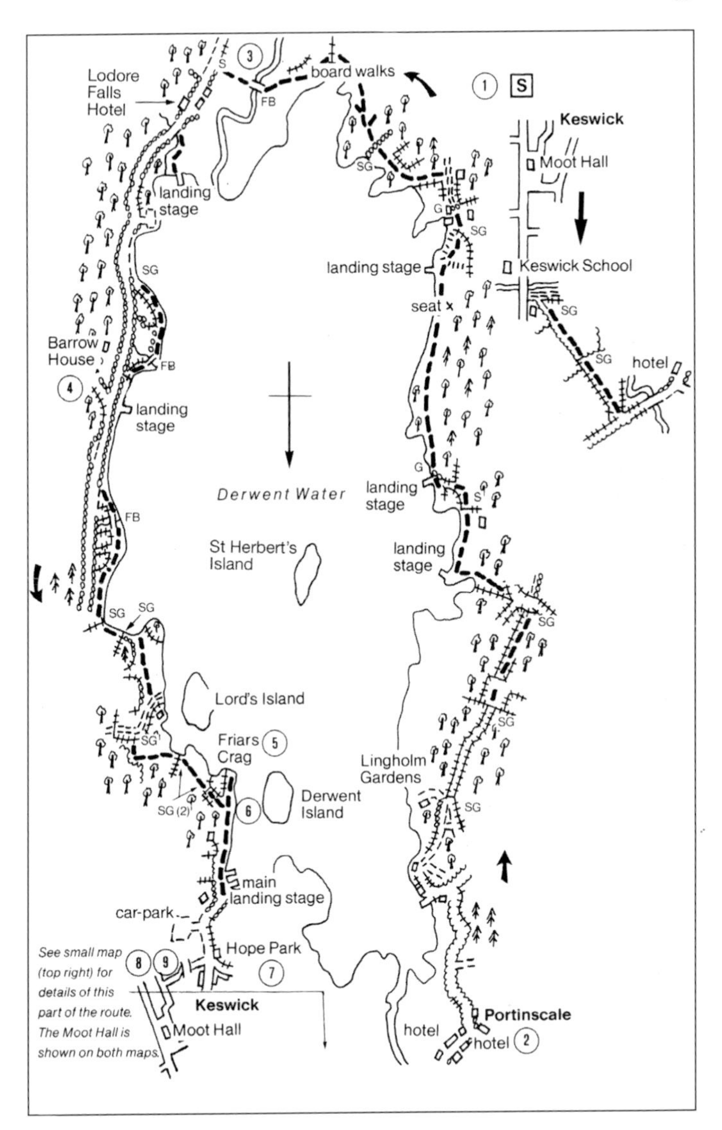
3
board walks
1
S
Lodore
Falls
Hotel
FB
Keswick
Moot Hall
SG
landing
stage
G
SG
landing stage
Keswick School
SG
seat
SG
Barrow
House
FB
SG
hotel
4
landing
stage
G
Derwent Water
landing
stage
S
FB
St Herbert's
Island
landing
stage
SG
SG
SG
Lord's Island
SG
SG
Friars
Crag
5
Lingholm
Gardens
SG (2)
6
Derwent
Island
SG
main
landing stage
car-park
Hope Park
See small map
(top right) for
details of this
part of the route.
The Moot Hall is
shown on both maps.
8
9
7
Keswick
Moot Hall
Portinscale
hotel
hotel
2

Map 14

The path to Cat Bells from the shores of Derwent Water

up to the right – see ④ Barrow House. Continue on road for further ¼ mile (400m) and then (where wall ends) turn L into woods. Follow path through woods, at end swinging R to wall. Do not go into road but continue to follow path by shore through two small gates. After second gate, path goes half R across field to reach drive. Go R on drive and follow past house. Just before it re-enters wood, turn L through small gate, entering through trees. The path is now very clear, later crossing footbridge and swinging L to reach shore at small gate. Continue along path close to shore, passing Friars Crag which has strong associations with John Ruskin. A path to the L after a small gate will take you up to the crag. A monolith to Ruskin's memory will be found surrounded by undergrowth a few yards from the crag

– see ⑤ the Ruskin Monument. Follow path back to Keswick, passing the 'Theatre by the Lake' and turning R through the subway at the end of Hope Park. Many of the features of interest on this route are crowded into the last half-mile or so – see ⑥ to ⑨ below.

① The Moot Hall, Keswick (89–266234)

The word 'moot' means 'to argue, plead or discuss' and hence a Moot Hall was a 'discussion hall' or, as we would say nowadays, a town hall or Council Chamber. The Moot Hall in Keswick was built in 1813 on the site of an earlier building. The outside was once covered with white plaster, but this has been stripped away to reveal the original stonework. It served as a town hall until the new council offices became available. The ground floor which had open arches – now closed – served as a market until 1971, and is now used as an Information Centre. The main hall above is used regularly for lectures. An interesting feature is the clock which has only a single hand.

② *Wells in Portinscale (90–252236)*

A short diversion up the road to the right at the junction in Portinscale leads to two fine examples of village wells. The one on the left is Dorothy Well; the one on the right has the inscription:

> Whosoever drinketh of this water shall thirst again,
> But whosoever drinketh of the water that
> I shall give him shall never thirst.

③ *Rock-climbing around Derwent Water*

Although some attention had been paid to Borrowdale by the early pioneers, rock-climbing in the valley was largely neglected up to about the Second World War. Since then, however, the situation has changed dramatically and the valley has become one of the most popular climbing centres in the Lake District, offering a wide variety of climbs of all standards. It is generally accepted that most credit for this should go to Bentley Beetham, a schoolteacher who had been a member of the very famous Everest expedition of 1924 on which Mallory and Irvine lost their lives. His first discoveries in the valley were made in 1921–2, but the main thrust of his explorations took place during and after the War when he was already over the age of fifty.

④ *Barrow House (90–200269)*

The large building, a short distance up the hill-slope to the right as the small peninsula on the east shore of Derwent Water is rounded, is Barrow House, which has been a youth hostel since 1961. It was built by Joseph Pocklington, a highly eccentric character who lived previously on Derwent Isle. Building began on 26 March 1787, for which his accounts record 'ale at laying foundations 5/-'. The house was occupied ten years later, on 10 January 1797 – on which day Joseph Pocklington wrote, 'Quitted my island this day and arrived safe at Barrow after a very rough voyage.'

The final cost of the house and grounds was £1,655 3s 6¾d (which says a lot about inflation since 1797). There is a beautiful Adam room, and the extensive grounds contain a waterfall 100 ft (30m) high, the result of a stream diversion when the house was built.

In the 1930s it was run as a guest house by Bob Graham (see page 257).

⑤ *The Ruskin Monument (90–264223)*

The tall monolith by Friars Crag on the shore of Derwent Water is a monument to John Ruskin. It has the inscription:

> John Ruskin
> MDCCCXIX – MDCCCC
> The first thing which I
> remember
> As an event in life was being
> taken by my nurse to the brow of
> Friar's Crag on Derwentwater.

Ruskin was born at Holborn, London in 1819, the son of a wealthy wine merchant. During his early years he travelled widely with his parents both in this country and abroad, visiting Keswick on several occasions, the one recounted above occurring when he was five years old. In 1848 at Perth he married Euphemia Chalmers Gray and returned to Keswick for his honeymoon. The marriage was not successful. He lived in London and Oxford until the age of fifty-two, when he bought Brantwood, a mansion on the eastern side of Coniston Water, where he lived until his death in 1900. He is buried in the churchyard at Coniston.

His output, both in quantity and in range of subject, was prodigious. He was an authoritative art critic, the first Slade Professor of the Fine Arts at Oxford, essayist, poet, lecturer and philanthropist – he gave away a fortune inherited from his father. But in addition to that, he will be remembered as a great economist and social reformer. His words: 'I hold it indisputable, that the first duty of a State is to see that every child born therein shall be well housed, clothed, fed and educated, till years of discretion', written in 1867, reveal his deep humanity.

Friars Crag is widely regarded as one of the finest view-points in the Lake District; at its best on warm, still, clear, summer evenings, when one can linger to absorb its beauty, but superb at almost any time. By tradition it is associated with St Herbert and St Herbert's Island on Derwent

Water, and its name is thought to have been derived from this.

⑥ *Canon Rawnsley (90–264224)*

Alongside the path to Keswick just past Friars Crag is a memorial tablet to Hardwicke Drummond Rawnsley, who was vicar of Great Crosthwaite – to the north-west of Keswick – from 1883 to 1917. A tireless worker, he became a County Councillor and a Canon of Carlisle Cathedral, played a part in the foundation of the School of Industrial Art at Keswick which still flourishes, of Keswick School, and of the Blencathra Sanatorium (now the Blencathra Centre). He was also a busy lecturer, prolific author, and champion of local rights: he revived the Keswick and District Footpaths Association and led it in a successful campaign to preserve access to the summit of Latrigg which had been threatened with closure. He was also instrumental in the publication in 1902 of The Tale of Peter Rabbit, *which was the first of Beatrix Potter's books.*

But by far his most important achievement was the foundation of the National Trust in 1895 with Miss Octavia Hill and Sir Robert Hunter. He was Honorary Secretary of the Trust from its inception to his death in 1920. It was during his secretaryship that the important National Trust Act of 1907 was passed which made the Trust a statutory body with the power to declare its land and buildings inalienable. It is perhaps fitting that the Trust holds more land in Cumbria than in any other county. Friars Crag, Lord's Island and a part of Great Wood were given to the Trust in 1922 by subscribers 'who desired that his name should not be forgotten'. He is buried at Crosthwaite church.

⑦ *Hope Park*

The Park was donated to the people of Keswick in 1974 by Sir Percy and Lady Hope.

⑧ *The Abraham Brothers*

The premises on the corner of Lake Road and Borrowdale Road in Keswick formerly belonged to two brothers, George Dixon Abraham

View across Derwent Water

and Ashley Percy Abraham, who played an important part in the early days of rock-climbing both by their own exploits in discovering new routes and by publicizing the sport through their photography.

Both professional photographers – as was their father, who founded the family business in Keswick – they began to climb by about 1890. They climbed together until 1936, George – by far the lighter and more nimble of the two – in the lead. They also formed a very strong team with Owen Glynne Jones, the most dynamic climber of the 1890s, for three years until his death in 1899. The Keswick Brothers' Climb on Sca Fell is named after them, and they were also responsible for other first ascents.

It is, however, primarily as mountain photographers that they will be remembered. Their photographs were used to illustrate a succession of guide books written and published by them, of which their British Mountain Climbs *was re-issued as late as 1948; and for the preparation of postcards which enjoyed enormous sales. Ashley died in 1951 and George in 1965.*

⑨ *The George Hotel, Keswick*

The George Hotel on St Johns Street is the oldest inn in Keswick, going back to at least the sixteenth century. Originally named 'The Bunch of Grapes' it became 'The George and Dragon', and then 'The George' on the accession of George I in 1714. It served as an official counting-house and revenue office during the reigns of Elizabeth I and James I, where German miners paid dues on production of silver. It is also said to have been a centre for a black market in ore and plumbago stolen by the miners. The third Earl of Derwentwater, who lived on Lord's Island on the lake, called here briefly for a tankard of ale before riding off to join the 1715 rebellion of the Old Pretender. It would probably have been better for him if he had stayed longer, for he was beheaded on Tower Hill in London later that year. In the late eighteenth century the front of the building – by now a coaching inn – was rebuilt in a Georgian style.

ROUTE 15 | Harter Fell via Hardknott Castle

Harter Fell is an isolated peak between the Duddon Valley and upper Eskdale (there is another Harter Fell south of Mardale Head). To the south and east it has received some attention from the Forestry Commission, but the rocky summit slopes have mercifully remained clear. It is best climbed by a grassy path coming out of Eskdale from the foot of the Hard Knott Pass, whose excellence will be the source of many happy memories long after the walk is completed.

The most vivid memories, however, will be of Hardknott Castle – the Roman fort of Mediobogdum – both seen at a distance from the summit of the fell in a wonderful aerial view, and passed close by during a detour away from the Hard Knott Pass road. Apart from Hadrian's Wall, which is in a class by itself, few other remains evoke so vividly the tremendous power and vitality of the Roman empire.

Length: 7½ miles (12km) | Ascent: 2,450 ft (750m) | Starting and finishing point: A small car-park in the Duddon Valley just past Birks Bridge on the road from Seathwaite (96–235995) | Maps: Landranger 90 and 96; Explorer OL6

ROUTE DESCRIPTION (MAP 15)

From the car-park cross the wooden footbridge and turn R to follow the river on its L bank and a fence. Where a small forest ends on the L, cross the fence at a stile and continue in the same direction. Pass a prominent rocky hill (Castle How) on your L, keeping close to the river pass through four gates, and then head half

L across a field towards a farm (Black Hall). Do not enter farmyard through the gate but turn L across a stile in a fence and cross field half L to gate in a wall by a small rock outcrop. Turn L and follow path to R of wall. After 90 yds (80m), at a junction go R up the hill away from the wall. Continue to the forest wall – the path disappears as you climb. Go up the hill keeping to the R of the forest, crossing a wall at a ladder stile, and eventually reaching the top of the ridge. Go ahead over a stile and down the far side on a path to road, where turn L.

Where the road swings sharply and steeply down to the L, leave to the R on a faint path. Follow this path to pass the parade ground of the fort (a relatively flat rectangular area) and the ruins of the fort itself (see ① Hardknott Castle) to the R. At the far end of the fort turn L, and drop down the path to the road.

Continue down the road to a young conifer wood on the R and a cattle-grid. Just before the grid turn L and cross a small bridge (PBS 'Dunnerdale 3 miles'). Follow the clear path which passes through two small gates and rises up the hillside. Higher by a stream cross the wall at a small gate and continue up a superb grassy path with magnificent views to L and behind. Later recross wall through a small gate and follow path to L of fence. Ignore paths via stiles to the R, continuing to follow the fence.

Eventually reach forest. Do not enter, but turn L and climb up hill with the forest fence to your R. From the corner of the forest continue along a path away from the fence and up the fellside. Eventually you reach the summit of Harter Fell. (The summit is marked by three spires of rock, of which the centre is marginally the highest.) Move across the summit for a few yards to the north (i.e. to the L of your approach) for a superb view of Hardknott Castle.

On the way up Harter Fell

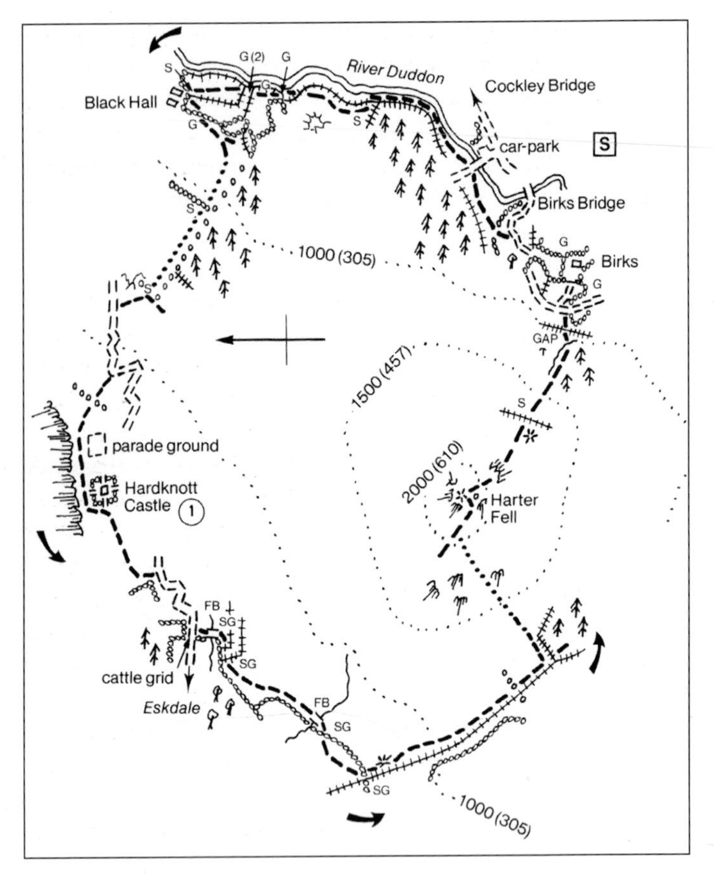

Map 15

Continue beyond the summit, bending to the R from your approach route (133° magnetic). The path is faint and soon descends across boulders. Beyond the boulders the path becomes much clearer and drops to a stile and small gate in a fence. Continue descending in the same direction towards a steep section in a recently deforested area. The path goes over boulders, loose stone and dirt, close to a stream, before emerging at a farm road. Turn L and then soon R, down towards a farm (Birks). Go through a gate and cross to L of buildings, where go through a second gate. Cross to lane opposite. Go down short lane to gate and continue beyond along farm road. At the river do not bend R but go ahead along a path on the L bank to the bridge and car-park where you started.

① *Hardknott Castle (Mediobogdum) (90–218015)*

Built towards the end of the first century AD, or early in the second, the Roman fort at Hardknott was intended to safeguard the great road which ran from Ambleside to Ravenglass, at a strategic point where it passed over the high ground between the valleys of the Duddon and the Esk. It is one of the finest of all Roman remains in Britain.

Situated on a narrow spur coming down from the high fell, with difficult ground on three sides and stone walls 5 ft (1.5m) thick, it would have been formidably difficult to capture, although it would have been regarded primarily as a secure base for offensive operations rather than for defence. Almost square in shape, with a turret at each corner and a gateway along each side, it was very similar in layout to other forts of its size. The main street – the Via Principalis – ran from the north-east gate to that on the south-west side, forming a T-junction with another from the south-east. Along the Via Principalis were the three main buildings of the fort: the granary, the Principia (the headquarters building) and the Praetorium (the house of the Prefect who commanded the fort), while behind and in front were the long barrack-blocks of the ordinary soldiery. Outside the fort, to the north-east, an area was levelled to provide a parade-ground, at the head of which the Prefect's podium can still be distinguished; also outside, and to the south, was the bath-house.

Hardknott was manned by a cohort of auxiliary troops from Yugoslavia, 500 strong, although it is likely that some local Britons would have been recruited into its ranks. Auxiliary troops were drawn from tribes friendly to Rome and were not themselves Roman citizens, although they would be made so on discharge at the end of their service or as a result of some particularly meritorious action. Forts and frontiers were normally manned by them, the legions being kept back in reserve at strategic centres.

The fort wall has been partly restored, the extent of the restoration work being indicated by a narrow slate course. Below the course the wall is original, merely treated to prevent collapse; above it the wall has been reconstructed from fallen Roman facing stones to a height of not more than 6½ ft (2m), which was the maximum height of original work found in position.

ROUTE 16 | Loughrigg

The climb up Loughrigg Terrace, for the wonderful view over Grasmere, is one of the most popular walks of the Ambleside area; an ideal place for a short evening stroll with long pauses for quiet contemplation of the beauty before you. The hilltop itself is a maze of paths over which it is easy to lose your way. This route is circular, reaching the summit from the Terrace, crossing the top before dropping down into Ambleside. The return route is through Rydal Park and by the northern slopes of the fell, passing impressive caverns left by early mining activities.

Length: 9 miles (14km) | Ascent: 1,450 ft (440m) | Starting and finishing point: Old Quarry car-park at the western end of Rydal Water on the A591, 2½ miles (4km) from Ambleside towards Keswick (90–349066) | Maps: Landranger 90; Explorer OL7

ROUTE DESCRIPTION (MAP 16)

From the car-park cross the road and go down the steps (National Trust sign 'White Moss Common'). By the stream turn R and walk past the bridge, passing through a small gate. Keep to the R of the stream through a wood, passing through two small gates and continuing on to reach a footbridge over the outlet of the lake of Grasmere. Go up the steps ahead; at the top turn L and follow the path up to the top of the ridge by a seat just below you. Turn back half R up the Terrace and enjoy the lovely views.

At a wall at the top of the Terrace turn L, climbing up the steep slope. Follow the path to the summit of Loughrigg. From the top

Bluebells on Loughrigg Terrace

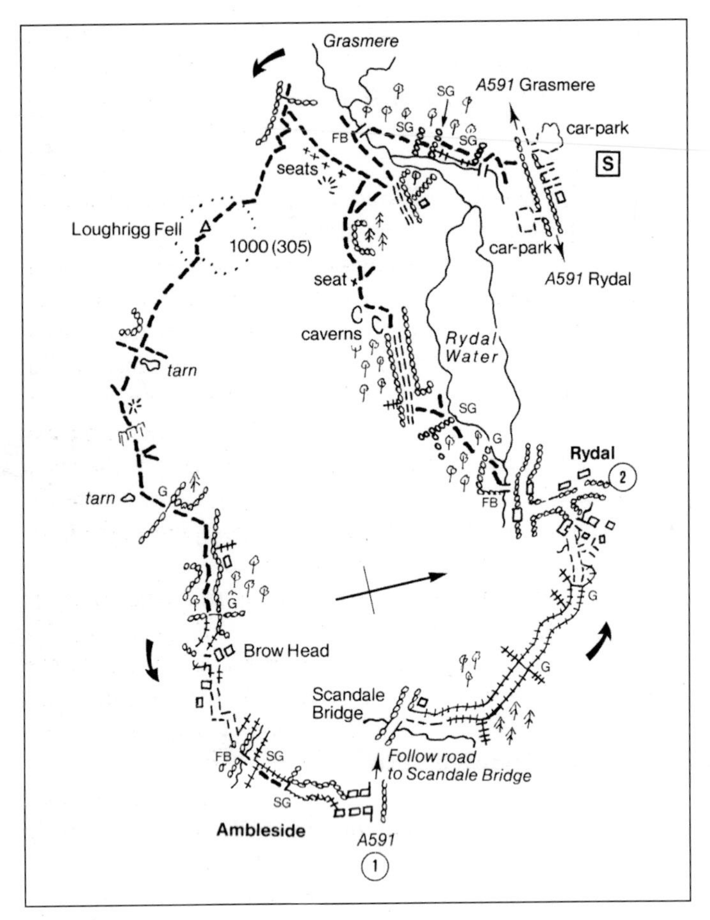

Map 16

you can see lakes Grasmere, Windermere, Elter Water, Esthwaite Water and Loughrigg Tarn, with Rydal Water just hidden. Continue in the same direction, descending into a hollow at a path junction. Keep straight ahead along the obvious path which bends down L into a small valley. Turn R down the valley (cairns). Later the path passes to the L of a wall and then to the R of a small tarn. Continue in the same direction over a ridge and down a lovely grassy path to reach a crossing track after a marshy area. Turn L. After 450 yds (410m) pass a very small tarn on the L. Cross a stream and climb the ridge ahead. The path then bends to the L and goes to a gate in a wall corner.

Continue descending, with the wall on your L. When the wall bends L, stay on the path to a further wall, where go R, following a slate sign for Ambleside. Keeping the wall on your L, pass over a stream and eventually reach a gate at the end of a lane. Go down this lane on a farm road, passing Brow Head Farm, to reach a road by a stream. Turn R, then L, over a bridge. Go straight on through a small gate and along the footpath to reach the main road in Ambleside (A591). It is worth diverting to the R here for a few yards to visit one of the best-known buildings in the Lake District – see ① the Bridge House, Ambleside.

Turn L and walk along the road to a bridge (Scandale Bridge). Immediately after the bridge turn R through large gates (PFS 'Rydal Hall'). Follow the farm road through two gates, and after 1 mile (1.6km), before a bridge, go R towards a house, part of the ecumenical centre at Rydal Hall. Go L between buildings, up past a tea shop, and down a lane to a road. A few yards up the road to the right is Rydal Mount, Wordsworth's home for 37 years: see ② Rydal Mount. Turn L and descend hill to the main road (A591), past the pretty church of St. Mary's. Turn R.

After 130 yds (120m), opposite the Badger Bar, go L down to a footbridge. On the opposite side turn R and follow a path to a gate, and beyond to a small gate. Take the L-hand path at a junction. This climbs slowly to a wide path by a wall. Turn R between woods. Soon pass a large cavern. After this, bend L up the hill to an even larger cavern. Turn R, cross the flat top of a spoil heap. At a path junction by a seat take the L fork, and follow the clear path to the

L of a wood and to the bottom of Loughrigg Terrace. Return to the car-park by the route used earlier.

① *The Bridge House, Ambleside (90–376047)*

The small but enchanting Bridge House which spans Stock Ghyll beside the A591 was built in the early sixteenth century as part of the estate of Ambleside Hall, situated up Smithy Brow to the east. The estate was very extensive, continuing down to the stream, with orchards and pastures on the opposite side. The Bridge House was built with two floors, probably as a summer house, apple store, and to provide a means of crossing the stream. Later, it was used for many purposes: as a tea-room and weaving shop, as a dwelling house for a family of the name of Rigg (who, it is claimed, raised a family of six there!), as a cobbler's shop, pigeon loft, as a store for leather and finally – until its present use – as an antiques shop. It was purchased by public subscription in 1928 and given to the National Trust, becoming the first Information Centre for the Trust in 1956.
In days gone by it was covered with ferns and rock plants and shielded by trees, presenting an even more charming picture than it does today. Rydal Road, which runs past the house, was constructed in 1843.

② *Rydal Mount (90–364064)*

On the first day of May 1813 William Wordsworth with his wife Mary and their three children, and accompanied by his sister Dorothy and sister-in-law Sara Hutchinson, moved into Rydal Mount from their previous home in Grasmere. Wordsworth was to stay there for the rest of his life.

Wordsworth's income up to that point had been fairly limited, but his appointment earlier in that year as Distributor of Stamps for the County of Westmorland – a sinecure providing considerable income but demanding attention to relatively few duties (i.e. the kind of job that most of us dream about) – enabled him and his family to live there in comparative comfort. His reputation as a poet was already established in 1813, but during his time at Rydal Mount

Looking over Grasmere

his fame grew considerably, sufficiently for him to be given a state pension in 1842 and to become Poet Laureate, succeeding Robert Southey, the following year. Wordsworth died at Rydal Mount on 23 April 1850. He was buried in the churchyard at Grasmere.

His sister Dorothy, who lived with him for most of her life, was a writer of considerable talent, best remembered for her journal which she kept from 1798. This is of particular interest for her descriptions of their life at Dove Cottage and Rydal Mount. As with the rest of her work, it was published only after her death.

The house dates from at least 1574, but substantial additions were made to it in the middle of the eighteenth century and again during Wordsworth's time. The garden of 4½ acres – from which there are superb views to the south – was designed by him and is still substantially as he left it. The house has been open to visitors since 1970 and now attracts around 70,000 a year.

ROUTE 17 | Place Fell and Ullswater

A number of writers have commented on the exceptional beauty of the lake shore walk from Sandwick to Patterdale; combined with a crossing of Place Fell, it gives one of the best medium-length walks in Lakeland. The ascent of the Fell – despite a 'false' summit about ¼ mile (400m) before the real one – is fairly short, and the descent is along a path of superlative quality, a perfect combination. The lake shore section is not as easy as might be expected, being rough in places and undulating. This is a walk that will stay in your memory long after the details of some longer and tougher ones have gone.

Length: 8 miles (13km) | Ascent: 2,250 ft (690m) | Starting and finishing point: Patterdale at the southern end of Ullswater (90–394161). The nearest car-park is at Glenridding. There is a hostel about ½ mile (800m) away – see ① Patterdale Youth Hostel
Maps: Landranger 90; Explorer OL5

ROUTE DESCRIPTION (MAP 17)

Go down the farm road to the L of the George Starkey Hut (Club Alpin Suisse), PFS 'Howtown, Boredale', a few yards from the church, as far as Side Farm. Go through the farmyard, and in the lane beyond turn R (PFS 'Angle Tarn Boredale Hause'). Go through a gate, and beyond a cottage go through a second gate. Immediately turn L through a further gate, and follow the obvious path which bends R up the hillside. After ½ mile (800m) reach the col of Boredale Hause. This has been, and is still, a key point in a number of activities – see ② Boredale Hause.

By a sheepfold and a metal cover go half L on a faint path. Follow this path, which grows more distinct, past a second fold and up the hill ahead. Rise up to the prominent cairn on Round How after a short scramble near the top and continue along the ridge to the OS obelisk on the summit of Place Fell.

Go half R on a path dropping down to the L of a small tarn. No difficulty should now be found in following the path to the end of the ridge, and then more steeply down to a sheepfold on a col (Low Moss). Here take the R-hand path which rises and then runs along the slopes high above Bore Dale. About ½ mile (800m) from the fold and near the end of the ridge, leave the edge on an obvious path dropping down to the R. Follow this beautiful path down to a wall in the valley, where turn L. Follow to a metalled road in Sandwick. Turn L.

After 75 yds (70m), go half L on a bridleway (signed 'Bridle-path to Patterdale'). This bridleway runs along the east side of Ullswater back to Side Farm, about 4½ miles (7.5km). Ullswater is one of the most beautiful lakes within the Lake District. It is also one of the most unusual – see ③ Ullswater. No difficulties should be found in following the path. From Side Farm return to Patterdale.

① Patterdale Youth Hostel (90–399167)

The original building was one of the first hostels in the Lake District, opening in 1931. It closed in 1967 and was demolished, making way for the present building which opened three years later. One interesting feature reminiscent of some buildings in Scandinavia is the grass roof on part of the building, which is regularly mowed during the summer.

② Boredale Hause (90–408157)

The col, Boredale Hause, between Patterdale and Bore Dale once carried a pack-horse trail between the two dales; it is now a meeting-place for

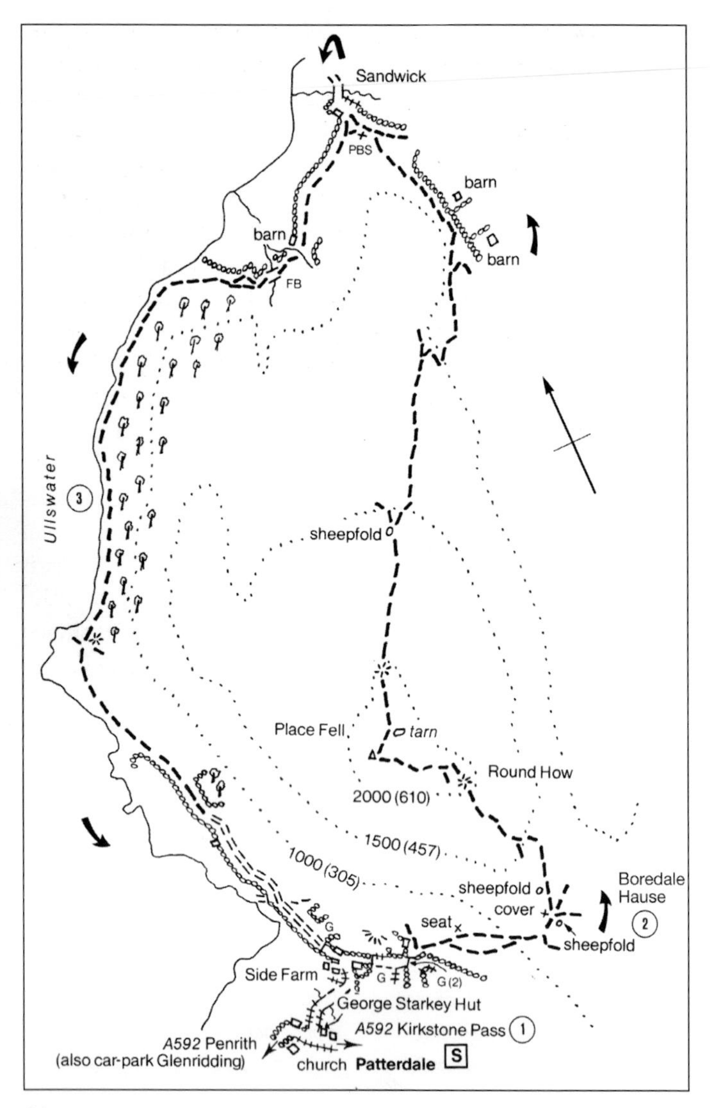
Sandwick
PBS
barn
barn
barn
FB
Ullswater
3
sheepfold
Place Fell
tarn
Round How
2000 (610)
1500 (457)
1000 (305)
sheepfold
cover
seat
Boredale Hause
2
sheepfold
G
Side Farm
G
G (2)
George Starkey Hut
A592 Kirkstone Pass
1
A592 Penrith
(also car-park Glenridding)
church
Patterdale
S

Map 17

walkers' routes to Place Fell, Bore Dale, Martindale and Angle Tarn. The ruin on the Hause is said to be that of a small chapel.

③ *Ullswater*

The shape of Ullswater – consisting of three distinct sections defined by sharp changes of direction opposite Birk Fell and Hallin Fell – is highly unusual for the Lake District. The area of the lake on both its eastern and western sides is a meeting-place between the beds of Skiddaw Slate and rocks of the Borrowdale Volcanic Series. The shape of the lake is certainly due to the action of a glacier which had greater eroding effect against the slate than against the volcanic rocks. The lakeside cliffs of Hallin, Birk and Place Fells are formed from the latter. The lake is at its deepest – 205 ft (63m) – towards the eastern shore near Birk Fell.

ROUTE 18 | Great Gable from the Climbers' Traverse

Most walkers ascend Great Gable either from Windy Gap (reached from the Honister Pass or up Aaron Slack) or directly from the Sty Head Pass. Both routes, however, miss out the main glory of the mountain – the Napes Ridges, which lie on the Wasdale Face. The Climbers' Traverse, starting at the Sty Head Pass, traverses the face below the Napes around to Beck Head. Although steep and rough in places, with some scrambling that may be found difficult, it is a route of superlative quality giving good views not only of the Napes, which include the Napes Needle, but also down into Wasdale. Some walkers may also find the rocky approach to Sty Head by Taylor Gill Force difficult, in which case an alternative route by Stockley Bridge is recommended.

Length: 7 miles (11km) | Ascent: 2,700 ft (820m) | Starting and finishing point: Parking area just before Seathwaite at head of Borrowdale (89–235123) | Maps: Landranger 89; Explorer OL4

ROUTE DESCRIPTION (MAP 18)

Walk up the road towards Seathwaite and go between the buildings. Just before the café on the L, turn R through a gated archway and along a walled lane to a bridge. Immediately after the bridge turn L through a small gate in a wall and follow a path to the R of the river. When the river bends L, continue in the same direction following the clear path up the hillside. Eventually after nearly ¾ mile (1.2km) the paths swings R and goes up broken

On the way up Great Gable

rocks to the R of a large waterfall (see ① Taylor Gill Force). After scrambling up the rocks, keep on the same side of the river to Sty Head Tarn. Continue along the path to the R of the tarn to the Mountain Rescue box on the summit of the Sty Head Pass. The site of this box was obviously well chosen, for the Pass is a key point of the central fells, with no less than seven major walking routes leading from it, and near to several important climbing faces – see ② Sty Head Pass.

At the box, turn half R up a rising path, and after about 150 yds (140m) at a path junction by a cairn take the path half L. (Between here and Beck Head the route passes some major climbing faces – see ③ Crags on Great Gable and ④ the Napes Needle, for identification and information about these.) Follow the path across the hillside past the large cliff (Kern Knotts) and then across the scree chute of Great Hell Gate. Beyond, follow the path below the Napes Ridges. The Napes Needle should first be seen from below. The path can now be followed all the way across the hillside to Beck Head, passing over some difficult patches, or, for the best view, go up the gully immediately beyond to the base of the Needle and then climb up the well-worn rocks on the L to a small ledge known as the Dress Circle. From there continue with care, choosing a suitable line to traverse along until beyond the Napes Ridges and into the further scree chute of Little Hell Gate. Here descend carefully to pick up a lower path, where turn R. Follow this path around the flanks of the mountain to a grassy col (Beck Head).

Just before the col, take the path half R rising over a small ridge. Descend half R on the far side by a line of posts to a stream in the valley. On the opposite bank turn R and climb to the L of the stream on a steep path up to a col (Windy Gap). Here turn R and follow the path which rises steeply to the summit of Great Gable. The area around the summit is a very special place to both walkers and climbers – see ⑤ the War Memorial Area. Return by the same route to Windy Gap.

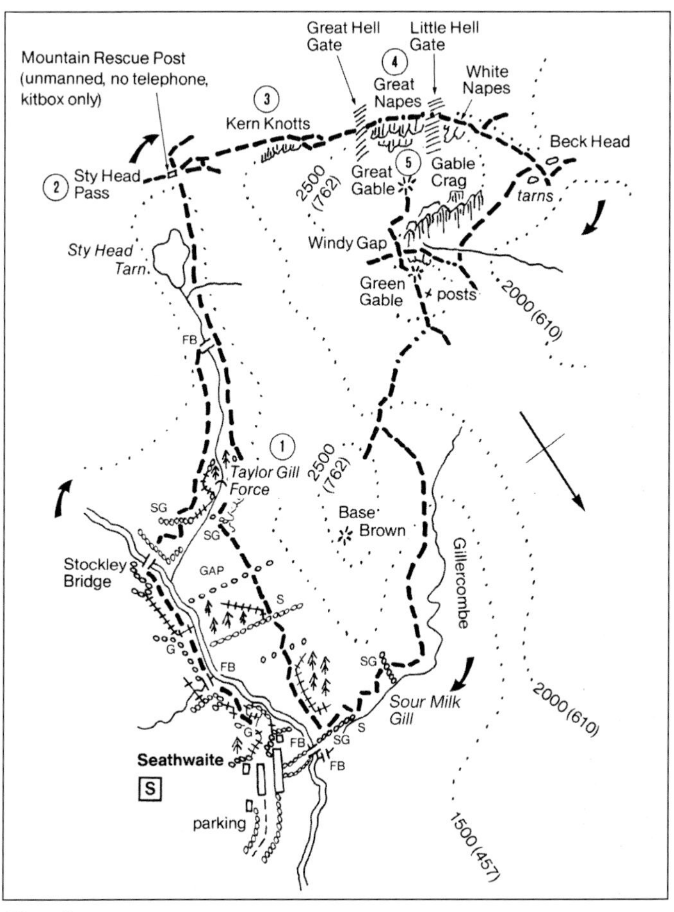

Map 18

Cross the gap and rise up on the opposite side from Great Gable to reach the summit of Green Gable. By the shelter turn R and follow the prominent path marked by cairns. Where the path bends L after about 300 yds (275m), leave half R to pick up a faint path after a few yards. Soon the path grows more distinct, and later, at a col, drops down steeply to the L. (Do not take the faint path half R just before this, which rises up to Base Brown.) Follow the path through the valley (Gillercombe). Where the path meets the stream, turn R to descend steeply on the R bank, back to the footbridge at Seathwaite.

① *Taylor Gill Force (89–229109)*

The head of Borrowford above Seathwaite contains two superb waterfalls: the first on Sty Head Gill (Taylor Gill Force) and the second on Sour Milk Gill. Each marks the edge of a hanging valley produced at the end of the Ice Age *(see page 37)*

② *Sty Head Pass (89–218094)*

The track from Borrowdale to Wasdale over the Sty Head Pass was an important pack-horse trail connecting the two dales, and for that reason was always kept in good repair. On the top of the pass there was a shelter for the drovers. Walkers will be horrified to learn that proposals were made for a road over Sty Head around the turn of the century; there were provisions in the will of John Musgrave of Wasdale Hall, who died in 1912, for the 'construction and maintenance' of the road. Proposals were submitted again in 1934 by Cumberland County Council. Providentially, these schemes were not successful.

③ *Crags on Great Gable*

The Climbers' Traverse from Sty Head across the Wasdale face of Great Gable passes some of the most famous climbing-crags in the Lake District. The first major cliff encountered, about ¼ mile (400m) from Sty Head, is Kern Knotts Buttress, easily recognized by the corner and large vertical wall facing you as you reach it. The wide and prominent Kern Knotts Crack on the left of this wall is a classic route, first climbed unaided by Owen Glynne Jones in 1897, although only after an ascent with top rope protection the previous year. The main difficulty occurs in the middle immediately above the lower wide section, known as the Sentry Box. The thin crack to its right is another classic, the Innominate Crack.

Beyond Kern Knotts is the wide scree chute of Great Hell Gate, flanked on its far side by the steep face of Tophet Wall. The steep and impressive ridges further along still are the famous and immensely popular Great Napes. In order, as they are met from Sty Head, they are Needle Ridge (with Napes Needle at its foot), Eagle's Nest Ridge, Arrowhead Ridge (so called because of the rock shaped like an arrowhead near the top), and Sphinx Ridge (named after a rock at its base which resembles the head of the Sphinx when seen from the east). The scree slope beyond the Napes is called Little Hell Gate. The first ridge to be climbed was Needle Ridge by Walter Parry Haskett Smith solo in 1884, two years before his famous ascent of the Needle. Eagle's Nest Ridge Direct, climbed in 1892 in a superb lead by Godfrey Solly, was the first climb made which is still classified as Very Severe.

Towards the summit of Great Gable above the Napes is Westmorland Crag, and beyond Little Hell Gate are the broken rocks of the White Napes. Finally, on the Ennerdale side is Gable Crag, a considerable cliff but one which is less popular than the Napes Ridges.

④ *The Napes Needle (89–209100)*

This famous rock pinnacle, about 60 ft (18m) high, stands at the foot of Needle Ridge on the Wasdale face of Great Gable. The first ascent by Walter Parry Haskett Smith at the end of June, 1886, is regarded as the beginning of rock-climbing as a sport in itself (as distinct from mountaineering generally, in which rock-climbing is merely a constituent skill). In truth, however, a number of other ascents had been made in the five or so years previously, both in the Lake District and elsewhere, which showed a similar attitude. The real importance of this ascent lay in the appearance of the Needle, which was very spectacular and extremely photogenic. The great Owen Glynne Jones – the self-styled 'Only Genuine Jones' who played a major part in raising the standard of British rock-climbing in the 1890s – told how he was attracted to Cumberland by a photograph of the Needle in a shop window in the Strand. 'By that evening a copy of the Needle hung in my room; in a fortnight Easter had come round and I found myself on the top of the pinnacle'. George Sansom, who was to climb Central Buttress on Sca Fell with Siegfried Herford in 1914, was also directed in a similar manner to Lakeland by an article describing an ascent of the Needle. Its importance, therefore, can hardly be overestimated. It attracted new men into climbing and those men to the mountains of Cumberland.

The route taken by Haskett Smith – known as the Wasdale Crack – is classified as Very Difficult, but there are now several other routes up to Hard Very Severe standard. In 1936, to mark the fiftieth anniversary of the first ascent, Haskett Smith, at the age of 76, returned to climb the Needle for the last time. Before an audience of around 300, the old man was led up the climb by R.S.T. Chorley and G.R. Speaker. He died ten years later.

⑤ *The War Memorial Area*

see page 123.

ROUTE 19 | Dale Head and Robinson

Dale Head owes its name to its commanding position at the head of the Newlands valley, Robinson to its purchase by a Richard Robinson in the sixteenth century. The finest way up the latter is undoubtedly by High Snab Bank, and up the former by a thin path which climbs its northern flank from the Newlands Beck. This route combines them both, with the magnificent ridge of Hindscarth and Littledale Edges in between. Famous mines – the Goldscope, Castlenook and Dale Head, first worked by the Company of Mines Royal in the late sixteenth century – are on the way.

Length: 7½ miles (12km) | Ascent: 2,800 ft (860m) | Starting and finishing point: Small car-park and roadside parking spaces by Chapel Bridge near Little Town in the Newlands Valley to the east of Derwent Water (89–231194) | Maps: Landranger 89; Explorer OL4

ROUTE DESCRIPTION (MAPS 19A, 19B)

Walk up the road towards Little Town, turning back half R through a gate by a seat before the first cottage on the R. Follow the old mine road, eventually with a wall on the R. After ¾ mile (1.2km) pass prominent spoil heaps on the hillside to the R which mark the site of the first and the most famous of the three mines on the route, the Goldscope Mine. They are not safe to explore (See ① Goldscope.) Half a mile (800m) further, pass the climbing hut of the Carlisle Mountaineering Club. Soon after, the wall on the R ends. Continue past some more spoil heaps (the Castlenook Mine) and at a fork keep R by the stream. Where the track comes close to the stream (just past an obvious tributary coming down

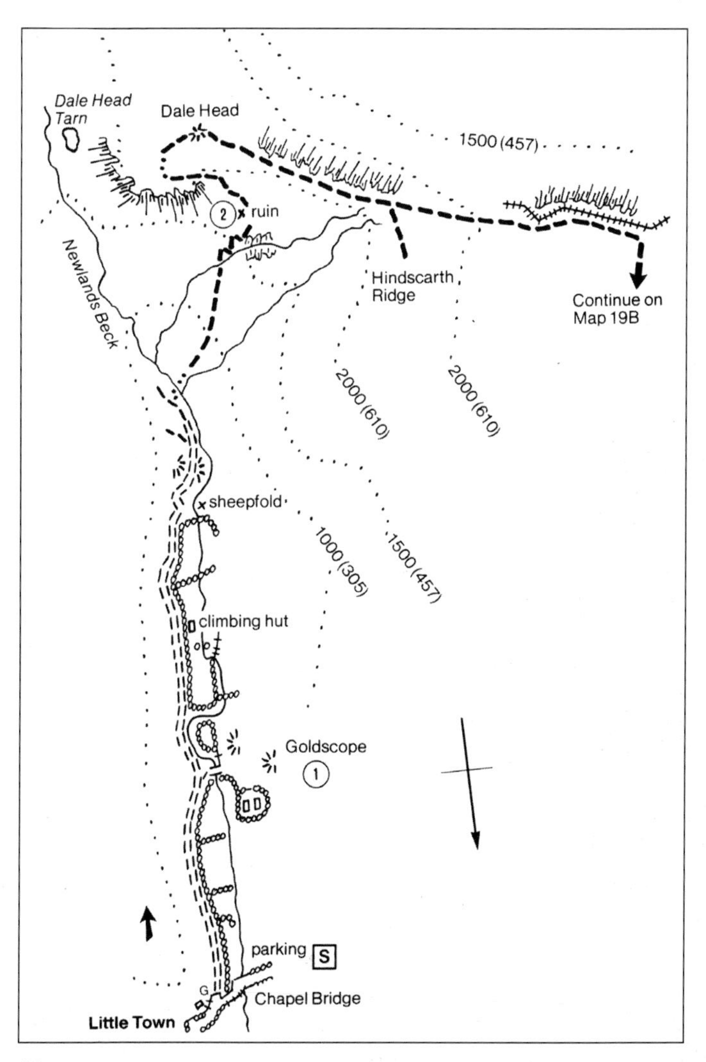

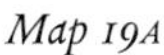
Map 19A

Looking up from Newlands

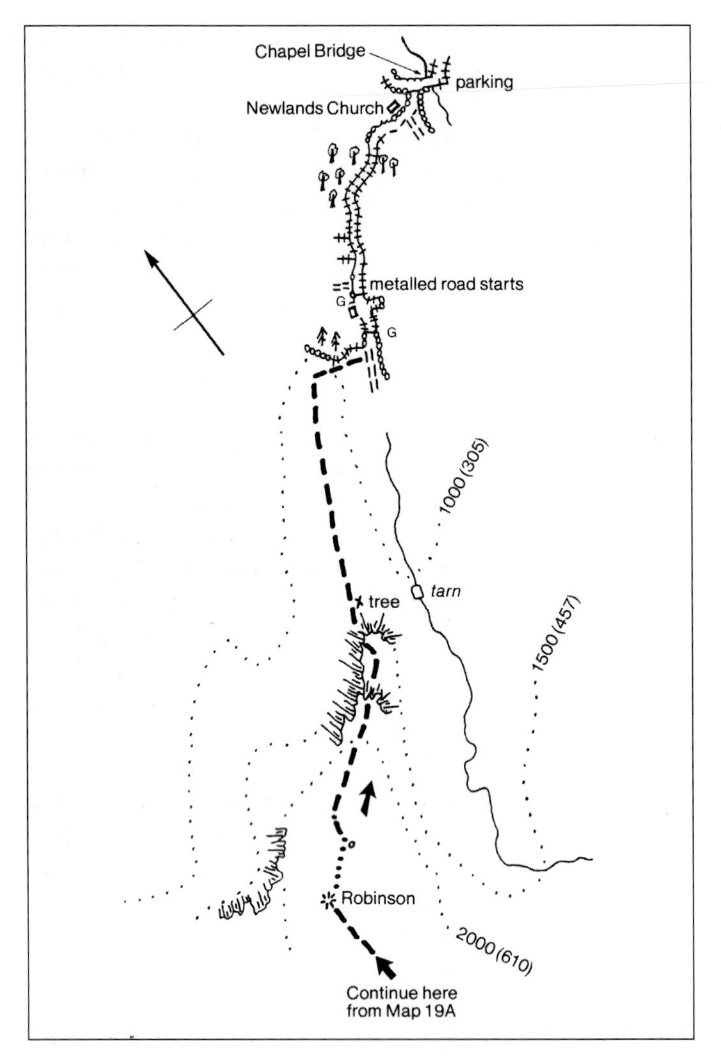
Chapel Bridge
parking
Newlands Church
metalled road starts
G
G
1000 (305)
tarn
tree
1500 (457)
Robinson
2000 (610)
Continue here
from Map 19A

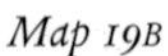
Map 19B

from a ravine on the opposite side) cross, and follow the obvious path which slopes up the hillside (i.e. half R to your original direction).

Much higher the path crosses a stream (Far Tongue Gill) below a ravine; beyond, follow the zig-zag path to the R of a small ruin (the Dale Head Mine – see ②). Continue up the path past the ruin (cairns). The path soon bends L and crosses a steep slope with scree to the R and a cliff down to the L. It is narrow and rough in places. At the end of the traverse, past a cairn, bend R up grass slopes to the summit of Dale Head.

Continue beyond the summit, soon dropping down to a wide grassy col. Rise up on the opposite side over a ridge (the end of Hindscarth ridge), ignoring the R hand path fork, and descend again to a second col (fence now on L). Rise up on the opposite side with a fence to the L and at the top, at a large cairn and bend in fence, take path to the R and follow to summit of Robinson.

Beyond the summit go slightly R following a path that is indistinct but with cairns at first, and which soon becomes more distinct. Continue down the steep ridge on an obvious path. Lower down, three short rock faces have to be negotiated, but after the small rowan tree overlooking a reservoir there will be no further difficulty.

Keep on the crest of the ridge (High Snab Bank) along a beautiful path. Eventually follow the path R down the east flank to a wall corner (small wood and wall to L during descent). At the bottom, turn L down lane between walls, soon going through a gate. Continue down the lane past another gate and cottages to a road and on past a small church (see ③ Newlands Church), then R at a junction back to the parking place.

① *Goldscope (89–229184)*

The spoil heaps on the eastern flank of Scope End, immediately beyond the farm of Low Snab, mark the site of the famous Goldscope Mine. Along with other mines in the Newlands area, it was worked by the Company of Mines Royal for about 100 years from 1565 until the middle of the following century. Its name is a corruption of the German 'Gotes Gab' – God's Gift. The ores produced by separate veins within the mine were galena (lead sulphide) and copper pyrites, the latter containing silver and a small amount of gold.

Although some mining of metal ores had taken place in the Lake District before the sixteenth century, it was probably on a relatively small scale. In 1564 the Company of Mines Royal was formed under an agreement between Elizabeth I, Thomas Thurland (Master of the Savoy) and Daniel Hechstetter (agent for Haug, Langnauer and Co. of Augsburg), whose purpose was to 'search, dig, try, roast and melt all manner of mines and ores of gold, silver, copper and quicksilver'. Shares in the Company were held by Haug, Langnauer and Co. and a number of individuals, while Elizabeth herself received a 10% royalty on the metal sales.

In the following year some 40 or 50 experienced German miners from the Tyrol and Styria were brought over by the Company, to be housed on Derwent Isle on Derwent Water, and operations began. Extraction of the ore was extremely arduous; the usual method in the early days of the mine involved by stope and feather, the 'feathers' being two iron plates and the 'stope' a thin tapering rod. A shallow hole was bored into the rock, into which the feathers were inserted; the stope was then hammered between the feathers, forcing them apart and causing the rock to split along a cleavage plane. The broken pieces of rock were removed to the surface, where they were sorted by hand before being carried to a stamp house where they were crushed into small fragments. Finally, the ore was smelted in a furnace to obtain the metal, using charcoal, coal or peat as fuel. A stamp house and several furnaces were in operation at Keswick soon after the opening of Goldscope and other Newlands mines.

A decline both in production and demand occurred in the seventeenth century, but the mine continued until the Civil War (about 1650) when it was closed down. The smelting furnaces of Keswick were also destroyed about this time. Apart from a short period at the end of the seventeenth century, there was probably no production at the mine until 1847, when a private company reopened it. The discovery of a rich lead ore vein a few years later made the mine highly profitable. Eventually, however, as the shaft went deeper, the waterwheel used for pumping out water was unable to cope and, to avoid further heavy expenditure, the owners closed the mine for the last time in 1864.

There are levels, shafts and adits on both sides of the Scope End ridge.

② *The Dale Head Mine (89–222158)*

Dale Head Mine, on the northern slope of the mountain, was worked for copper in the sixteenth century by the Company of Mines Royal. There is a small ruin soon after the crossing of Far Tongue Gill and just before the final rise to the thin traverse above Gable Crag, a level above the path before the Gill, and further workings down the slope towards Newlands Beck. The bright green veins found in some of the spoil around the small ruin are copper malachite; this was produced by weathering of the original ore, copper pyrites.

③ *Newlands Church (89–230194)*

The small but charming church, which is passed towards the end of Route 19, was formerly a school built by the parishoners of Newlands in 1877. It closed in 1967, and was converted into a church.

ROUTE 20 | The Traverse of the Langdale Pikes

The skyline of Great Langdale is one of the most exciting in the Lake District, the most spectacular section being that of the Langdale Pikes (the word 'pike' is derived from an old Norse word 'pik', meaning 'a sharp summit'). The Pikes themselves have also become famous as the site of an important centre for axe-head manufacture in Neolithic times. This route reaches the eastern end of the Pikes by Stickle Tarn and traverses them, finally descending from the Stake Pass along the line of the Cumbria Way. Except perhaps for some route-finding problems – particularly in mist – over the moorland section beyond Pike o' Stickle, no particular difficulties should be encountered.

Length: 8 miles (13 km) | Ascent: 2,450 ft (750m) | Starting and finishing point: The National Trust car-park by the New Dungeon Ghyll Hotel in Great Langdale (90–295064) | Maps: Landranger 90; Explorer OL6

ROUTE DESCRIPTION (MAP 20)

Before starting, see page 129 for information about Great Langdale. Go to the far end of the car-park (i.e. towards the hotel), turning L before the toilet (PFS). Turn R through a small gate then L through a gap in the wall, and follow the path up the hillside to the L of the stream (Stickle Gill). Soon cross a footbridge and continue climbing on the R bank of the stream. Much higher, cross the stream once more (no footbridge) and reach the dam of Stickle Tarn.

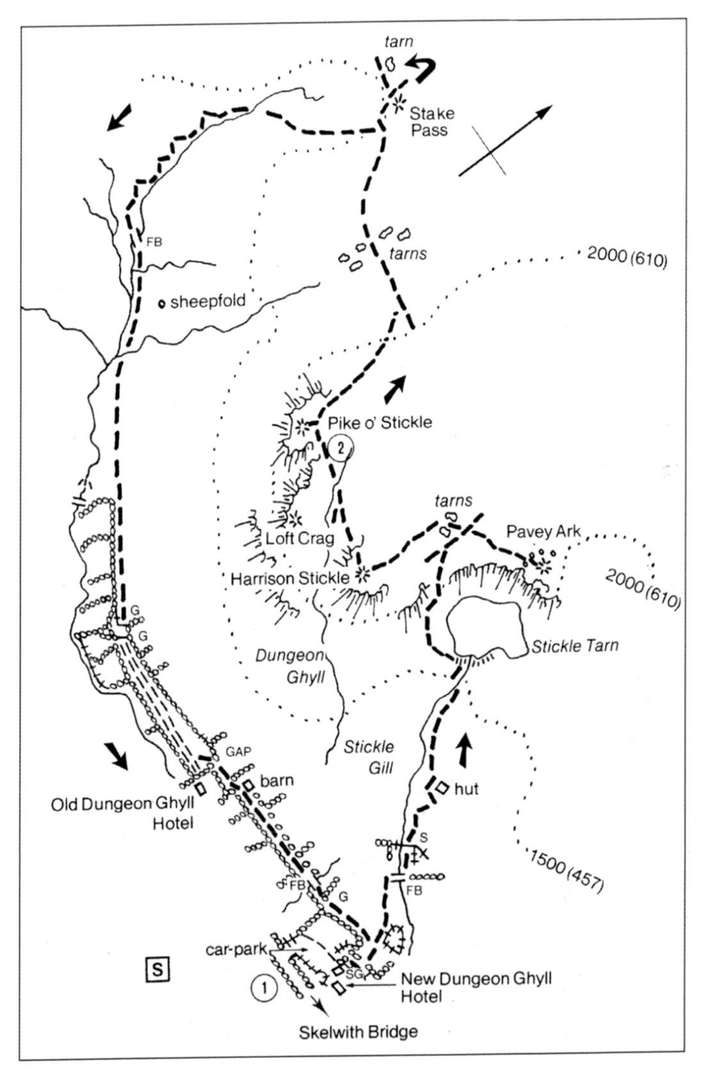
tarn
Stake
Pass
FB
tarns
2000 (610)
sheepfold
Pike o' Stickle
2
tarns
Pavey Ark
Loft Crag
Harrison Stickle
2000 (610)
G
G
Stickle Tarn
Dungeon
Ghyll
Stickle
Gill
GAP
barn
hut
Old Dungeon Ghyll
Hotel
S
1500 (457)
FB
FB
G
car-park
S
SG
1
New Dungeon Ghyll
Hotel
Skelwith Bridge

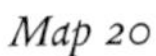
Map 20

The peak on the far side with the large cliff facing the tarn is Pavey Ark. Follow the path to the L of the tarn, soon going half L and up the slope to the L of the cliff. The ascent is rocky in parts, but marked by cairns. At the top of the ridge at a cross path, go R to the summit of Pavey Ark. There are great views down to the tarn and the valley.

Return to the junction and continue along the clear ridge path. Just after two small tarns the path bends L to the summit of Harrison Stickle. From the summit go half R to pick up a prominent path descending (with a short scramble) into a valley. (Here you can divert to the L for a fourth summit, Loft Crag, before continuing to Pike o' Stickle.) Cross the stream in the valley and rise up on the far side to Pike o' Stickle. The great scree gully falling away to the left immediately before Pike o' Stickle was the site of an axe-head factory: see page 193.

On the Pike, descend the summit crags by the way you came up, and at a cairn on the grassy ridge turn back half L on a path (i.e. half R to your approach route). The path becomes faint, slowly descending Martcrag Moor over slightly marshy ground. Lower down, the path goes between several small tarns. Approach a wide col area (Stake Pass) with stream heads to L and R. Here, just before a large cairn, turn L along a path which descends slowly (if you reach a small tarn on your R before finding this path, then you have overshot). The path slowly descends the hillside on the L side of the valley. Where the hillside steepens, the path crosses to the far side of the stream and descends on the R bank. Descend to a footbridge and continue down a clear path to the L of the stream for nearly 2 miles (3km) to the Old Dungeon Ghyll Hotel. Follow the road back to the New Dungeon Ghyll Hotel and the car-park.

On the traverse of the Pikes

ROUTE 21 | A Traverse of Skiddaw (via Ullock Pike)

The vast majority of walkers who climb Skiddaw use the old traditional route by Latrigg and Jenkin Hill. A much better route, however, comes over Ullock Pike and along the airy arête of Longside Edge, approaching the south summit of Skiddaw from Carl Side. The traditional route can then be used for the descent.

The only disadvantage to this is that the starting and finishing points are separated, and a car, taxi or bus has to be used to link them together. (Stronger walkers will find it possible to link them by footpath through Ormathwaite, Applethwaite, Millbeck, the Thornthwaite Forest and Mire House, although this adds about five miles to the total distance.)

Length: 8 miles (13km) | Ascent: 2,700 ft (820m) | Starting point: Ravenstone Hotel on A591, Keswick-to-Bothel road, 5 miles (8km) from Keswick (89–236297). Cars should not be parked in the vicinity of the hotel. Finishing point: Keswick | Maps: Landranger 89; Explorer OL4

ROUTE DESCRIPTION (MAPS 21A, 21B)

Go through a small gate to R of hotel (i.e. on Keswick side) and climb very steep path through wood between fences. Leave wood at stile by a small gate to meet a grassy track. Take a few steps to your R, then continue up the stony path in the same direction. Go through a further small gate, and continue along path with fence to L. At a fork in the path, turn half R up a path across open ground. In late summer, the sight and smell of heather accompanies you as

Looking across Bassenthwaite Lake

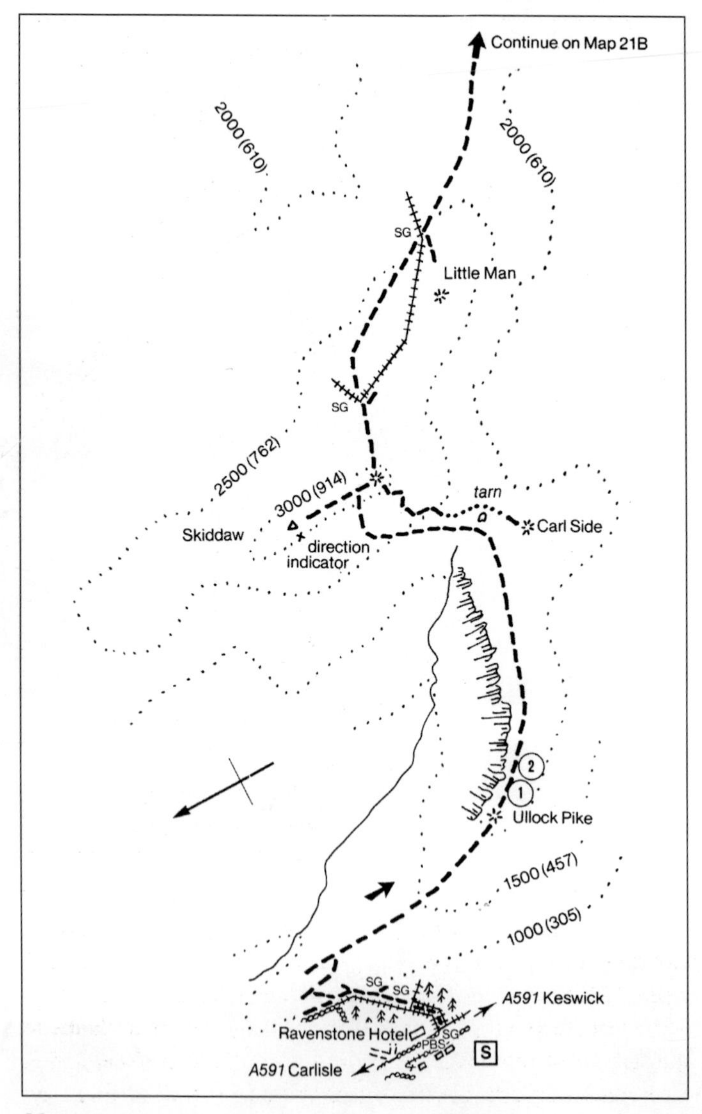

Continue on Map 21B
2000 (610)
2000 (610)
SG
Little Man
SG
2500 (762)
3000 (914)
tarn
Skiddaw
Carl Side
direction indicator
2
1
Ullock Pike
1500 (457)
1000 (305)
SG
SG
A591 Keswick
Ravenstone Hotel
SG
PBS
S
A591 Carlisle

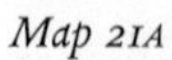
Map 21A

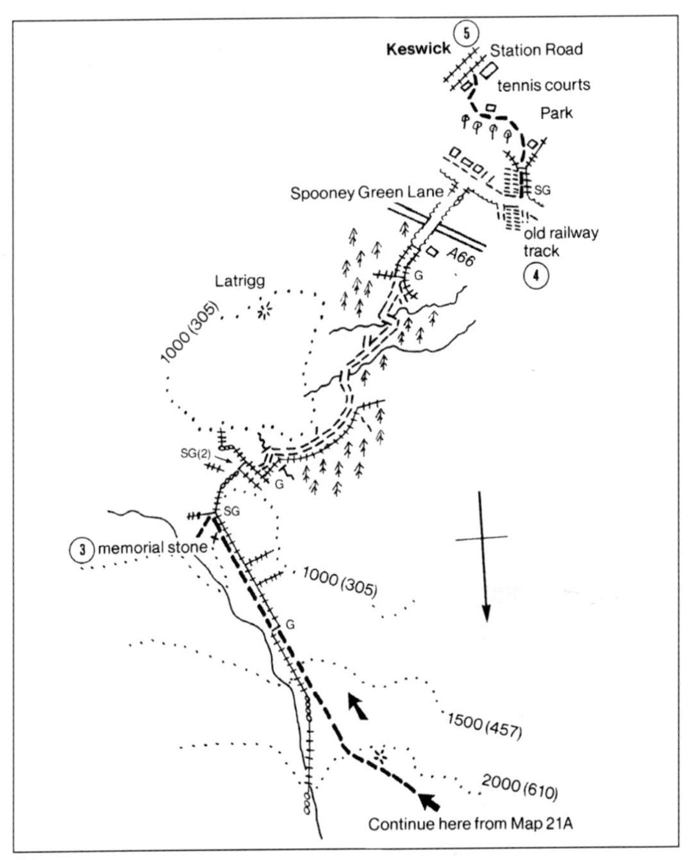

Map 21B

you climb. After 300 yds (275m) meet crossing track and turn R. Continue to top of ridge and, at another crossing track, turn R again. Ullock Pike can soon be seen directly ahead. The path is very clear, keeping more or less on the ridge top as it climbs to the summit of the Pike. The views L (over Southerndale) and R (over Bassenthwaite Lake) are magnificent. The large forest on both sides of Bassenthwaite Lake, well seen from this ridge, is

Thornthwaite Forest, one of the earliest of the Forestry Commission. It still contains some of the first plantings, now more than 80 years old – see ① Thornthwaite Forest.

Beyond the summit, continue along the arête, dipping slightly before rising to the next summit of Longside Edge, with fine views over Keswick to Derwent Water and Borrowdale beyond. The low but prominent peak rising above the forests on the opposite side of the valley, above the end of Bassenthwaite Lake, is Barf, long famous locally for its ecclesiastical connections – see ② the Bishop of Barf. Further along still, the path keeps to the L of the ridge top, dropping down grass slopes to a wide col. On col path swings L and rises steeply to a path which can be clearly seen running diagonally across scree slopes to the summit ridge of Skiddaw. Here turn L along ridge path to OS pillar and stone shelter on Skiddaw Man.

For the return route, go back along the summit ridge to a cairn at the far end (south summit). Just beyond this, turn half L to pick up prominent path which descends steeply to gap in fence with a stile and small gate. At this point the energetic could take a brief excursion to the top of Little Man. No difficulty whatsoever will now be found in following this very clear path, slowly descending around the flanks of Little Man with gently folding slopes to the L to a small gate in a fence. Beyond, continue slowly to descend along path to a cairn, where path swings L before falling steeply to the R. Follow path down to gate in fence; cross, and continue to descend with fence on R. Just before the next gate and only a few yards from the path is a stone raised in honour of two pioneer breeders of Herdwick sheep – see ③ Memorial Stone. Eventually, at small gate, follow wall to reach road end (Gale Road).

Go R through a small gate into road and soon go L through another. Follow the wide path around the flanks of Latrigg, and when you reach a fork go R, ignoring the gate to the L, and continue down. Cross the bridge over the A66 to reach the road in Keswick. Turn R, and immediately after site of old railway bridge (see ④ the Cockermouth, Keswick and Penrith Railway) turn back half L along path. At the path end turn R into Fitz Park and then L across park, entering Station Road by large gates. By this time most walkers will be increasing speed, eager to quench their thirsts in Keswick, now barely 200 yds (180m) away. Spare a few minutes, however, to pay your respects to Sir John Bankes, who will be found just inside the Park on the opposite side of the road – see ⑤. Turn R for the centre of Keswick.

① *Thornthwaite Forest*

The first trees of Thornthwaite Forest were planted on the summit of Whinlatter Pass on 9 December 1919, missing by one day the honour of being the first of the Forestry Commission, which had been established earlier that year. Some of these – Sitka spruce – can still be seen in the forest. Many of the early plantings were European larch and Norway spruce which have not proved entirely satisfactory and have been replaced by Japanese or Hybrid larch and Sitka spruce respectively. Blocks of many other species can be found in the forest, planted in the early days on an experimental basis. There is a Visitor Centre at Whinlatter.

② *The Bishop of Barf (89–219265)*

The craggy hill rising above Forestry Commission plantations directly across the head of Bassenthwaite Lake from Longside Edge, known as Barf, is readily identified by a prominent white object on its lower slopes. This is a pinnacle of rock, about 7 ft (2m) high, known as the Bishop or the Bishop's Rock, its colour arising not from the natural rock, which is dark grey Skiddaw slate, but from whitewash applied every year by the nearby Swan Hotel. Lower down on the slopes below the Bishop is a second pinnacle known as the Clerk. Both are marked on 1:25000 Ordnance Survey maps. On closer inspection the main pinnacle bears some resemblance to a Bishop standing in a pulpit.

③ *Memorial Stone (89–283257)*

The stone cross on the lower slopes of Skiddaw just before the Gale Road is reached was erected in 1891 to the memory of '... two Skiddaw shepherds Edward Hawell of Lonscale, born October 21st 1815, died June 2nd 1889, and his son Joseph Hawell of Lonscale, born December 24th 1854, died February 20th 1891. Noted breeders of prize Herdwick sheep ...' and to Robert Walker Hawell, born 16 March 1851, died 29 December 1911.

④ *The Cockermouth, Keswick and Penrith Railway*

The railway line from Penrith to Cockermouth, which opened for mineral traffic on 4 November 1864 and passenger traffic on 9 January of the following year, was built primarily to serve the iron-ore industry of west Cumberland. Ore and pig-iron smelted at local blast furnaces were carried to Penrith where they were transferred to the North-Eastern Railway for the remainder of their journey to steelworks in Durham and South Yorkshire; in return, smelting coke was carried in the opposite direction from the Durham coalfield to west Cumberland.

From Penrith the railway followed a tortuous path around Newbiggin – for the benefit of local quarries – before crossing the line of the present A66 beyond Penruddock. It crossed again at Threlkeld where there were quarry sidings, and passed north of Keswick and Braithwaite and along the western side of Bassenthwaite Lake to Cockermouth.

The railway company became part of the London Midland and Scottish Railway in 1923, and of British Railways in 1948. As elsewhere, however, both mineral and passenger traffic declined considerably and the line was finally closed on 4 March 1972. The old station at Keswick is now part of a nearby hotel.

⑤ *Sir John Bankes*

By Jenkinson's Gates just inside Fitz Park is an exceptionally fine bust of Sir John Bankes. Sir John, who was born at Castlerigg in 1589, became Attorney General in 1634 and Lord Chief Justice of the Common Pleas in 1640. He died at Oxford in 1644.

ROUTE 22 | The Claife Heights

The Claife Heights is the long hill to the west of Windermere, to the north of Belle Isle and the ferry crossing. Its name, derived from the Old Norse word 'kleif' meaning a 'steep slope', is very apposite, for its eastern flanks, largely covered by mixed forest, fall sharply down to the lake. Over the brow of the hill rows of conifers – Japanese larch, European larch, Sitka spruce and similar species – hold sway. It is a walking area *par excellence*; a fact recognized by both the Park Authority and the National Trust which have waymarked walks within it. It is marked 'The White Post Route', white-tipped posts showing the way to the summit of Latterbarrow.

This walk falls into two distinct and very unequal parts. The outward leg over the Heights to Latterbarrow and down to Belle Grange on the shore of Windermere is essentially a forest walk; the return leg back to the starting point near Ferry House by Far Sawrey keeps close to the lake shore throughout.

Length: 10 miles (16km) | Ascent: 1,550 ft (470m) | Starting and finishing point: A small car-park by the B5285 road to Hawkshead, 600yds (550m) from the western end of the ferry across Windermere (97–388954) | Maps: Landranger 96 or 97; Explorer OL7

ROUTE DESCRIPTION (MAP 22)

Although no sites are actually visited on this walk, the general area crossed was famous in medieval times for the smelting of iron ore – see ① the Bloomeries. Facing away from the lake, leave the car-park at the far R-hand corner (PFS 'Ferry and Latterbarrow

via Claife Station'). Follow the path, and just before reaching the road turn L at PFS 'West's Station, Claife Heights, Latterbarrow', climbing steeply through zig-zags towards a ruin. This has a connection with the large house at the end of the ferry crossing – see ② the Ferry House. Meet a cross path before the ruin and go L through an archway; beyond continue to follow the path up to a fence. Here go R with the fence on your L (PFS 'Hawkshead'). Continue in the same direction when the fence ends, across open ground, soon going between a fence and a wall. At the end go through a small gate into a lane and turn L. After 350 yds (320m) turn R (PFS 'Latterbarrow, Hawkshead') up a lane between walls. Keep on the clear farm road, soon passing through a gate. Continue with a wall on your R over open ground and later with a fence on the L having passed through a gate. Later go L up a hill. At the top continue through a wood to PFS; here go L (i.e. to Hawkshead). Follow this splendid path through the forest. No real difficulty should be encountered, as the path is amply provided with white markers. Soon reach a view-point of surrounding fells, slightly obscured by the forest, at an OS pillar. Shortly afterwards the path goes L and reaches a forest road. Turn R past Brown Stone Tarn.

After 110 yds (100m) turn L (PFS 'Hawkshead') along a path. Continue through the forest, eventually meeting a wall where turn R. At the wall end (at the end of a forest road), turn L ('PFS Hawkshead') and follow path to meet further forest road. Turn R and follow for 650 yds (600m) to PFS 'Hawkshead' on the L. Turn L here along a path. Go through a gate and continue ahead, with a fence on the L, past a small tarn. Beyond the tarn the path widens a little. Continue along this for ⅝ mile (1km) to a metalled road. Turn R for nearly ½ mile (800m).

Just after a minor road on the L, go R through a gate (PFS 'Latterbarrow'). Follow the obvious path, at the start of a coniferous

Woodland on Claife Heights

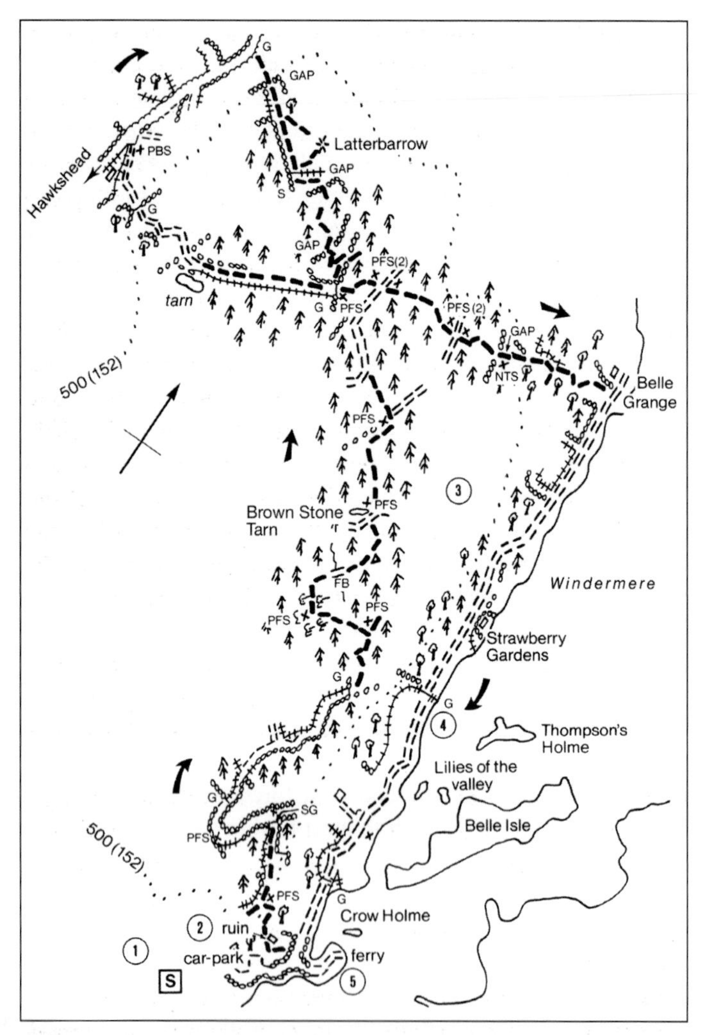
G
GAP
Latterbarrow
GAP
S
PBS
Hawkshead
G
GAP
PFS(2)
tarn
G
PFS
PFS (2)
GAP
NTS
Belle
Grange
500 (152)
PFS
3
PFS
Brown Stone
Tarn
FB
PFS
PFS
Windermere
Strawberry
Gardens
G
G
4
Thompson's
Holme
Lilies of the
valley
G
SG
Belle Isle
PFS
500 (152)
PFS
G
Crow Holme
2
ruin
1
car-park
ferry
S
5

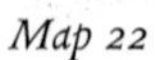
Map 22

wood on the R, leaving half L up a side path to the summit of Latterbarrow. There are wonderful views all around from here.

At the summit turn R and descend on a prominent path to a wall. At the wall turn L over a stile. Follow the path, passing through a gap in the wall and following the white markers through the forest. After ½ mile (800m) bend R at a wall, going through a gap L after 70 yds (65m). Go down a steep path to a second wall. Here turn R. Follow the wall to end of lane reached earlier. Return L along the path to the forest road.

Go down the path directly across (PFS 'Belle Grange'). No difficulty should now be found in following this path, which goes for 1 mile (1.6km) in the same direction with signs to Belle Grange and Lakeshore. (A warning to the curious – see ③ the Crier of Claife!)

At the lake turn R (PFS 'Windermere, Ferry, and Far Sawrey') along a wide track which follows the shore for 2¼ miles (3.6km) to the road by the Ferry House. Go R along the road back to the car-park. For information about features of interest during the final mile see ④ Belle Isle, and ⑤ the Windermere Ferry.

① *The Bloomeries*

The area of Furness between Windermere and Coniston Water, and also to the west of Coniston Water, has many remains of smelting sites – called bloomeries – which date back to medieval times. It is likely that this region was chosen because of the proximity of rich haematite deposits further south in Low Furness to the local woodlands which served as a source of fuel. The smelting was carried out in small bowl-shaped hearths, lined with stone and possibly clay, using charcoal as fuel and blown by hand-operated bellows. The iron-ore would thus be reduced to iron, impurities being run off as a liquid slag. Under these conditions it is unlikely that the iron would melt, and it would be removed as a soft mass to be shaped by hammering.

The practice caused such widespread denudation of the woodlands that it was banned in 1565, although it is likely that it continued well beyond that date.

② The Ferry House (97–391957)

The large building at the western end of the Windermere ferry crossing is the Ferry House, built as a hotel in 1879 on the site of an earlier inn, but now the headquarters of the Freshwater Biological Association which moved there in 1950. The Association was founded in 1929 to foster research into the biology of freshwater environments. The small ruin passed early in the walk belonged to the Ferry House when it was run as a hotel: it was a 'station' or classic viewing-point, in this case over the lake, and was also used for parties and dances. It was described in Guide to the Lakes *written by Thomas West and published in 1778.*

③ The Crier of Claife (96–386981)

Observant owners of maps of the Windermere area will notice the name 'Crier of Claife' given to a small area of steep hillside on Claife Heights directly down from the TV mast towards the lake. It is supposedly the spot on which the Crier, a particularly restless spirit, is imprisoned. His speciality consisted of calling across the lake on stormy nights for the ferry, which in those days was kept on the opposite shore. Investigation of this phenomenon by the locals was not, apparently, without its dangers. Walkers on Route 22 will be relieved to learn, however, that eventually the Crier was exorcized and is now safely buried on the Heights. In 1962 he became the property of the National Trust, to whom, presumably, any reports of his return should be directed.

④ Belle Isle (96/97–394967)

The largest island of Windermere is Belle Isle, owned by the Curwen family for more than 200 years and occupied until 1993. The house upon it was built for a Mr English in 1774, but was purchased seven years later by Isabella Curwen. The grounds were landscaped by her and her husband, who also gave the island its present name. Originally it was called Longholme. The house is extremely unusual in that it is circular in plan, with a dome and lantern, and an imposing white portico of

Dawn over Windermere

four columns on the east side. It stands on the site of a Roman villa. House and grounds are open to the public.

⑤ The Windermere Ferry (96–394958)

The ferry service across Windermere has operated for at least 500 years. The early ferries were all man-powered with oars, but large enough to convey horses or a horse and cart across the lake. The first steam-powered ferry was introduced in around 1860. The one operating at the turn of the century had drop ends, with the boiler and engine to one side, and could carry a coach and four with a full complement of passengers without difficulty. The present ferry is called the Mallard.

ROUTE 23 | Crinkle Crags

The ridge of Crinkle Crags, which forms a great barrier nearly a mile long across the head of Oxendale, is unique in Lakeland. Its challenge lies in the multiplicity of small rocky peaks separated by steep-sided cols, each of which must be negotiated in turn. On this route the end of the ridge is reached from Great Langdale by an ascent of the Band, which rises between Mickleden and Oxendale; and the return is by Red Tarn around the flanks of Pike o' Blisco. The 'crux' of the walk occurs during the descent of the highest top when a short rock chimney, with a drop to the left, has to be negotiated. A common error during the traverse of the ridge, particularly in mist, is to overlook the change of direction towards the end: this has caused many walkers to descend into Moasdale to the south-west. Choose a fine day for this walk and do not attempt it in mist, when navigation is difficult and the views are missed.

Length: 8 miles (13km) | Ascent: 2,800 ft (850m) | Starting and finishing point: The National Trust car-park by the New Dungeon Ghyll Hotel in Great Langdale (90–295064). The walk can be shortened at either end by starting at the Old Dungeon Ghyll Hotel instead | Maps: Landranger 90; Explorer OL6

ROUTE DESCRIPTION (MAPS 13, 23)

Follow Route 13 as far as the second bridge after the Old Dungeon Ghyll Hotel. Cross the bridge to the road and immediately turn R through a gate. Follow the metalled farm road to Stool End. (Although not visited on this route, there is from here – and from higher on the Band – a superb view of the site of the Neolithic axe-head factory on Pike o' Stickle. See ① the Langdale

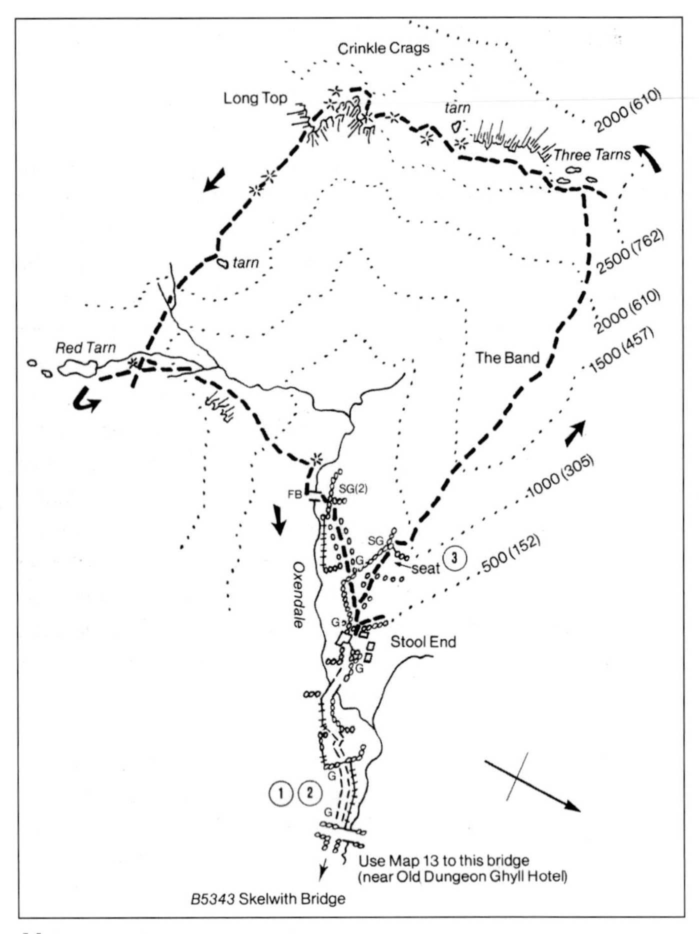

Map 23

axe-head factory, and also read ② Great Langdale.) Go through the farmyard and through a gate to the L of the white cottage. Take the L fork beyond. After a short distance take the very obvious path going half R up the ridge and soon passing through a small gate – see ③ Memorial seat on the Band. Follow this path (the Band) as it slowly climbs for about 2 miles (3km) to a col with three small tarns.

Turn L on the col and follow the path up and along the ridge traversing the minor summits. The path is indistinct in places, but follow the cairns to pick your way over the rocks. It is important to notice that the ridge swings to the L after the highest top. The only difficulty occurs during the descent from that top, when a short chimney – with a considerable drop to the L – has to be descended, either by dropping down behind the chockstone or by climbing down the L wall of the chimney. After the tops, descend steeply and then more slowly on the obvious path across the moor.

After 1 mile (1.6km) of descent, reach a cross track near a tarn (Red Tarn). Turn L. The reddish path soon descends steeply between two streams along a narrow ridge. Just before the end of the ridge, turn R over the stream and follow the path descending across the hillside. Descend for nearly 1 mile (1.6km) – the last part steeply – to reach a footbridge across the river (Oxendale Beck). On the opposite bank turn R, soon passing through two small gates to the R of a sheepfold. Follow the obvious track which leads back to Stool End. Return along the farm road and the main road back to the car-park.

① *The Langdale axe-head factory (90–274073)*

The great scree chute dropping down into Great Langdale from near the summit rocks of Pike o' Stickle was the site of a large and important factory for the manufacture of stone axe-heads in Neolithic (i.e. New Stone Age) times. The factory, discovered in 1947, was identified by the numerous flakes and discarded axe-heads on the scree, although its presence within that area had already been suspected. Other sites in the same general area have been discovered since then, below Harrison Stickle and near the summit of Scafell Pike.

The rock used was a fine-grained, but very hard, volcanic tuff, which can easily be shaped into a rough axe-head form by striking away flakes with a hard stone. It is thought likely that the roughly shaped axe-heads – probably produced during the summer months – were transported down to the coast, where they were finally shaped by grinding and polishing. Finished axe-heads from this site, identified by a close study of rock type, have been found in many areas of Britain well away from Cumbria, such as Hampshire, indicating a lively trade. The site may have remained in production until about 1400 BC.

② *Great Langdale.*

see page 129.

③ *Memorial seat on the Band (90–273058)*

A memorial plaque above the seat low down on the Band asks us to 'Rest and remember the work of S.H. Hamer Secretary of The National Trust 1911–1934.

ROUTE 24 | The Newlands Horseshoe

The predominant rocks of the north-western area of the Lake District National Park are the Skiddaw Slates, relatively homogeneous rocks with only limited resistance to erosion. It is an area therefore of long narrow ridges and rounded conical peaks, with smooth grassy flanks deeply cut by long stream valleys. Where occasional crags do occur they tend to be loose and broken, the haunt of botanists and entomologists rather than of the rock-climber. Although lacking the dramatic scenery and exciting walking associated with the Borrowdale Volcanic Series further south, some of the finest ridge walks in Lakeland are to be found here. The Newlands Horseshoe, which takes its name from the Newlands valley running south through Little Town and Stair, is one of them.

Length: 10 miles (16km) | Ascent: 3,000 ft (910m) | Starting and finishing point: Walkers: Hawes End landing stage, reached by launch from Keswick (89–251213). Car-owners: One of the small car-parks at 89–247213. Take the Swinside road from Portinscale, going L at each of two junctions. The first car-park is ½ mile (800m) beyond the second junction, near a cattle-grid where the road bends sharply; the second is a short distance beyond, along the Skelgill road | Maps: Landranger 89; Explorer OL4

ROUTE DESCRIPTION (MAPS 7, 24)

Follow Route 7 as far as the col beyond the summit of Cat Bells, and see ① the Newlands valley, for the origin of the name of the valley which lies to the right of the Cat Bells ridge. Continue in the same direction, rising up the prominent path ahead. The path rises

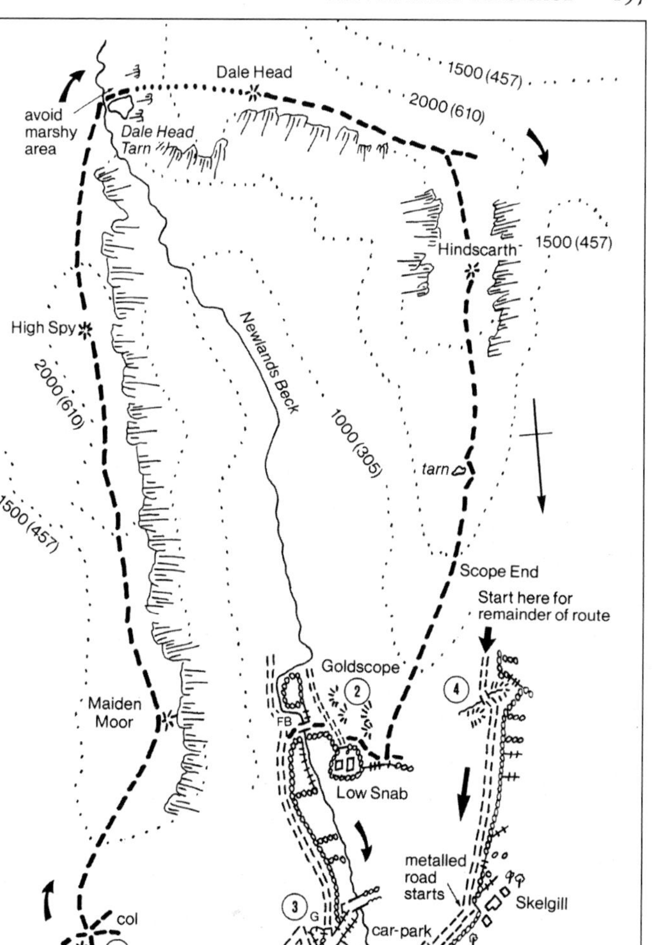

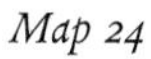
Map 24

The Newlands Horseshoe

steadily over grassy slopes (occasional cairns), eventually reaching the edge of a cliff on Maiden Moor overlooking the Newlands valley to the R. Continue along the ridge, keeping to the L of the cliff edge, to a prominent cairn on High Spy (2 miles, 3km from col). Beyond the summit continue in the same direction, descending, and later bending slightly R to reach a stream on col. Cross and pick up a clear path up the hillside, passing a tarn on the L. If the stream is heavy, it may be easier to cross a little further up. Continue up the hill slope ahead, picking the best route through the small crags. At the top go over to the tall summit cairn of Dale Head.

Continue in the same direction beyond the summit, dropping down to a broad grassy col (occasional old fence posts by path). Where the rise begins on the opposite side, take a path half R. This goes along a side ridge to the summit of Hindscarth.

Keep in the same direction beyond the summit, down scree, passing a large cairn. Descend down the ridge, the path running below the crest of the ridge, and further down descending steeply on the crest of Scope End. Eventually, very low down, meet a cross track by a wall and turn R. The spoil heaps to the R mark the site of one of the most famous mines in Lakeland – see ② Goldscope. Follow this track down and along a wall, soon turning L to a footbridge (signed 'Footbridge Dalehead or Little Town'). Cross and go up to old mine road. Turn L and continue for just over ½ mile (800m) to gate at Little Town. Walkers who read all the information given for Route 7 used earlier in the day will remember that Little Town was the home of Lucie who met Mrs Tiggy-Winkle. Those who didn't have a second opportunity – see ③ Beatrix Potter.

Go through gate and along metalled road for a few yards. Just after cottage on R (PBS 'Hause Gate Leading to Catbells footpath'), turn R to gate. Go up old mine road, which soon bends back half L. Continue to follow this broad path, soon passing a second mine (see ④ Yewthwaite Mine) with wall on L for 1½ miles (2.5km) to metalled road at Skelgill. Turn R along the road to car-parks (or Hawes End landing stage).

The ridge over Cat Bells towards Derwent Water

① *The Newlands valley*

A shallow tarn (Husaker or Uzzicar Tarn) situated in the wide and now relatively flat valley to the north-west of Cat Bells was drained around the thirteenth century to provide further cultivatable land. Known as Neuland in 1323, the name means 'newly cleared land' or 'newly acquired land'. The name of the tarn is also commemorated in Farm Uzzicar, which lies to the west of the area.

② *Goldscope*

see page 169.

③ *Beatrix Potter*

Beatrix Potter, whose books have been read and loved by children from many countries, is more usually associated with the village of Near Sawrey on the ferry road between Windermere and Hawkshead, where she owned a farm, Hill Top, which was her home for many years. Most of her books published after 1905 were based upon Hill Top and Near Sawrey, but several of the earlier ones drew their background from the area around the Newlands valley and Derwent Water, where Beatrix Potter spent several summers before 1903. The Tale of Squirrel Nutkin *(1903) was inspired by the red squirrels which still frequent the woods on the shore of Derwent Water, Owl Island where Old Brown lived in the story being St Herberts Island; while the illustrations for* The Tale of Benjamin Bunny *(1904) were prepared from sketches made at Fawe Park which overlooks the western shore of the lake. The connection is strongest, however, in* The Tale of Mrs Tiggy-Winkle *(1905). This story is about a small girl called Lucie who lives at Little-Town in Newlands. One day she meets washerwoman (or washerhedgehog!) Mrs Tiggy-Winkle, who works in a kitchen behind a small door on the side of Cat Bells. There is reference in the story to Skelghyl and Gatesgarth, which are both local places. The real Lucie was a daughter of the Vicar of Newlands whom Beatrix Potter met on her visits there.*

From 1901 to 1913 Beatrix Potter was very prolific, having one, or more usually two, books published each year; but after her marriage her output declined considerably. She died in 1943. About half of the village of Near Sawrey, including Hill Top, and other properties elsewhere, were left to the National Trust in her will.

④ *Yewthwaite Mine (89–239194)*

The spoil heaps about Yewthwaite Gill just after Little Town mark the site of Yewthwaite Mine. Working probably began in the second half of the eighteenth century and ended towards the end of the nineteenth. Copper and zinc ores were extracted.

ROUTE 25 | The ascent of Helvellyn (via Striding Edge)

The crossing of Striding Edge is probably the best-known walk in the Lake District, familiar even to those who have never set foot on a fell. Lacking some of the difficulty of Sharp Edge on Blencathra further to the north and a little of the sheer grandeur of the Crib-goch Ridge in the Snowdonia National Park, it gives nevertheless a wonderful airy traverse high above flanking coves. It is a popular route and often busy, but best avoided in very cold weather when ice can make it treacherous. The best return route is along the adjacent arête of Swirral Edge. If you follow this route, do not fall to the temptation of by-passing Catchedicam (Catstye Cam), for a bonnier little peak you will never find anywhere. It is also, incidentally, the tenth highest in the Park.

Length: 8½ miles (14km) | Ascent: 2,850 ft (870m) | Starting and finishing point: Car-park at Glenridding on the A592 to the west of Ullswater (90–386170) | Maps: Landranger 90; Explorer OL5

ROUTE DESCRIPTION (MAP 25)

Leave the car-park into the road and turn R over the bridge. Immediately turn R up a lane to the L of the river. Go past the Public Hall and farm; a short distance beyond go L at a junction (signed 'Public Bridleway Helvellyn'). Where the lane ends just past two cottages, turn L over a small bridge and follow the path steeply up the hill. Just beyond the fences (erosion control), turn R and go along the path to a small gate in a wall; do not go through this, but turn back half L (signed 'Striding Edge, Grisedale') and continue climbing over the hill and down to a

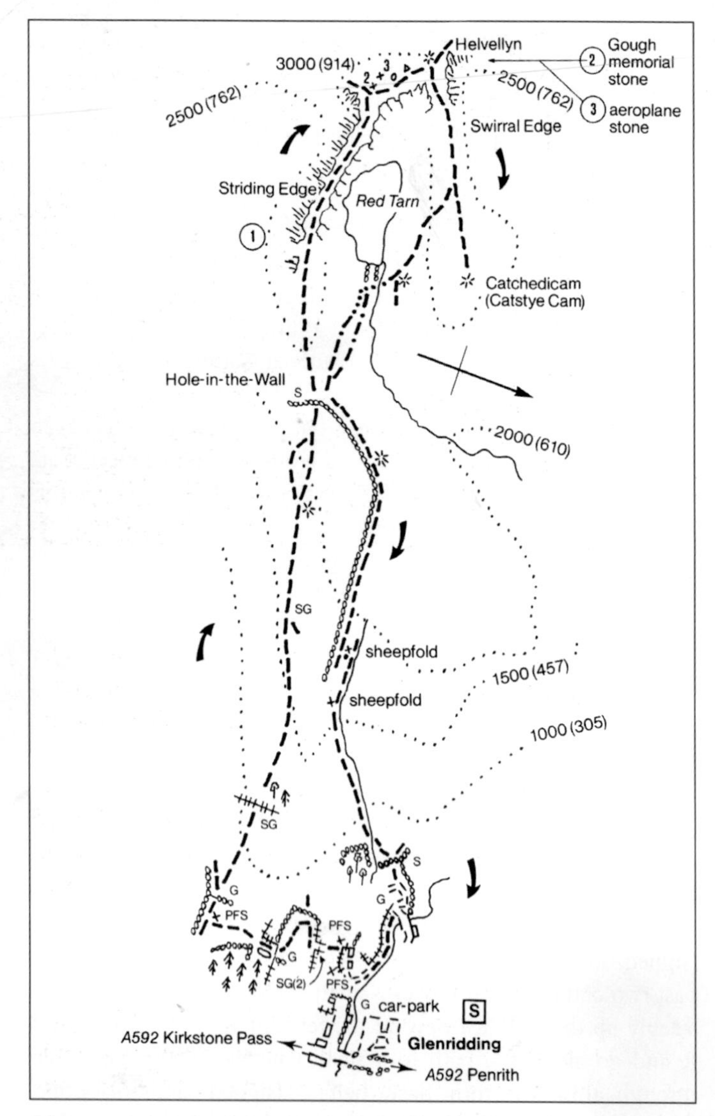
Helvellyn
Gough memorial stone
aeroplane stone
3000 (914)
2500 (762)
2500 (762)
Swirral Edge
Striding Edge
Red Tarn
Catchedicam (Catstye Cam)
Hole-in-the-Wall
2000 (610)
SG
sheepfold
sheepfold
1500 (457)
1000 (305)
SG
PFS
PFS
PFS
SG(2)
car-park
S
A592 Kirkstone Pass
Glenridding
A592 Penrith

Map 25

Striding Edge from Helvellyn

gate in a wall. Cross, and take the path past the tarn. At the far end continue in the same direction, descending steeply to a cross track by a wall. Take the R hand path, and after a short distance go through a gate (i.e the right-hand of two gates).

Follow the very clear path as it slowly climbs for 1¾ miles (3km) to a stile in a wall (Hole-in-the-Wall). Follow the path beyond along the ridge (i.e. do not cross the ladder-stile or take any paths to the R). The ridge is broad but soon narrows to a splendid rocky arête (for facts about its formation see ① the Helvellyn Ridge). Continue along the arête, treading carefully, and at the end climbing directly up the shattered rocks and scree to the summit ridge. Turn R to the shelter, and beyond to the OS obelisk. Helvellyn is more richly endowed with memorials than any other mountain in the Lake District, and two of them are near the summit cairn – see ② the Gough Memorial Stone and ③ the Aeroplane Stone.

Looking north up Ullswater

Continue beyond the obelisk for 140 yds (130m) to a cairn at the end of the summit plain. Turn R and descend steeply over broken rocks to the end of Swirral Edge. Go along the Edge to a path junction. (A short and worthwhile diversion can be made along the L-hand path to the summit of Catstye Cam, returning back to the junction by the same route.) Take the R-hand path down to a cairn in the valley; at this junction turn R and cross below the tarn (no path) to pick up one of two paths going to the

L down the valley on the far side of the stream. These lead back to a ladder stile by Hole-in-the-Wall.

Do not cross here, but turn L with the wall on your R. Follow this for ½ mile (800m) to where it turns R. Continue to follow the wall as it descends steeply. After about 700 yds (640m) – just before the wall levels out, and with a small valley on the L – bear L to pick up a parallel path near a sheepfold. Turn R, soon passing a further sheepfold. Low down by a wood cross the stream and continue to descend on the opposite bank to a gate at a wall corner. Go through, and follow the wall down to a farm road. Turn L then L again on to a metalled road further down. Just before a bridge turn R along a lane (signed 'Path to car park'). Follow the lane through the campsite back to Glenridding.

① *The Helvellyn Ridge*

The two flanks of the main ridge through Helvellyn, which runs approximately north-south, are of very different character. The western slopes are smooth and uninterrupted, whilst those to the east are broken by a line of superb coves (cirques). There is no doubt that these coves were produced by glacial action towards the end of the Ice Age. In those immediately to the east of the Helvellyn summit, the action of adjacent glaciers on the separating walls was so severe that only the narrow rock ridges of Swirral Edge and Striding Edge were left. Between these two edges is Red Tarn, which was formed when water collected in the hollow of the deep cirque basin. The difference between the two slopes of the Helvellyn ridge is probably accounted for by the greater tendency of snow to collect and remain on the eastern slopes, owing to the prevalent wind direction, and to the slightly north-facing inclination of the ridge.

② *The Gough Memorial Stone (90–344150)*

This stone is to be found on the main summit ridge near the top of the rise from Striding Edge. Beneath the spot on which the stone stands were found in 1805 the remains of Charles Gough, who was killed by a fall from the rocks. It is recorded on the stone that his dog was found still guarding the body, which had been reduced to a skeleton. It is sad to have to note that some people – no doubt of a suspicious and cynical nature – have suggested that the dog may not have been entirely innocent with regard to the condition of the body.

Walter Scott described the event in his poem 'I climbed the dark brow of the mighty Helvellyn'. Wordsworth also recorded it in his lines on fidelity, which conclude:

> The dog which still was hovering nigh,
> Repeating the same timid cry,
> This dog had been through three months' space

A dweller in that savage place.

How nourished here through
such long time,
He knows, who gave that love
sublime,
And gave that strength of feeling
great,
Above all human estimate.

The stone was erected in 1890, in memory of that love and strength of feeling.

③ *The Aeroplane Stone (90–343151)*

The small square stone about 50 yds (45m) south of the shelter commemorates the landing of an aeroplane on the summit of Helvellyn in December 1926. This was claimed to be the first landing on a mountain in Great Britain. After a short stay the plane took off safely.

ROUTE 26 | Wetherlam and the Old Man of Coniston

Despite its scarred appearance to the south and east, the Old Man of Coniston is a well-loved mountain and a great favourite with visitors to the Coniston area. Its name is derived appropriately from the dialect word 'man' which means 'a huge cairn', for the one which at present graces its summit is equalled in size only by that on the highest point of Scafell Pike. The direct ascent from Coniston, which uses the quarry road, is not to be recommended, however, by comparison with an approach from Wetherlam which gives several miles of superb ridge walking and the opportunity to cross several other fine tops along the way. The way down by Goat's Water is longer than the direct descent to Coniston, but far nicer.

Length: 7½ miles (12km) | Ascent: 3,825 ft (1,170m) | Starting and finishing point: The National Park Authority car-park in Coniston (96–302976). There is also some free parking on the steep hill on the L after the R turn at the garage crossroads (see below) | Maps: Landranger 90 and 96; Explorer OL6

ROUTE DESCRIPTION (MAPS 26A, 26B)

Go into the road from the car-park and turn L past the church. Cross the bridge and walk along the main road. At the crossroads just past the garage, turn R. At a junction go L and up a very steep hill. Where the road bends back half L, go through a stile ahead, ignoring the gates to the L of this (PFS 'Coppermines Valley and Miners Bridge'). Go R to a small gate in a corner. Cross the stream over a footbridge beyond and follow a path to the R by a wall.

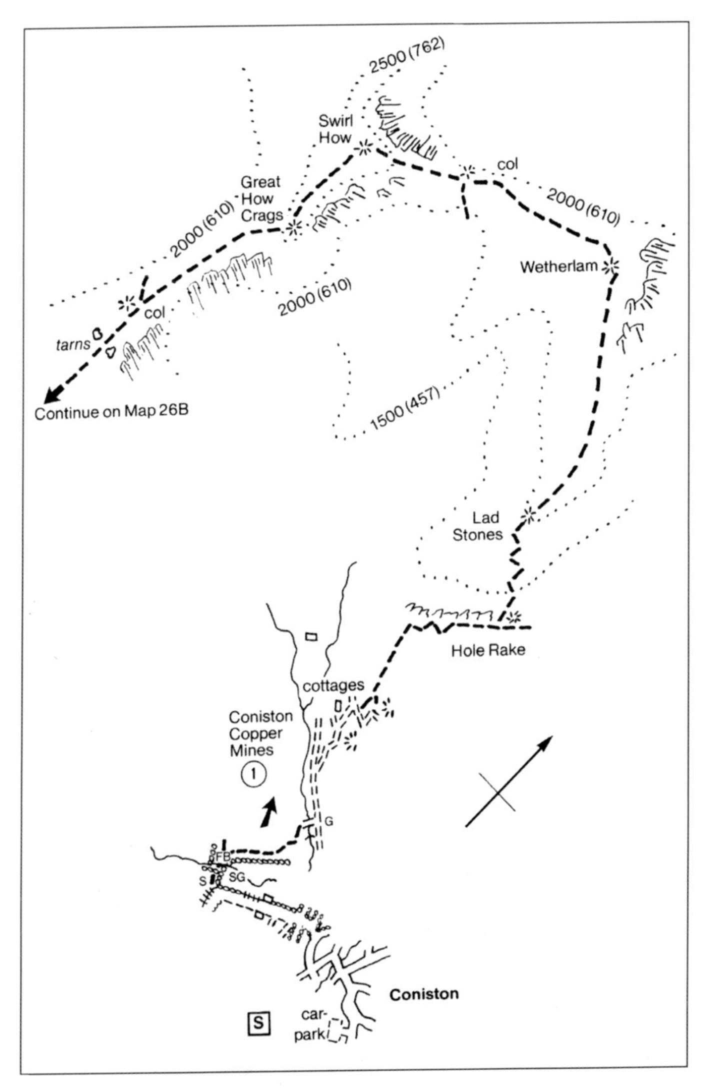
2500 (762)
Swirl How
col
Great How Crags
2000 (610)
2000 (610)
Wetherlam
2000 (610)
col
tarns
Continue on Map 26B
1500 (457)
Lad Stones
Hole Rake
cottages
Coniston Copper Mines
1
G
FB
S
SG
Coniston
S
car-park

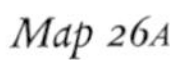
Map 26A

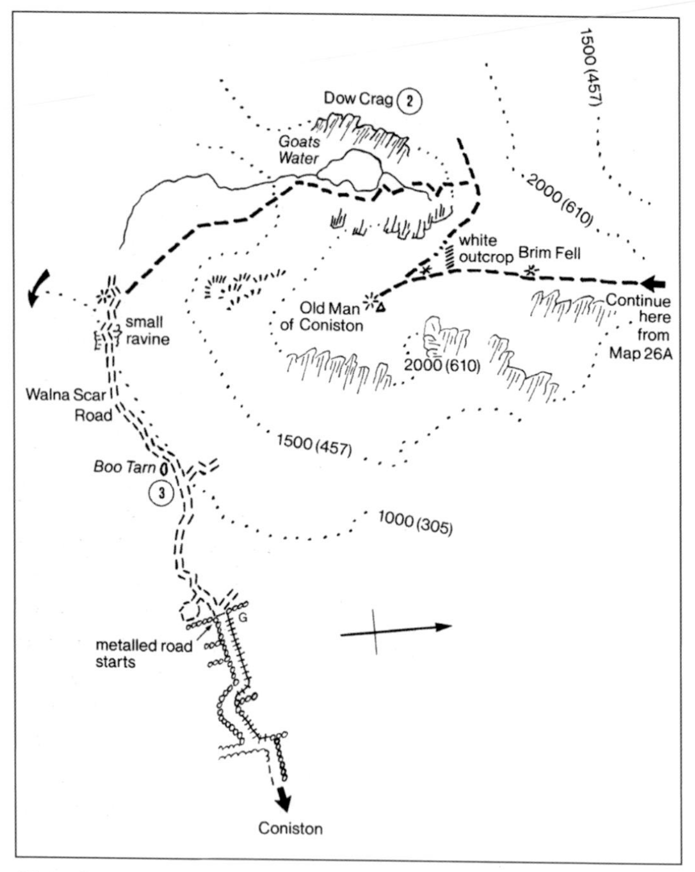

Map 26B

This beautiful path curves to the L and eventually drops down to Miners Bridge over Church Beck. On the far side, turn L along the quarry road. The best-known mine in Lakeland is now directly ahead – see ① Coppermines Valley.

After 200 yds (180m), at a junction take the R-hand branch. At a further junction just ahead of a cottage go R again, and at a third junction R once more. At a cairn just before the quarry on the L, go L up a path. Follow the path, climbing steadily, soon with a small valley (Hole Rake) on your L. Almost at the top, where the valley levels out, take a faint path half L. Follow the path which climbs steadily (but at some length!) to the summit of Wetherlam.

From the summit go half L, picking up cairns and a path which soon descends on the R side of the ridge down to a col. After a large cairn, climb steeply up the opposite side (Prison Band) to the summit of Swirl How. Hardy souls may here make a diversion to Great Carrs and even Grey Friar, but ordinary mortals will turn to the L, i.e. due south, and enjoy nearly 2 miles (3km) of first-rate ridge walking to the summit of the Old Man. Route-finding instructions should be superfluous.

From the summit, return 250 yds (230m) to a path junction; here take the L-hand lower path. After 225 yds (210m), at a band of whitish rocks go L to pick up a path after a few yards. Descend to a marshy col (Goat's Hawse). Turn L and descend on a path to the L of a large tarn (Goat's Water). Walkers on this route will have to be in dense mist to fail to notice at this point a very large cliff on the opposite side of Goat's Water. One of its attractions is a remarkably clear echo – see ② Dow Crag. Pass the tarn on the L and follow the path which soon swings to the L past the spoil heaps of an old quarry. Drop down to a wide crossing track (the Walna Scar Road). Turn L. A small tarn, Boo Tarn, to the right of the track further along may easily be missed, so watch for it – see ③ the Banniside Burial Site. After 1¼ miles (2km) reach a metalled road through a gate. Follow this for 1 mile (1.6km) back to Coniston, soon picking up the route used earlier.

① *Coppermines Valley (96–287989)*

Two veins of copper ore, the Bonser and the Triddle, cross the valley of the Red Dell Beck to the south-east of Levers Water. Extraction of this ore on a substantial commercial basis began about 1599 by the Company of Mines Royal, who were already

Goat's Water on the way down from the Old Man of Coniston

operating in the Newlands valley, and mined here until the time of the Civil War. Mining continued on a sporadic basis throughout the following two centuries, the most productive period being in the middle of the nineteenth. The final decline began, however, about 1875; it was caused by the increasing cost of pumping from the deep levels, and by the availability of cheap supplies of copper from overseas. The mine finally closed shortly after the First World War. The nineteenth-century processing shops for sorting, crushing and washing the ore were in the area of the present youth hostel.

② *Dow Crag (96–263978)*

The large cliff on the opposite side of Goat's Water from the Old Man is Dow Crag, one of the most impressive and important climbing faces in the Lake District. The first climb on the cliff was made by W.P. Haskett Smith and J.W. Robinson in 1886; owing no doubt to its accessibility, it grew rapidly in popularity so that by 1914 more than 20 routes had been devised and more still were added after the First World War. Several new and very hard routes have since been worked out. A very clear echo can be obtained from the opposite side of Goat's Water.

③ *The Banniside Burial Site (96–285967)*

A stone circle about 250 yds (230m) to the south-east of Boo Tarn – marked as an 'enclosure' on the Ordnance Survey's Explorer OL6 Map – was the site of important discoveries made during excavation by W.G. Collingwood in 1909. Two urns containing bone ash and the teeth of a small child were discovered within the circle, buried after cremations carried out in the Middle Bronze Age about 3,000 years ago. Of particular interest was a small fragment of woven cloth, one of the earliest samples to be found in the British Isles.

ROUTE 27 | The Red Pike Ridge

The south-west boundary of the Buttermere valley is defined by a magnificent ridge running from Red Pike to Hay Stacks (although the ridge can be extended further – see Route 40) which offers one of the finest walks in Lakeland with superb views down into the flanking valleys. The route described here reaches the summit of Red Pike from the north-west corner of Buttermere via Bleaberry Tarn. A return to the starting point can be made along the northern shore of the lake.

Length: 9½ miles (15km) | Ascent: 3,450 ft (1,050m) | Starting and finishing point: The Fish Hotel in Buttermere village (89–174169). There is further parking by the church nearby | Maps: Landranger 89; Explorer OL4

ROUTE DESCRIPTION (MAPS 27, 10, 5)

Go down the farm road to the L of the Fish Hotel (signed 'Public Bridleway Buttermere Lake'), soon bending L. After 150 yds (140m) go through a gate ahead and follow the farm road half R. (Do not go through the gate to the R which leads to Scale Force.) Go through a small gate near to the lake shore and turn R, walking down to a small footbridge. On the far side continue up a path half R to a small gate, and cross the higher of two footbridges over a stream coming down the steep hillside (Sour Milk Gill). Immediately cross a wall over a ladder stile (by a gate) and go ahead on the wide track just below. After 50 yds (45m), at a cairn turn R up a rough track.

Climb through the wood (path and cairns) to leave it at a stile in a fence. Continue to climb on the clear path (cairns) which

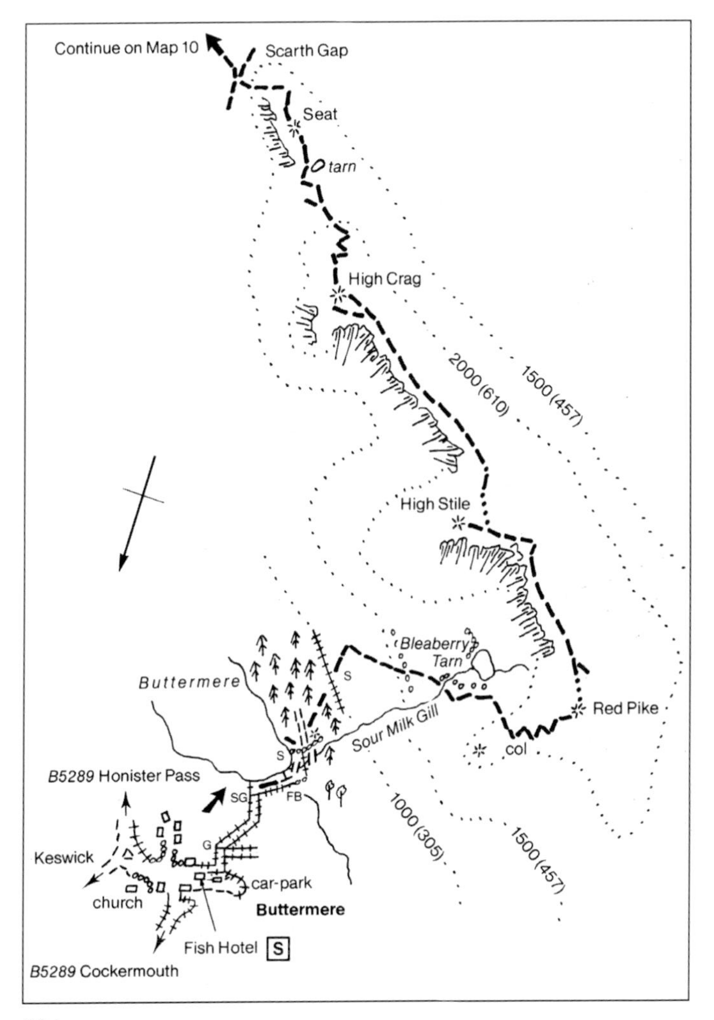
Continue on Map 10
Scarth Gap
Seat
tarn
High Crag
2000 (610)
1500 (457)
High Stile
Bleaberry Tarn
Buttermere
S
Red Pike
Sour Milk Gill
col
S
B5289 Honister Pass
SG
FB
1000 (305)
1500 (457)
G
Keswick
car-park
church
Buttermere
Fish Hotel
S
B5289 Cockermouth

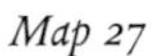
Map 27

Looking across Buttermere to Fleetwith Pike

soon bends R. Higher, cross a ruined wall and then a stream. The path then bends to the L and goes parallel with a wall and the stream to a tarn (Bleaberry Tarn). The path passes to the R of the tarn, through a broken wall, and climbs half R up to a prominent col. From the col continue to climb steeply L to the summit of

Red Pike, the final stretch being something of a scramble over scree – though the views down reward you for the effort.

From the summit cairn go half L and cross the top, to pick up a faint path which soon reaches another coming in from the R. Turn L along the path and follow it along the ridge (there is an intermittent line of old metal fence posts along the ridge top by the path). Soon reach the large cairn at the summit of High Stile, ¾ mile (1.2km) from Red Pike (an earlier point is almost as high).

Go back about 200 yds (180m) to pick up line of posts which goes back half L. Follow these, soon pick up a path and cairns, and descend to col. Cross the col over minor rises, and at the far end take the clear R-hand path following posts to rise to the summit of High Crag.

Continue beyond the summit on a very clear path, soon descending on steep scree then grass to a small tarn on a col. Beyond rise up to the small summit of Seat. Again continue in the same direction, down steep scree to a grassy col (Scarth Gap).

Hay Stacks is now in front of you. See Route 10 for route from here to Gatesgarth Farm – depending on your energy levels this route can take you back either directly or via Hay Stacks and two tarns – and Route 5 from there back to Buttermere. For information about features of interest along the way, see Routes 5 and 10.

ROUTE 28 | Sca Fell from Wasdale

Although separated from Scafell Pike by a mere ⅔ mile (1.1km), and therefore temptingly close when viewed from that peak across the connecting col of Mickledore, the summit of Sca Fell is by comparison both quiet and little frequented. The crowds who climb Scafell Pike because it is the highest mountain in England rarely go further once they have attained it, leaving Sca Fell – which is only 46 ft (14m) lower – to the few (usually rock-climbers and seasoned fell-walkers) who know of its attractions. The formidable defences of the mountain towards the Pike, and the long distances to be covered out of Upper Eskdale where access is easy, are additional factors in its isolation.

The classical route up Sca Fell is by Lord's Rake, and this is the one described here. It must be stressed, however, that the upper reach of the first (and main) section of the Rake is now badly eroded, and some will find it both difficult and unpleasant. Lord's Rake also becomes blocked by landfalls at times – signs on the ascent will alert you to this – forcing you into another way up. The best alternative is to cross Mickledore and then make the ascent by Foxes Tarn, but even this should not be regarded as an easy route.

Length: 8½ miles (14km) | Ascent: 3,950 ft (1,200m) | Starting and finishing point: National Trust car-park near Brackenclose at the head of Wast Water (89–182075) | Maps: Landranger 89; Explorer OL6

ROUTE DESCRIPTION (MAPS 28, 32B)

Leave the car-park and turn L down the farm road through a gate ahead. Immediately after the bridge turn L (PBS 'Eskdale/ Mitterdale, Scafell Massif') along a footpath to the R of the river.

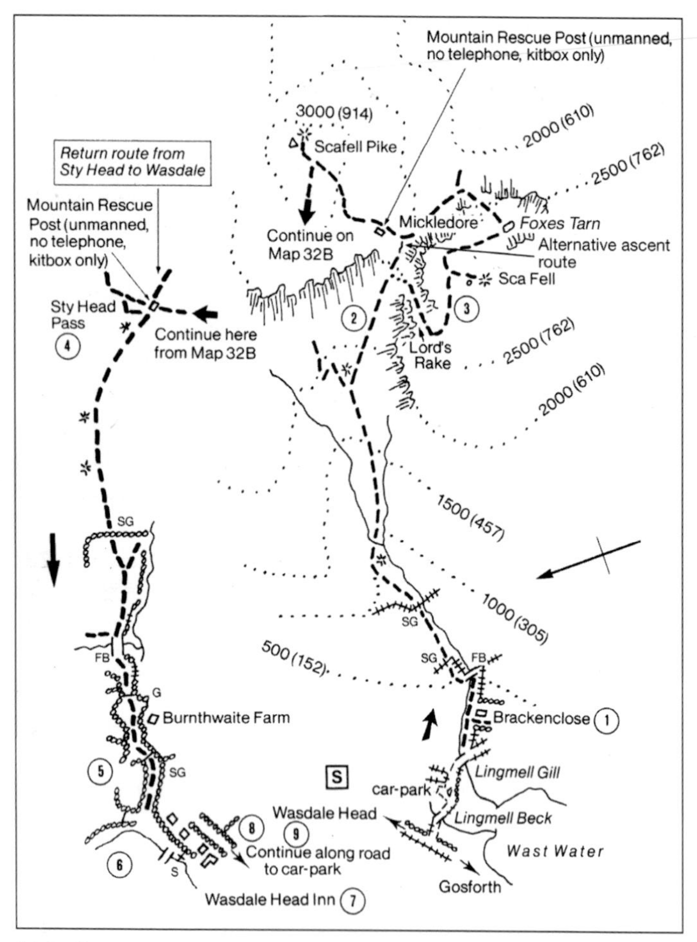

Map 28

Go to L of a small building and soon over a footbridge. The building just passed is a club hut of the Fell and Rock Climbing Club – see ① Brackenclose. Continue to rise on the L bank of the river, crossing a fence at a small gate, and later a second fence at another small gate. After a large cairn at the junction of two stream tributaries the path crosses the L-hand stream and continues to rise by the R-hand one. Towards the top of the steep rise where the path forks, take the R-hand path.

The scene before you at this point is one of the most dramatic and exciting in the entire Lake District. The col of Mickledore is now directly ahead, with Scafell Pike to the L and Sca Fell to the R. The great cliff to the right of Mickledore is Scafell Crag, the scene of some of the greatest triumphs but also one of the most terrible disasters in British rock-climbing – see ② Scafell Crag. Note that at times, as during the update of this book in 2005, Lord's Rake can be blocked by falling boulders or bad weather. In this case, it is best to ascend directly ahead to Mickledore. Here, turn L to pick up the path to Scafell Pike or, if you don't want to miss Sca Fell, reverse the directions from Mickledore below. It is a considerable detour to the top though.

On approaching Mickledore, a fan-shaped scree slope will be seen on the R coming down to the R of the main cliff. If the Lord's Rake route is clear, climb this to the bottom of a deep and steep cleft going up to the R. This is Lord's Rake. Climb the cleft carefully to a small col. Descend a few feet, and then rise to a second col. Descend on the far side and again climb up the slope ahead. At the top, bend L up the slope, eventually reaching the summit of Sca Fell. It should be helpful to remember that there are three ascents and two descents all in the same direction along the Rake before the final turn to the L. You should approach the summit along a cairned path from about NNE. (The name of H.H. Symonds is an honoured one within the Lake District. It was appropriate, therefore, that a small rock peak on Sca Fell was named after him – see ③ Symonds Knott.)

Retrace your steps for about 200 yds (180m) along the path to the NNE, to a path fork. Go R and follow the cairned path steeply down scree to Foxes Tarn. This is a very small pool which can disappear completely in dry periods. Go half L, descending to the L of a small stream which is the tarn outflow. Lower down, continue to descend through a ravine in which a small stream flows. At the bottom turn L up steep scree below the cliff to the col of Mickledore.

Turn R across the col to the Mountain Rescue box. Beyond, take the cairned path across boulders to the summit of Scafell Pike. Follow the Corridor Route (see Route 32) back to the Mountain Rescue box at Sty Head (see ④ Sty Head Pass). Here turn L and follow the very clear path as it descends steadily across the flanks of Great Gable into Wasdale. Eventually, after 1¾ miles (3km), at Wasdale Head pass the farm of Burnthwaite and go down the lane directly ahead, crossing over a succession of small footbridges. (Walkers who have read the section on drystone walls on page 27 should by now be extremely impressed by those in view – see ⑤ Drystone walls at Wasdale Head.) Continue past the old bridge (see ⑥ Pack-horse bridge at Wasdale Head) to the Inn (see ⑦ the Wasdale Head Inn). The first objective of most walkers on completing Route 28 is likely to be Ritson's bar at the Inn, and no pleasanter place could be found throughout the whole of the Lakeland fells for a quiet hour of recovery and the exchange of the day's memories over a good glass of ale.

From here, follow the road for about 1 mile (1.6km) back to the car-park. Alternatively, take the footpath which starts directly opposite the Inn to pass by the small church – see ⑧ St Olaf's Church, Wasdale Head. For information about the progress of civilization towards Wasdale Head, see ⑨ Electricity at Wasdale Head.

ALTERNATIVES FOR THE RETURN ROUTE:

(1) From Mickledore the shortest way is directly ahead, dropping down the slope ahead to the bottom of the scree slope below Lord's Rake, and then back along the approach route.

(2) An exciting alternative is to use the east side of Piers Gill instead of the longer route by Sty Head. Follow the Corridor Route down as far as Piers Gill. On the *far* side take the path which goes to the L along the R side (i.e. the east side) of the Gill. Follow down by the Gill, eventually reaching the bottom where the Gill stream joins the main valley stream (Spouthead Gill). Here cross, and follow the path to the L on the far side which, before Wasdale Head, joins the path described in the main route. Do *not* attempt to descend on the L side (i.e. the western side) or within the Gill itself.

① *Brackenclose (89–185073)*

The building of Brackenclose at the head of Wast Water was the first club hut of the Fell and Rock Climbing Club. It was opened officially on 3 October 1937, and provided a much-needed and healthy stimulus to the Club's development. It was established mainly through the initiative of W.G. Milligan, President 1933–35.

② *Scafell Crag (89–208068)*

This magnificent precipice on the north side of Sca Fell is one of the most important climbing-faces in the Lake District. The main cliff lies between Mickledore, the col which separates Sca Fell and Scafell Pike, and the slanting groove of Lord's Rake. It is made up of four buttresses: from left to right, Central Buttress, Pisgah, Scafell Pinnacle, and Deep Ghyll Buttress (the last of these is directly over Lord's Rake). The three gullies which separate them are Moss, Steep and Deep Ghylls respectively. Below Lord's Rake is Shamrock Buttress.

The first climb of note on the cliff is considered to be the ascent of the Pinnacle by Slingsby's Chimney on 15 July 1888 by a team of W.P. Haskett Smith, W.C. Slingsby, G. Hastings and E. Hopkinson. This involved 355 ft of climbing, and is now graded Hard Difficult. The ascent of Central Buttress in April 1914 by S. Herford and G.S. Sansom was considered the hardest climb in Britain for many years.

The terrible tragedy of 1903 (see page 227) took place on Scafell Pinnacle: a large cross carved on the rock face near the foot of Lord's Rake commemorates this accident.

The main cliff can be turned by easier routes on both flanks. That on the left, above Mickledore, is Broad Stand. It cannot be emphasized too much or too often that this is classified as a rock-climb, although Moderate in standard, and has a long history of accidents, some of which have been fatal. On the right is Lord's Rake which, although now badly eroded, does offer a route for walkers. The crag on the opposite side of Mickledore is Scafell East Buttress.

③ *Symonds Knott (89–206067)*

The rocky outcrop to the north-west of the summit of Sca Fell was named after the Reverend H.H. Symonds. In Walking in the Lake District, *published in 1933, he suggested the formation of 'some thoroughly national group of Friends of the Lake District to supply the emotional impetus without which skill and knowledge win no victories'. Such a group was formed at an open-air meeting at Keswick on 17 June 1934 and was named The Friends of the Lake District in the following September (see page 323).*

④ *Sty Head Pass (89–218094)*

see page 162.

⑤ *Drystone walls at Wasdale Head*

Visitors to Wasdale Head cannot fail to be impressed by the abnormal thickness of some of its drystone walls, made mainly from rounded stones. These are the result of extensive field clearances carried out several hundred years ago. The most convenient method of disposing of the stones was to build them into walls. Similar walls can be found in other dales, e.g. Eskdale.

⑥ *Pack-horse bridge at Wasdale Head (89–187089)*

Behind the hotel at Wasdale Head is a superb pack-horse bridge. There are a number of similar bridges around the Lake District, evidence of

At Wasdale Head

the importance of this form of transport for linking together the lonelier dales. They are narrow, with a single arch and low parapets, built of local stone, probably 1660– 1760.

⑦ *The Wasdale Head Inn (89–187087)*

It is impossible to overestimate the importance of the Wasdale Head Inn in the early years of British rock-climbing. Superbly situated within walking distance of the important climbing-faces of Scafell Crag, the Napes Ridges of Great Gable and Pillar Rock, it became and remained the centre for Lakeland climbing up to the First World War. Undoubtedly some of its early popularity was due to the strong personality of the first landlord, Will Ritson, who was born at the farm of Row Foot in 1808. In due course he inherited the farm and began to accommodate visitors – as is still commonly done today – in 1856 obtaining a licence for the inn trade. Named originally the Huntsman's Inn (it became the Wastwater Hotel later, and is now the Wasdale Head Inn), it soon began to attract walkers and climbers. Most of the important developments in climbing took place, however, during the tenancy of Ritson's successor, Dan Tyson.

The community of climbers which gathered at Wasdale Head in the early days was closely knit. Some of them had family ties, such as the four Hopkinson brothers, the two Abrahams, the Bartons and the Broadricks; many of them had climbed together in North Wales, Scotland, the Alps and even further afield; but, most of all, they came without exception from the same band of society – university professors, businessmen, solicitors: affluent middle-class figures sufficiently prosperous to have both the time and the money for their pursuits.

The community was also almost exclusively male. Hard climbing on the local fells was followed by evenings of loud, lively and thrusting debate around the dining-table, by energetic games of billiard fives or by attempts on one of the in-house climbs: the Barn Door Traverse, the Billiard Room Traverse or the 'passage of the Billiard Table leg'. Restricting and softening female influences did not intrude upon this male preserve.

The terrible tragedy on Sca Fell in 1903 (see below), the First World War which took away several leading climbers, the development of climbing crags in other parts of the Lake District, and finally the formation of climbing groups such as those in Snowdonia at the Pen-y-Gwryd and the Gorphwysfa Hotels, were all factors which contributed to the eventual end of that brilliant and romantic era.

The hotel remained – and still is – a busy and important centre for fell-walkers and climbers, its superb setting amid some of the finest mountains of Lakeland acting as guarantor for its popularity. There is now a Ritson's Bar – as there is a Ritson's Force higher up Mosedale Beck – and a Barn Door Shop supplying climbing equipment, mountaineering publications and food. But much is as the pioneers knew it, and if they could return – as perhaps they do in spirit – no doubt they would find it still to their liking.

⑧ *St Olaf's Church, Wasdale Head*

The church of St Olaf at Wasdale Head, set among a few trees in a small walled enclosure, is reputed to be the smallest parish church in the country. Although small and simple, it is nevertheless a building of considerable charm. It was built about 1552, but probably as a fairly primitive construction. Even 300 years later it was said to have had no door – a thorn bush was used to keep out the sheep – bracken on the floor, and only two pews.

In the small graveyard (right of burial there was granted in 1889) are the graves of several climbers who were killed on the surrounding fells. Of greatest interest is the common grave of three men: Henry L. Jupp (aged 29), Algernon E.W. Garrett (27) and Stanley Ridsdale (26), who lost their lives with R.W. Broadrick (31) on Sca Fell (spelt Scawfell on their gravestone) on 21 September 1903. This accident was the worst in British climbing until the 1950s, and indeed the first to involve the death of any member of a roped party (as distinct from solo climbers or scramblers). The party was apparently attempting to reach Hopkinson's Cairn on Scafell Pinnacle by a direct ascent from Lord's Rake. The cairn was so called because it was built by Charles, Edward and Albert Hopkinson in

1887 on a ledge about 250 ft (75m) above the base which they had reached with a cousin, W.N. Tribe, by a descent from the top of the Pinnacle. The actual fall was unobserved by any other party, but it was caused by Garrett slipping either when he was in the lead or about to take over from Broadrick. Three men were found dead at the foot of the crag, and the fourth, Ridsdale, died shortly afterwards. The climb was completed by S.W. Herford and G.S. Sansom in 1912 and is now graded Severe.

Other well-known climbers buried there are G.R. Speaker, a President of the Fell and Rock Climbing Club, and C.D. Frankland, who both died on Great Gable.

⑨ *Electricity at Wasdale Head*

Wasdale Head was one of the last areas of the Lake District to receive electricity (in 1977). The cable was laid on the bed of Wast Water and underground, so that there was no damaging effect to the environment. The area is still without TV or mobile phone reception, something of which the Wasdale Head Inn is very proud.

More Strenuous Routes

ROUTE 29 | The Fairfield Horseshoe

The Fairfield Horseshoe is one of the great classics of the Lake District. As the name implies, the route follows the long horseshoe ridge – whose centre 'nail' is the summit of Fairfield – which runs around the valley of the Rydal Beck to the north-west of Ambleside. The route can be taken in either direction, but clockwise is better as it involves a shorter ascent. To make a circular route, as described here, it is best to start at Ambleside, where there is a large car-park, and walk to Rydal through Rydal Park.

Length: 11 miles (18km) | Ascent: 3,300 ft (1,000m) | Starting and finishing point: Ambleside (90–376045). There is also parking at Rydal Hall, where the walk can be joined | Maps: Landranger 90; Explorer OL7 and OL5

ROUTE DESCRIPTION (MAPS 29A, 29B, 29C)

From Ambleside walk along the A591, Grasmere-Keswick road (see ① the Bridge House, Ambleside and ② Charlotte Mason and St Martin's College for features of interest along the way). After about ½ mile (800m) go over Scandale Bridge and turn R through large gates (PFS 'Rydal Hall'). Go along a farm road between fences. After ½ mile (800m) go through a gate, and after ¼ mile (400m) through a second gate. Pass small camp-fire area, and before a small bridge turn R towards a large house. Go between the buildings (Rydal Hall), over a bridge and along a lane to reach the road in Rydal.

Bridge House, Ambleside

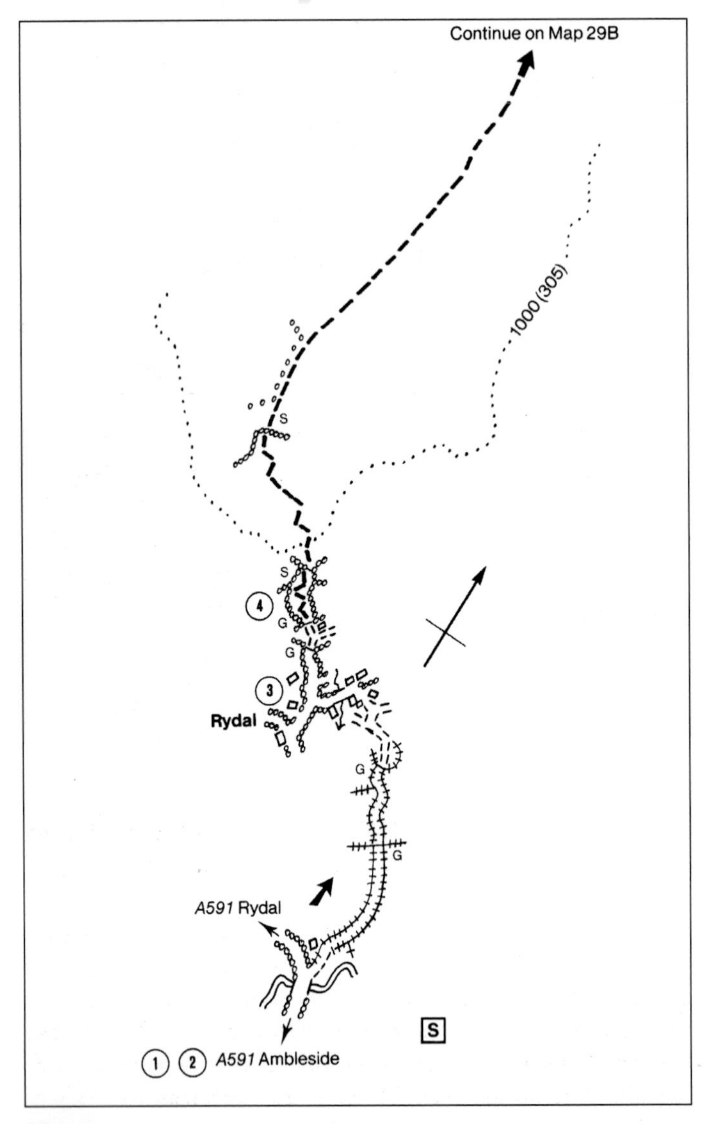
Continue on Map 29B
1000 (305)
S
S
4
G
G
3
Rydal
G
G
A591 Rydal
S
1
2
A591 Ambleside

Map 29A

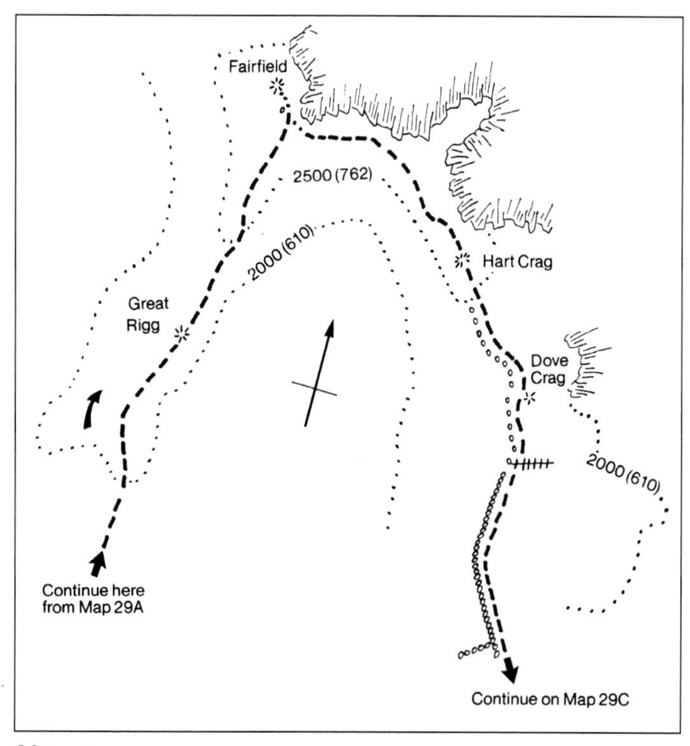

Map 29B

Turn R up the hill. Pass Rydal Mount, occupied by William Wordsworth from 1813 to his death in 1850 (see ③ Rydal Mount), and go up the lane between walls (PFS). Cross a gate in front of you and take the farm road to the L to a second gate. Continue up hill on very obvious path between walls, soon going through zig-zags; considerable work has been done on this hillside to reduce the effects of erosion (see ④ the Lake District National Park Authority). By a conifer wood cross ladder stile. Rise up the open fell on a clear path (cairns) to a second ladder stile in a wall corner. Beyond continue on the path,

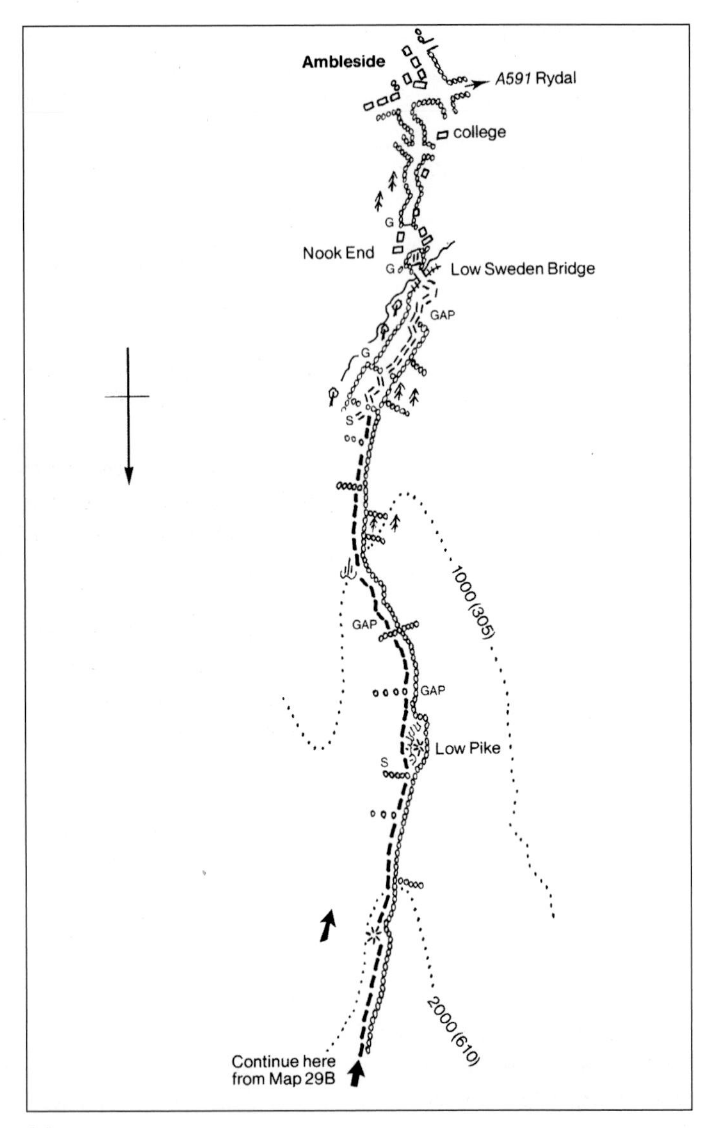
Ambleside
A591 Rydal
college
G
Nook End
G
Low Sweden Bridge
GAP
G
S
1000 (305)
GAP
GAP
Low Pike
S
2000 (610)
Continue here
from Map 29B

Map 29C

which is clearly marked by cairns. No problems should now be encountered in following the path along the ridge, rising over Great Rigg and on to the summit of Fairfield, about 3 miles (5km) from the last ladder stile.

From the summit shelter turn half R (147° magnetic) along the ridge, soon picking up a very obvious path marked by cairns. After a few yards this bends half L, still keeping on the ridge, then later half R descending over boulders to a col; beyond, ascend steeply to the summit of Hart Crag. Continue in the same direction, descending a boulder slope and soon reaching a broken wall. Follow the path to the L of this wall for 2¾ miles (4.5km), crossing Dove Crag, High Pike and Low Pike, leaving the wall to continue on the clear path further down.

Eventually, very low down the path becomes a farm track, passes through a gate, and then continues down to a bridge (Low Sweden Bridge) and through Nook End farmyard to road. Continue down the road back to Ambleside.

① *The Bridge House, Ambleside*

see page 150.

② *Charlotte Mason and St Martin's College (90–375049)*

The College at Ambleside was founded by Charlotte Mason in 1892 for the training of governesses. Initially at Springfield house, it moved to Green Bank three years later. Until 1890 Green Bank had been the home of Mrs Dorothy Benson Harrison, who was the daughter of Robinson Wordsworth, a relation of William Wordsworth. Green Bank was later renamed Scale How. Charlotte Mason remained as Principal until her death in 1923. The College was a private institution until 1961, when it was sold to Westmorland County Council. The site is now known as St Martin's College and its library is named in her honour. The nearby Armitt Museum houses her archives.

③ *Rydal Mount*

see page 150.

Down the Fairfield valley towards Ambleside

④ *The Lake District National Park Authority (90–362066)*

As in other popular mountain areas, such as Snowdonia or the Yorkshire Dales, the problem of footpath erosion is now a serious one for the Lake District. It is caused by the tremendous increase in walking which has taken place since the Second World War, and the natural concentration of walkers along certain routes. It was against this background that the National Park Authority set about repairing the paths.

Much work has already been done. Resurfacing with hard and durable materials, re-alignment of paths, provision of better drainage and the erection of short lengths of fence to keep walkers to the common route are some of the methods used. New paths have also been created where this was helpful, and the Nab Scar path from Rydal on to Fairfield Horseshoe has been among the beneficiaries.

Inevitably, as elsewhere, such work has attracted criticism. But the alternative of disfigured hillsides giving increasingly rougher and less satisfactory walking is one that in the long term would please very few. Together with partners including the National Trust and English Nature, the Park Authority has launched a campaign to raise funds for more path repairs. Details of its work can be found online at www.fixthefells.co.uk.

ROUTE 30 | The Kentmere Horseshoe

The Kentmere Horseshoe is the great ridge in the shape of a horseshoe around the upper valley of the river Kent, the central 'nail' being the summit of High Street. Although long, and with considerable climbing, the walking is easy, good underfoot and along clear paths. The views, particularly on the return leg over Mardale Ill Bell and Harter Fell, are magnificent.

Length: 12 miles (19km) | Ascent: 3,650 ft (1,100m) | Starting and finishing point: A small parking area by the church in Kentmere, about 5 miles (8km) north-east of Windermere (90–456041). Park with care so that the road is not obstructed | Maps: Landranger 90; Explorer OL7 and OL5

ROUTE DESCRIPTION (MAPS 30A, 30B, 30C)

See ① Kentmere, before starting. Walk up the road from the parking area, away from the church. At the end of the road go R up a farm road (PFS 'Troutbeck via Garburn Pass'), which soon bends L to a gate. Continue up the farm road for about 1 mile (1.6km), climbing steadily. During the early part of this ascent there is a superb view over the wall to the left of Kentmere Hall – see ② the Pele Tower at Kentmere. Finally, near to the top of a wide col (Garburn Pass), go through a gate and immediately turn R. The path is indistinct and marshy at first, but soon becomes clearer by a wall.

Follow the wall for 1 mile (1.6km) to a ladder stile in a wall corner. Cross and go up the path on the R and ahead to the summit of Yoke. On the ascent the distinctive peak of Ill Bell can be clearly seen, and beyond that High Street. There are fine views

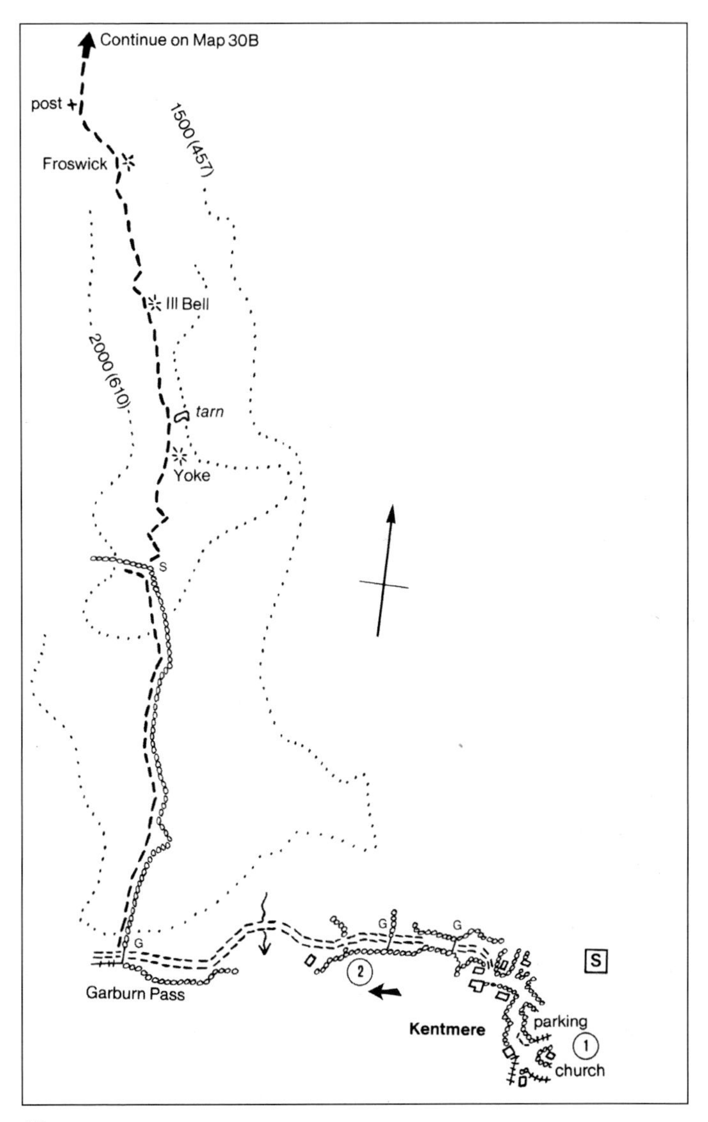
Continue on Map 30B
post
1500 (457)
Froswick
Ill Bell
2000 (610)
tarn
Yoke
S
G
G
G
2
S
Garburn Pass
parking
Kentmere
1
church

Map 30A

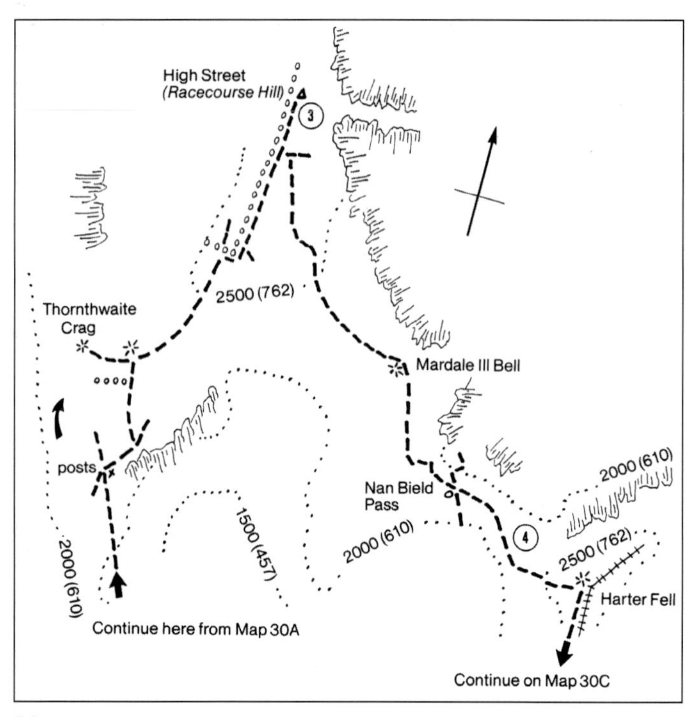

Map 30B

out to the west, on the L of the climb from Yoke. Continue along the ridge on a clear path, traversing Ill Bell and then, after a descent, Froswick. After about ⅔ mile (1.1km) from Froswick, at several posts and a path fork, take the R-hand fork (with a steep slope to the R; a short diversion to the L here will take you up to the top of Thornthwaite Crag with a distinctive 14 ft high cairn). A short distance beyond go L at a second fork away from the cliff edge. Reach the end of a broken stone wall. Keep in the same direction to a T-junction, where turn R. Soon reach a wall. Do not go through the gap but follow the wall to the R (soon turning L) to reach the summit of High Street, marked by an OS pillar. This

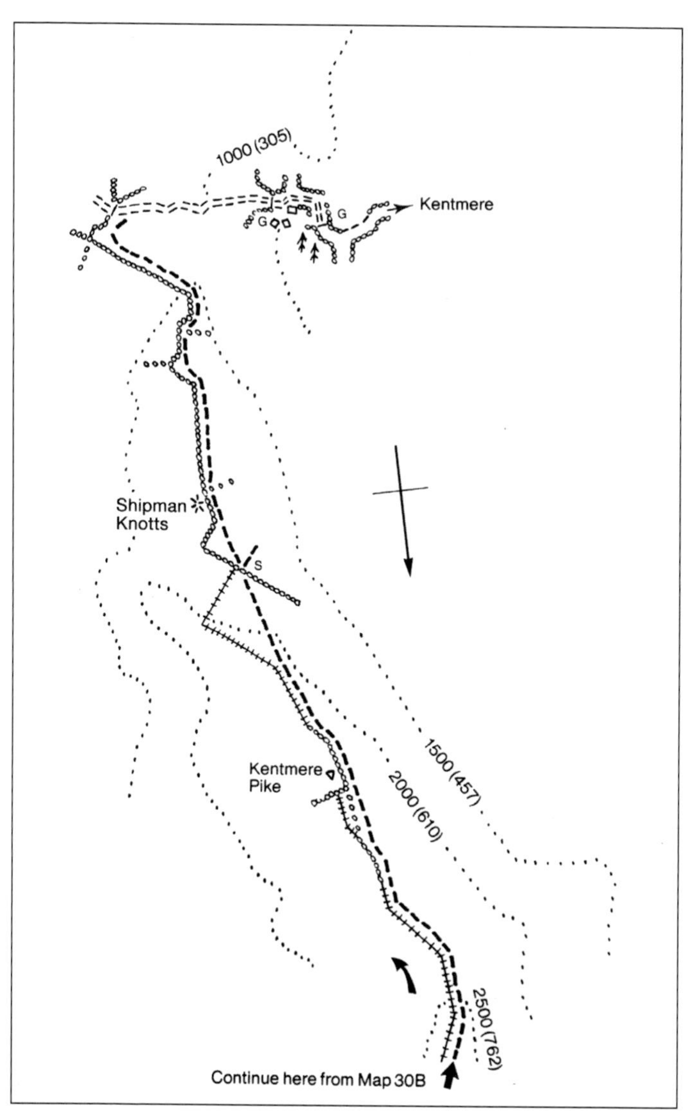
1000 (305)
Kentmere
G
G
Shipman Knotts
S
Kentmere Pike
1500 (457)
2000 (610)
2500 (762)
Continue here from Map 30B

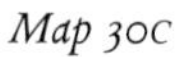
Map 30C

summit has a second (and very unlikely-sounding) name – see ③ Racecourse Hill.

Retrace your steps along the wall for 350 yds (320m) to a faint path going L (cairn). Follow this away from the wall, going R at a junction after a few yards, in a general south-east direction down a broad ridge, which later narrows, to the summit of Mardale Ill Bell. Follow the path beyond, which descends steeply to the shelter on the Nan Bield Pass.

Cross and continue in the same direction, rising to the summit of Harter Fell. (The summit cairn is unique, made up from the remains of several fence posts and stones.) A magnificent view of Haweswater can be obtained on a clear day by walking for a short distance along the ridge towards the north-east (see ④ Mardale). Turn R and follow the fence (later a wall) for 1 mile (1.6km) to the OS obelisk on Kentmere Pike, found opposite a cairn on the other side of the wall.

Keep in the same direction, descending from the Pike, for nearly ½ mile (800m). Where the fence bends to the L, go half R on a path across the moor to a ladder stile in a corner. Cross the stile and take the clear path half L, cutting the corner to a wall. Descend to the R of the wall for just over 1 mile (1.6km), passing over Shipman Knotts to meet a farm road near a gate in the valley. Turn R along it for ¾ mile (1.2km), to a metalled road. Turn L. At the first junction go R and soon at a T-junction R again, back to the parking place in Kentmere.

① Kentmere (90–457041)

The mere, or lake, which was situated on the very flat ground to the south of the village and from which the dale and village derive their names, was substantially drained in the second half of the nineteenth century.

② The Pele Tower at Kentmere (90–451042)

The inhabitants of Furness to the south of the National Park have an old proverb: 'Nowt good comes round Black Combe', and even today it strikes a slight chill. Its origin has been lost with the passage of time, but a plausible explanation is that it arose from the Scottish raids of the fourteenth century, which followed the crushing defeat of the English at Bannockburn in 1314. It is known that western Cumberland was sacked in 1315, and Furness in 1316 and again in 1322, the raiders coming southwards down the coastal plain and around the prominent hill of Black Combe.

In the face of this danger and in the absence of any effective outside help from an inept king, it is scarcely surprising that the inhabitants of the Lakeland area looked to their own defence, particularly on the outskirts of the upland dome where the threat was at its greatest. Beacons lit on suitable hills, such as Skiddaw and the Old Man of Coniston, provided an early warning of the approach of raiders; strategically placed dykes, robust stone towers on churches, and fortified tower-houses (pele towers) could then perhaps provide sufficient strength to withstand attack for a short period. This was all that would normally be required, for the raids were generally short and inclined towards the taking of easy booty.

A fine example of a pele tower is to be seen down to the left at Kentmere Hall on the rise out of Kentmere. It was built in the fourteenth century, and is attached to farm buildings of the sixteenth. Like most towers, it consists of three floors with a flat roof.

③ *Racecourse Hill (90–441111)*

see page 276.

④ *Mardale (90–476118)*

The building of a dam across Mardale which began in 1929 raised the water level of the lake there by 95 ft (29m) and produced a new reservoir about 4 miles (6.5km) long. During the rise, a small hamlet near the head of the dale was drowned. Its church, built in the sixteenth century and set among yew trees, was demolished, and the coffins from the churchyard were lifted and reburied in a small enclosure at Shap. With the church went several cottages, the school, and the Dun Bull Inn.

Occasionally, when the dam water drops to a very low level, the remains of the hamlet re-emerge immediately to the north of a wooded peninsula known as The Rigg. The field walls are still surprisingly intact, as are those that define the road which ran through the village as far as the Inn. It is also intriguing to see that the Mardale Beck resumes its original course under the old bridge.

But in most years only the memories remain in the minds of the very small – and diminishing – group of people who once knew Mardale. For the rest of us, there are a few old black-and-white photographs: one of Mardale Church in about 1920; another of Isaac Cookson of Gillhead, Bampton at the Mardale Shepherds' Meet which he attended on 64 occasions; and one of a party of hunt supporters outside the Dun Bull Inn. The observant will also notice on OS maps the line of the old corpse road – along which the dead were carried (before there was a right of burial at the church) from Mardale to the nearest consecrated ground at Shap – which disappears into the reservoir on its eastern shore.

ROUTE 31 | The Coledale Horseshoe

The Coledale Horseshoe is unquestionably the finest ridge walk of the north-western fells, an area that is rich with them. The route goes in a horseshoe around the valley of the Coledale Beck, hence its name. Strictly, perhaps, the return leg to the south should traverse Outerside and Barrow, which would also give a more direct route back to Braithwaite, but the Causey Pike ridge further to the south is both higher and finer. A worthwhile detour can be made to the summit of Grasmoor, but this will add more than 1½ miles (2.5km) to the total distance.

Length: 10½ miles (17km) | Ascent: 4,400 ft (1,340m) | Starting and finishing point: Small parking place on the L of the B5292, just out of Braithwaite towards the Whinlatter Pass (89–227238). It is found just before a sign for 'Parking, ½ mile' – if the smaller car-park is full, use this further space and walk back along the B5292 to the start of the route | Maps: Landranger 89; Explorer OL4

ROUTE DESCRIPTION (MAPS 31A, 31B)

Facing away from the road, go up some steps at the R end of the car-park. The path rises slowly, turning L before the forest. After crossing a stile, bear R and continue upwards. The path continues to rise well to the L of the forest and overlooking the Coledale Beck on the L. Higher, the ridge becomes much steeper and narrower. After 2¼ miles (3.5km) from Braithwaite, reach the summit of Grisedale Pike.

Continue on a clear path beyond, crossing a minor summit and, taking the R hand fork at a cairn, then rising to the L of a large crag (Hobcarton Crags) to the summit of Hopegill Head. This is

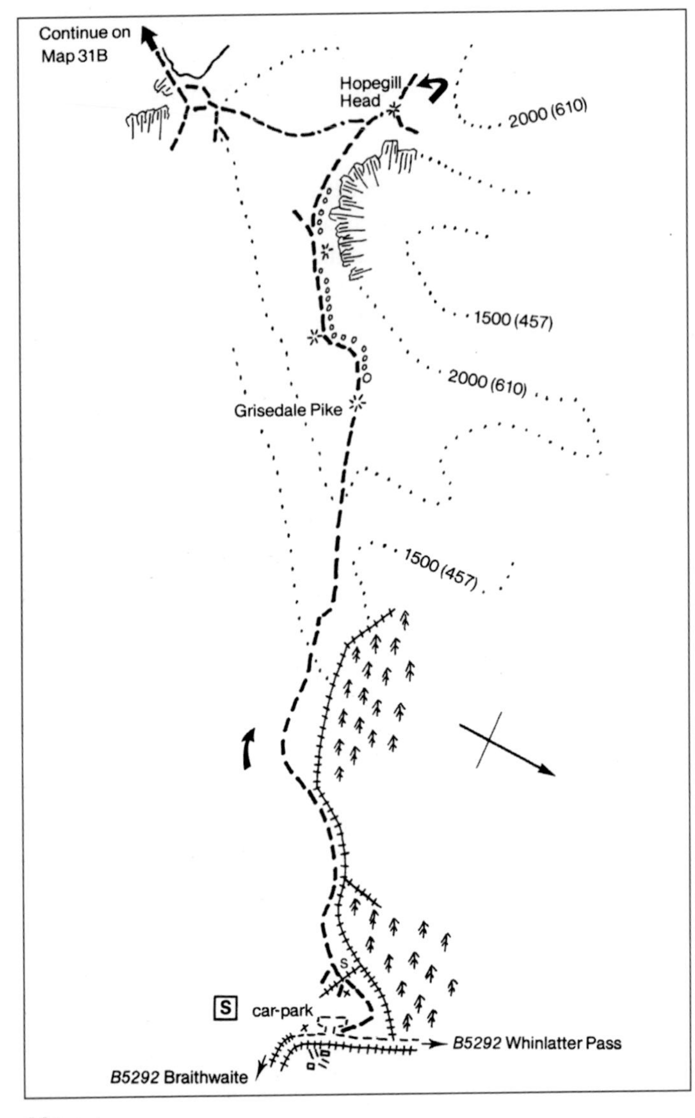
Continue on
Map 31B
Hopegill
Head
2000 (610)
1500 (457)
2000 (610)
Grisedale Pike
1500 (457)
S
S car-park
B5292 Whinlatter Pass
B5292 Braithwaite

Map 31A

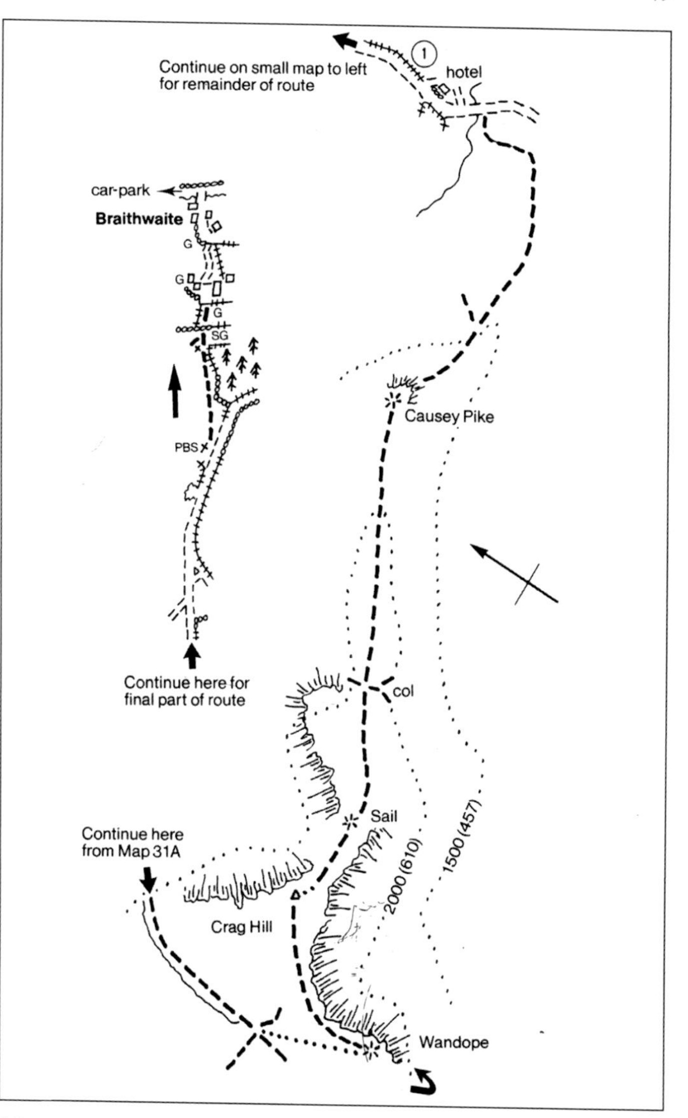
Continue on small map to left for remainder of route
1
hotel
car-park
Braithwaite
G
G
G
SG
PBS
Causey Pike
Continue here for final part of route
col
Sail
Continue here from Map 31A
2000 (610)
1500 (457)
Crag Hill
Wandope

Map 31B

The Coledale Horseshoe from the west

a magnificent view-point, the meeting point of three superb ridges. The lake you can see is Crummock Water.

Go back about 65 yds (60m) and then leave half R from the original path along a line of cairns and down a stony path. Soon the path drops further down grassy slopes to a wide col. On the opposite side at a fork take either path, to rise to an upper path where turn R. This path goes up a narrow valley to the L of a stream. When the stream ends, continue in the same direction to reach a prominent crossing place of two tracks at the highest point. From this go half L across open fell (no path) to the summit of Wandope (small cairn).

Turn L along the ridge and follow a path near to the edge (there is a steep slope and a cliff to the R). Descend to col and then rise to the summit of Crag Hill. Leave half L towards a cairn (no path). Just beyond, pick up a clear path called 'The Scar' and descend steeply, then rising to the next summit of Sail. Continue now on the ridge for 1½ miles (2.5km), crossing Scar Crags to the summit of Causey Pike. The view ahead to Derwent Water is beautiful. Continue in the same direction beyond the summit, descending rocks to a path. At a junction after an initial descent take the R path. Later, descend steeply and negotiate the maze of paths to bring yourself out at a bridge on a metalled road, clearly visible for much of the descent.

Turn L along the road (see ① the Newlands valley). After ¾ mile (1.2km), soon after a small quarry slope on the L, leave the road half L on a path (PBS). This goes past a wood and eventually down to a small gate in a wall. Go through and keep on the L side of a field by a fence to a stile. Go straight on between farm buildings to a gate. Beyond, follow the farm road to a gate and, further on, a metalled road. Turn L and go through the village (Braithwaite) and over a bridge to the B5292. Turn L for the car-park.

① *The Newlands valley*

See page 199 for derivation of name. A good view of the site of the old tarn is obtained from the road section following the descent from the Causey Pike ridge. Uzzicar Farm is just to the right of the road.

ROUTE 32 | Scafell Pike from Borrowdale

The ascent of Scafell Pike from Borrowdale over Glaramara and Allen Crags presents no particular problems, but the way is long and some walkers may therefore prefer to start at Seathwaite instead of Seatoller, which will reduce the total distance by 2–3 miles (3–5km). Although it attains the main objective of the Pike, this alternative omits the lovely high-level traverse over the two peaks mentioned above, using instead the much inferior approach via Sty Head. Nevertheless, both routes are of high quality. The Corridor Route – formerly called the Guides' Route – is used for the return to Sty Head.

Length: 10 miles (16km) | Ascent: 3,100 ft (950m) | Starting and finishing point: The car-park at Seatoller in Borrowdale (89–246137) | Maps: Landranger 89; Explorer OL4 and OL6

ROUTE DESCRIPTION (MAPS 32A, 32B, 18)

Leave the car-park into the road, and turn L. At the junction go L. Pass the Glaramara outdoor adventure and holiday centre and immediately after the bridge turn R down a lane (PFS 'Seathwaite'). (Before entering the lane read ① Bob Graham, and consider whether a short diversion is not in order.) Where the wall on the L ends, go L through a small gate and follow the path which soon bends R at a wall corner. About ½ mile (800m) further, go through a small gate, and after 300 yds (270m) go R at a path junction (there is a cairn at the junction and a sheepfold to the L across the stream).

Follow the path which rises steadily up the broad ridge. Just before the summit of Glaramara (i.e. 1½ miles (2.5km) from the

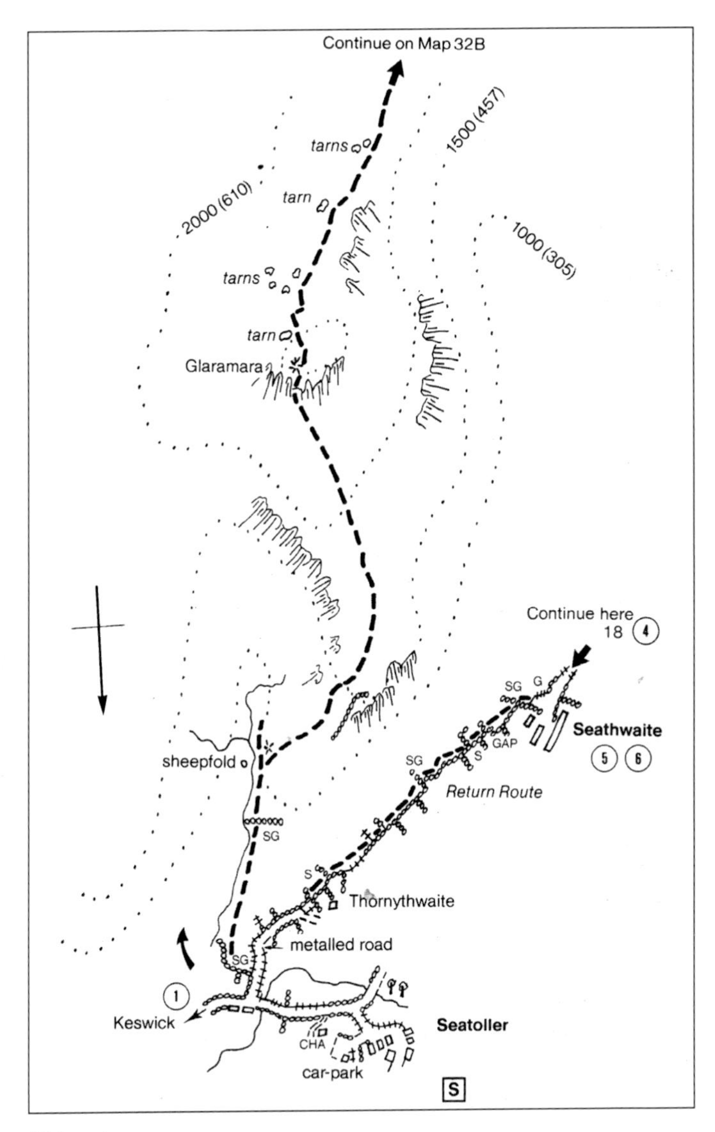
Continue on Map 32B
tarns
1500 (457)
2000 (610)
tarn
1000 (305)
tarns
tarn
Glaramara
Continue here
18 4
SG
G
Seathwaite
GAP
5 6
SG
S
Return Route
sheepfold
SG
S
Thornythwaite
metalled road
SG
1
Keswick
Seatoller
CHA
car-park
S

Map 32A

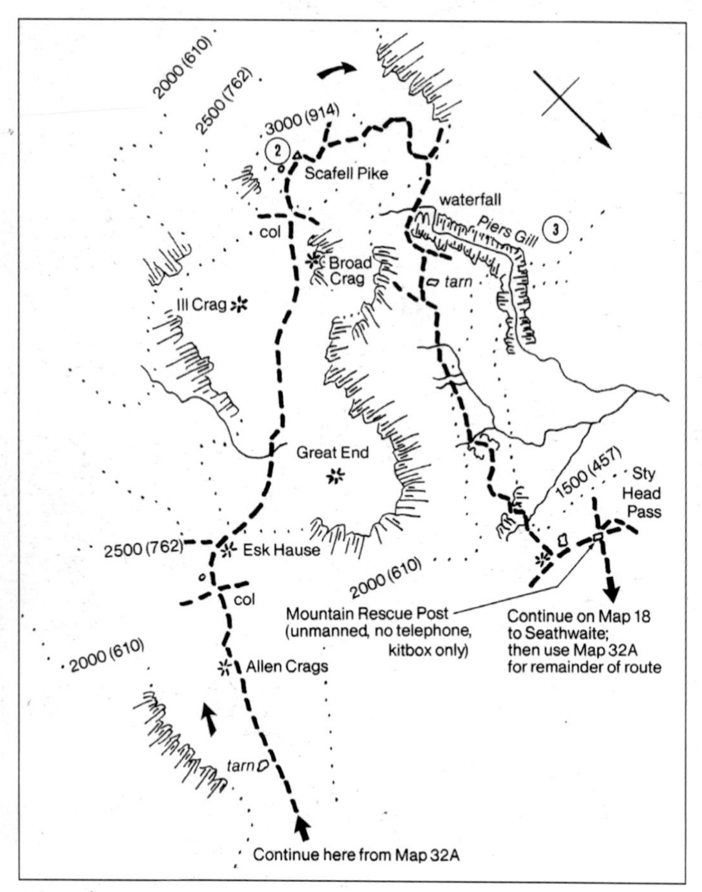

Map 32b

junction) a short scramble has to be negotiated. From the summit cairn go half R, soon dropping down a short rock face. From there pick up the path which goes along the ridge in a far-from-straight line, past several small tarns to Allen Crags about 1½

Frozen falls, near Piers Gill

miles (2.5km) away. Beyond the cairn of Allen Crags, drop down to a grassy col with a cross track.

Continue in the same direction past a shelter for 300 yds (270m), bending R at the end to a cairn. Continue along the path. After about 1 mile (1.6km) the path crosses boulders between two rocky summits (Broad Crag and Ill Crag), and then descends to a narrow col. From the col ascend to the summit of Scafell Pike, the last part over boulders with the path marked by a series of cairns. As with several other mountains and hills in the Lake District, such as Great Gable and Castle Crag, the summit of Scafell Pike was dedicated as a memorial to men who died in the First World War – see ② the summit of Scafell Pike: War Memorial.

From the summit cairn drop down to the R relative to your approach route, to pick up a path which soon bends L. About 75 yds (70m) from the bend at a fork, take the R-hand branch marked by many cairns. Soon descend steeply towards a grassy col (Lingmell Col). Just before the col, take a path to the R, indistinct at first but marked by cairns. Soon go around the head of a deep ravine with a waterfall on the L. This ravine is Piers Gill, the scene in 1921 of one of the most extraordinary walking accidents ever to have occurred in the Lakeland fells – see ③ Piers Gill. Do not take the path which goes to the L following the edge of the Gill on the far side; instead continue in the same direction. No difficulty should now be found in following the path for 1½ miles (2.5km) back to Sty Head, but make sure you do not descend too far – the path to Sty Head remains higher up the valley before descending to a col and rising. The path joins the Sty Head to Angle Tarn path at a T-junction; there turn L to the Mountain Rescue box.

At the box, turn R and follow the path past Sty Head Tarn. Cross the footbridge and follow the path to a further bridge (see ④ Stockley Bridge). Here, bear L on the path for about 1 mile (1.6km) back to Seathwaite. Walkers arriving in the village on those Lakeland days when the rain is coming down 'straight as stair rods' will not be surprised to learn that in Victorian times Seathwaite enjoyed the reputation of being the wettest place in England – see ⑤ Seathwaite.

Passing through the little village and a café, go L (PFS 'Thornythwaite'). Go through a gate and follow the path to the R of a wall. After a short distance go through a small gate on your L and along the footpath across the field. (The hillside across the valley at this point was the site of a famous mine serving the Keswick pencil industry – see ⑥ the Borrowdale Plumbago Mine.) At the end, go through a gap in a wall corner. Continue now for 1 mile (1.6km), keeping the wall on your L, to reach a metalled farm road. Turn R and follow this to the B5289, and turn L back towards the car-park.

① *Bob Graham (1889–1966)*

The small church at Borrowdale has the grave of Bob Graham, whose Bob Graham Round, named after his feat of more than 70 years ago, still remains one of the most demanding challenges of the Lakeland fells.

Starting from Keswick Moot Hall at 1 a.m. on Sunday 13 June 1932, Graham climbed 42 peaks, the vast majority being over 2,000 ft, before returning to his starting point in 23 hours 39 minutes. His route from Keswick led over Skiddaw, Great Calva and Blencathra to Threlkeld, down the long ridge to the south over Clough Head, Helvellyn, Dollywaggon Pike, Fairfield and Seat Sandal to Dunmail Raise, then south-west to the Langdale Pikes and on over Bow Fell and Great End to Scafell Pike. Broad Stand was crossed to Sca Fell, before a descent to Wasdale Head. The Mosedale circuit of Yewbarrow, Red Pike, Steeple, Pillar, Kirk Fell and Great Gable was then completed, followed by a traverse over Green Gable, Brandreth and Grey Knotts to Honister Hause. The final stretch was over Dale Head, Hindscarth and Robinson and back to Keswick: 27,000 ft of climbing over 72 miles! A remarkable feat by any standards. Strangely, his gravestone gives 32,000 ft and 130 miles, a considerable error particularly as regards the distance. Bob Graham's record stood for 28 years until

View from the rocky top of Scafell Pike

1960, when Alan Heaton completed the circuit in 22 hours 18 minutes.

In 1971 a Bob Graham 24 Hour Club was formed. Full membership is restricted to those who have completed the Graham Round – clockwise or anti-clockwise – of 42 peaks within 24 hours, or who have completed a similar round but including other peaks, which is regarded as 'a more meritorious achievement.' More than 1,000 men and women have now completed the remarkable feat. More details on the Round can be found online at www.bobgrahamround.co.uk.

The small headstone of green slate will be found to the south-east of the church.

② The summit of Scafell Pike: War Memorial (89–215072)

Forty acres (16 hectares) around the summit of Scafell Pike were given to the National Trust by the third Lord Leconfield as a war memorial for the Lake District. On 24 August 1921 a large cairn was built on the summit by men of the Ordnance Survey, who were there to erect a trigonometrical survey pillar. Into this was set a stone plaque – brought up by wheelbarrow from Seathwaite – which reads: 'In perpetual memory of the men of the Lake District who fell for God and King, for freedom, peace and right in the Great War 1914–18. This summit of Scafell was given to the nation, subject to any commoners rights, and placed in the custody of the National Trust by Charles Henry, Baron Leconfield, 1919.'

③ *Piers Gill (89–212082)*

Piers Gill is the fierce ravine to the east of Lingmell, which holds the main tributary of Lingmell Beck. In the early days of rock-climbing, the full and direct ascent of the Gill was considered by many to be impossible, but this was achieved in 1892. Twenty-nine years later, in 1921, it was the scene of a highly unusual accident. Three climbers attempting the first descent of the Gill during an exceptionally dry period came upon an injured man. The walker had lost his way in mist while descending to Wasdale Head and had fallen in Piers Gill, injuring both legs. He had lain there undiscovered, with practically no food, for twenty days, despite extensive searches of the surrounding area.

The zig-zag course of Piers Gill is caused by the stream water eroding along the shattered lines of several intersecting faults. The full ascent is a rock climb of Very Difficult standard, called Pilgrim's Progress, and should not be attempted by non-climbers.

④ *Stockley Bridge (89–235109)*

The bridge above Seathwaite was used on the old pack-horse road from Borrowdale to Wasdale. It has been badly damaged and repaired on several occasions after flooding caused by heavy rain.

⑤ *Seathwaite (89–236121)*

The farm at Seathwaite, about 1½ miles (2.5km) from Seatoller in Borrowdale, was long regarded as the wettest place in England. This reputation was based originally upon readings taken from a rain-gauge placed there by John Miller of Whitehaven in 1844, but owed as much to an ignorance of rainfall elsewhere as to the actual values recorded. Later work showed that higher rainfall occurred at greater altitudes in the central mountain mass, and in some areas outside the Lake District. However, Seathwaite with about 130 inches (3,300mm) of rain each year can still justifiably claim to be the wettest inhabited place in Britain.

⑥ The Borrowdale Plumbago Mine (89–232127)

The eastern slopes of Grey Knotts above Seathwaite are the site of old plumbago mines, whose produce was used in the early days of the Keswick pencil industry. Plumbago, originally also known as blacklead, black-cawke and wad, and nowadays called graphite, is a very pure amorphous form of carbon occurring in 'pipes' in the rocks of the Borrowdale Volcanic Series.

The first discovery of this source was probably made about the middle of the sixteenth century, for there is a mention of it in 1555 and the mine was worked, although spasmodically and at a low level, from then onwards. Around the middle of the eighteenth century, however, largely because of its use in the Keswick pencil industry, its price rose considerably. Despite stringent precautions at the mines and in its subsequent transport, a lively smuggling trade developed and in 1752 Parliament found it necessary to pass an Act making unlawful entry into a mine, or the stealing of wad, a felony punishable by hard labour or transportation. By the early years of the nineteenth century, however, output declined as the pipes were worked out and, faced with competition from foreign supplies, the mines were forced to close. The last graphite was mined about 1838. Keswick now has a popular and interesting pencil museum on Main Street.

Looking across the valley soon after leaving Seathwaite, the walker will see spoil heaps of the mines to the right of the Sour Milk Gill waterfalls. There are a number of shafts and levels in the area.

ROUTE 33 | Pillar by the High Level Route

No walker worth his salt should leave the Lake District without at least some acquaintance with Pillar Rock, arguably the most impressive climbing-face within the Park, although the summit of the Rock itself, High Man, is strictly for climbers. The High Level Route – justifiably regarded as the finest way to the Rock – runs from near Looking Stead, a minor peak on the long ridge between the Black Sail Pass and the summit of Pillar, to Robinson's Cairn, from where there is a magnificent view of the Rock. From there an exciting climb can be made to the top of the fell.

The ideal starting point for this walk – as for any walk in Ennerdale – must be one of the two youth hostels situated within the valley: Black Sail at the eastern end of the forest, or Ennerdale near High Gillerthwaite. Apart from these, the valley is totally devoid of any accommodation higher than the western end of Ennerdale Water. Nor are any unauthorized vehicles allowed. For those travelling by car, an approach must be made either from the car-park at Bowness Knott or from one of the adjacent valleys of Buttermere or Wasdale. The route described here starts at Buttermere, but will serve equally well for those staying at Black Sail.

Length: 11 miles (18km) | Ascent: 4,800 ft (1,460m) | Starting and finishing point: The car-park by Gatesgarth Farm at the eastern end of Buttermere (89–195150) | Maps: Landranger 89; Explorer OL4

ROUTE DESCRIPTION (MAPS 10, 33A, 33B)

From the car-park go into the road and turn R. Do not cross the bridge, but just before it turn L through a small gate and down a

footpath. At the end go through a small gate and cross the field ahead to a path between fences. Cross the footbridge, and go through the gate at the wall corner. Take the path directly ahead up the hillside to the R of a wall and fence. Shortly, the path goes L crossing the fence and climbs across the hillside. Higher, cross a further wall, eventually reaching Scarth Gap.

Cross the gap and descend on the far side, soon bending half L along the edge of the forest, now mostly cut down for replanting. At the forest road turn L and follow to Black Sail – see ① Black Sail Hut. (Those staying at the hostel will start here.) Pass the hostel, keeping by the edge of the forest (now partly cleared), soon crossing the stream at a footbridge. On the opposite side, follow the path up the hillside to the R of the stream. Keep climbing to Black Sail Pass. Turn R.

After nearly ½ mile (800m) pass the small summit of Looking Stead on your R and descend slightly on the far side. About 200 yds (180m) after the col at a cairn, take a path to the R away from the main ridge. Follow the clear path across the hillside for nearly ¾ mile (1.2km) to a prominent cairn, erected in honour of an early cragsman – see ② Robinson's Cairn. The magnificent precipice now directly ahead is one of the most famous climbing-faces in the Lake District – see ③ Pillar Rock.

Continue in the same direction towards the Rock, descending slightly. After about 400 yds (370m), the path turns L, later zigzaging up scree. At the rock face go to the R up a wide shelf across the cliff (Shamrock Terrace). Skirt around the top of a gully, and reach a tall, thin crag, Pisgah, at the rear of the Rock. Turn L and climb steeply up to the top of Pillar. Use Route 40 for the descent from Pillar to the lower forest road (see ④ Ennerdale Forest).

Turn R and follow the road for nearly 1 mile (1.6km) to a bridge over the river to the L. Cross, and turn R on the forest road

In Ennerdale

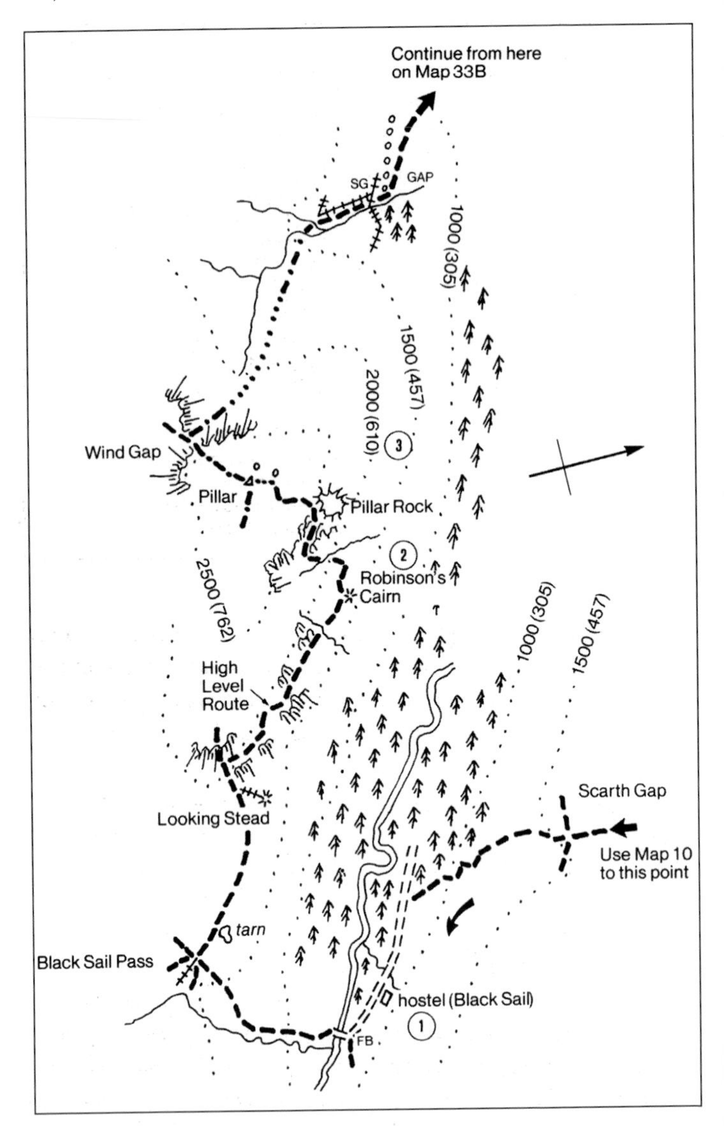
Continue from here
on Map 33B
SG
GAP
1000 (305)
1500 (457)
2000 (610)
3
Wind Gap
Pillar
Pillar Rock
2
Robinson's
Cairn
2500 (762)
1000 (305)
1500 (457)
High
Level
Route
Scarth Gap
Looking Stead
Use Map 10
to this point
tarn
Black Sail Pass
hostel (Black Sail)
1
FB

Map 33A

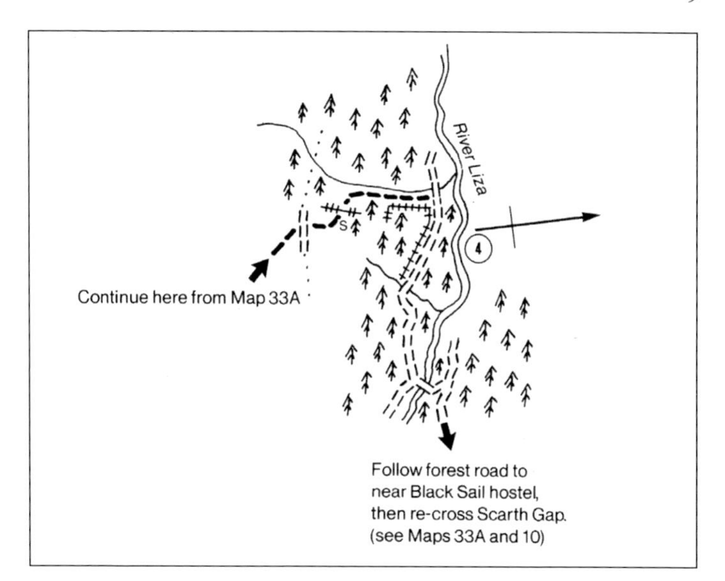

Map 33B

on the far side. Follow for 1¾ mile (3km) to the end of the forest. Turn L and follow the path over Scarth Gap back to Buttermere the way you came earlier. (If bound for Black Sail, continue further along the forest road for a short distance.)

① *Black Sail Hut (89–195124)*

Situated by the tree-line on the northern slopes of Ennerdale, immediately below the summit ridge of Hay Stacks, is Black Sail Hut, justifiably described by the YHA as one of the most isolated and excitingly situated hostels in England. Formerly a shepherd's bothy serving the Lowther Estates, it was leased by the YHA from the Forestry Commission in 1932. Thanks to a generous donation by Professor Trevelyan, it was adapted for use as a hostel and opened in 1933. It was an immediate success, the Annual Report of the following year noting that 'a great number of bookings had of necessity to be declined'. Of simple grade, it offers accommodation for 16 walkers (there is no access for cars) between

March and October and is among the favourites of YHA members. Its cosy facilities and its superb and isolated situation within easy reach of many of the finest mountains of Lakeland are among its attractions.

② *Robinson's Cairn (89–177123)*

The large upright cairn situated at a superb view-point on the High Level Route just before the sharp rise to the Shamrock Terrace was erected by members of the Fell and Rock Climbing Club to the memory of John Wilson Robinson (1853–1907), one of the pioneers of Lakeland climbing. He played a part in a number of first ascents, in particular Moss Ghyll on Sca Fell and Great Gully on The Screes. There is a small memorial plaque nearby.

③ *Pillar Rock (89–175124)*

This superb crag is situated on the northern slopes of Pillar, facing into Ennerdale. Both for its spectacular form and for the part that it played in the early days of British rock-climbing it must rank as one of the most important climbing-faces in the British Isles – in the Lake District, it is on a par with Scafell Crag and the Napes Ridges on Great Gable. Only its name does it less than justice, although perhaps somewhat better than 'the Pillar Stone', as the early dalesmen and cragsmen knew it.

Fashioned out of the excellent climbing rock of the Borrowdale Volcanic Series, it reaches a height of about 750 ft (230m). The actual summit is appropriately called High Man, while the prominent shoulder further down the main face is Low Man. To the east (i.e. on the left when facing it from Ennerdale) it is flanked by a dark cleft, Walker's Gully, which lies between it and a further rock face, the Shamrock. The shortest face is at the rear, where a deep cleft (the Jordan gap) separates it from a small cliff on the main mountain called Pisgah. (These names were all given by early climbers: Pisgah was the high place from which Moses viewed the promised land which lay across the Jordan; Walker's Gully was named after a young climber killed there in 1883; and Shamrock was so called because of the broken nature of the rock.)

The first recorded ascent to High Man was made by a local shepherd, John Atkinson, on 9 July 1826, probably up the west face to Low

The view to Ennerdale Water on the descent from Pillar

Man and then from there to the main summit. Although this feat was repeated by the end of the same year, ascents did not become common until after about 1850. In 1861 came the first ascent of the east face by the Slab and Notch Route.

One noteworthy visitor was the Reverend James Jackson, a retired clergyman who lived near Whitehaven. During his incumbency he had already earned a considerable reputation for eccentricity by climbing up his church steeple to repair the weathercock when local builders jibbed at the task. He climbed Pillar Rock twice, the first time in 1875 at the age of 79, and the second the following year. On the strength of these exploits Jackson, an extreme extrovert, dubbed himself 'Patriarch of the Pillarites'. He was killed in 1878 in a third attempt.

High Man can only be reached by a rock-climb, and is therefore out of the range of walkers.

④ Ennerdale Forest

see page 110.

ROUTE 34 | High Street

The long ridge running south between Penrith and Windermere is famous as the course of the important Roman road of High Street. It is also justifiably famous among the fell-walking fraternity as a superb walking route. Although the total distance to be covered is substantial, the amount of climbing involved is surprisingly low and the going throughout easy. For most walkers the main problem will be the return from Troutbeck to Pooley Bridge at the end of a long day – buses connect the two via Glenridding, but check times in advance.

Length: 16 miles (26km) | Ascent: 2,900 ft (890m) | Starting point: Pooley Bridge at the northern end of Ullswater (90–473245). There are two car-parks in the village | Finishing point: Troutbeck, just off the A592 road 3½ miles (5.5km) north of Windermere (90–411035) | Maps: Landranger 90; Explorer OL5 and OL7

ROUTE DESCRIPTION (MAPS 34A, 34B, 34C, 34D)

From the bridge over the River Eamont walk down the main street of Pooley Bridge (B5320). By the church leave the main road to the R up the Howtown and Martindale road. Soon at a crossroads continue ahead. By Roehead Farm the metalled road ends at a gate. Go through this and up the rough moor road beyond (PBS 'Helton'). At a crossing point by a large cairn after ⅔ mile (1.1km), turn R. After 500 yds (460m) reach a crossing track at an obvious stone circle (see ① the Cockpit). Turn R along a track, soon crossing a small stream. The moor to the left of this path has a particularly high concentration of barrows and cairns from the Bronze Age, many of which lie within a short distance of the track going up the moor from Roehead Farm. Most walkers, however, with 15 miles of fell-walking still in front of them, will think twice before making a diversion – see ② Moor Divock.

After ⅝ mile (1km), cross a stream with a wall to the R. Rise up on the L hand path on the far side and turn L up a broad grassy path for 1 mile (1.6km) to reach the top by a small hill (Arthur's Pike). Here the path bends L to join another track coming in from the L. Turn R and after 10 yds (9m) turn L to start rising again. Over the next 1¾ miles (3km) the path climbs up the moor and then swings around in a half-circle to the west of Loadpot Hill, to the remains of a shooting-lodge on the far side.

At this ruin turn R, and follow a path first descending slightly to the R side of a low broad col, and then rising to the summit of Wether Hill. Descend, pass through a broken wall and then cross a second summit, Red Crag, beyond, keeping in the same direction, and descend to a wall corner. Go through gap and across moor to a fence. Turn L. Follow fence for 1⅔ miles (2.5km). Where the fence turns R keep in the same direction for about 300 yds (270m), passing High Raise (the summit cairn is up to the L).

Past the summit keep in the same direction, descending to a col with a small tarn. Here the path bends to the R and rises to Rampsgill Head (crags to R). Keeping in the same direction, descend on the far side on to a clear path, and at a T-junction by a wall turn L. (Soon after this L turn, a path leaves half R through a gap in the wall. This is one of the more obvious and impressive sections of the Roman road which goes to the west of the summit – see ③ High Street.) Do not take this clear path, but follow the wall to the summit of High Street, where there is an OS obelisk (see ④ Racecourse Hill). Continue to follow the wall as it gently descends and where it bends R, turn with it. After 30 yds (25m), at a crossing track go L.

After 400 yds (370m) at a cairn and T-junction turn L onto a faint, grassy path, towards and past a broken wall (the large cairn on Thornthwaite Crag is directly ahead and worth a short

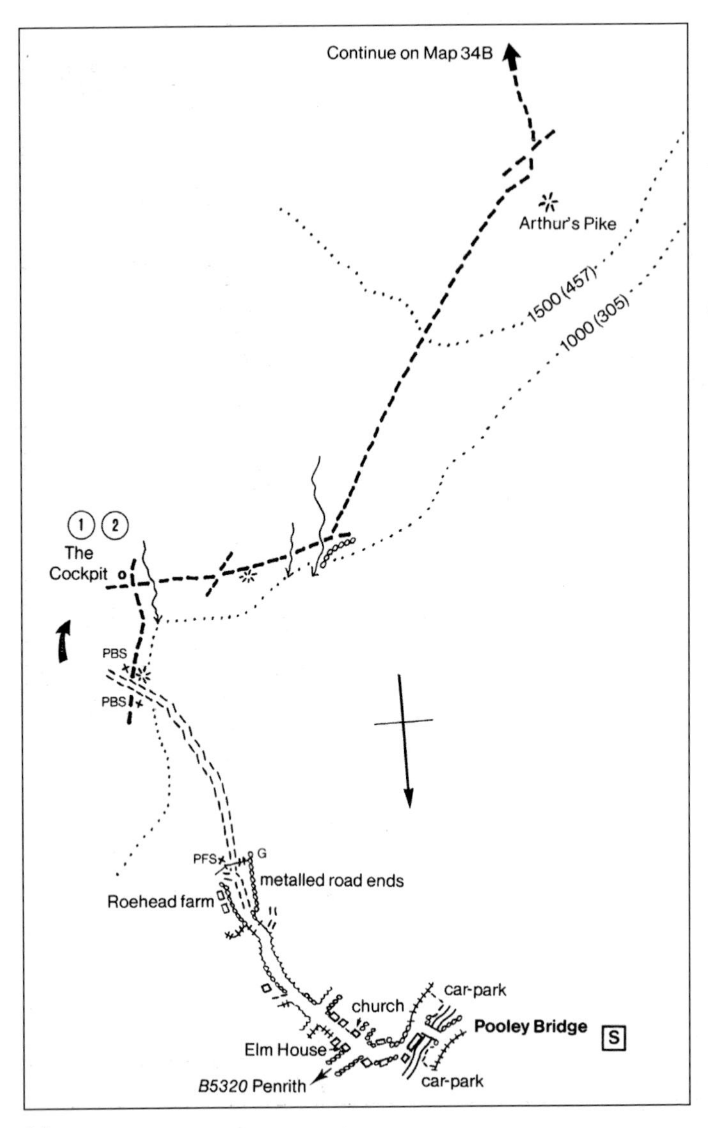
Continue on Map 34B
Arthur's Pike
1500 (457)
1000 (305)
The Cockpit
PBS
PBS
PFS
G
metalled road ends
Roehead farm
church
car-park
Pooley Bridge
S
Elm House
B5320 Penrith
car-park

Map 34A

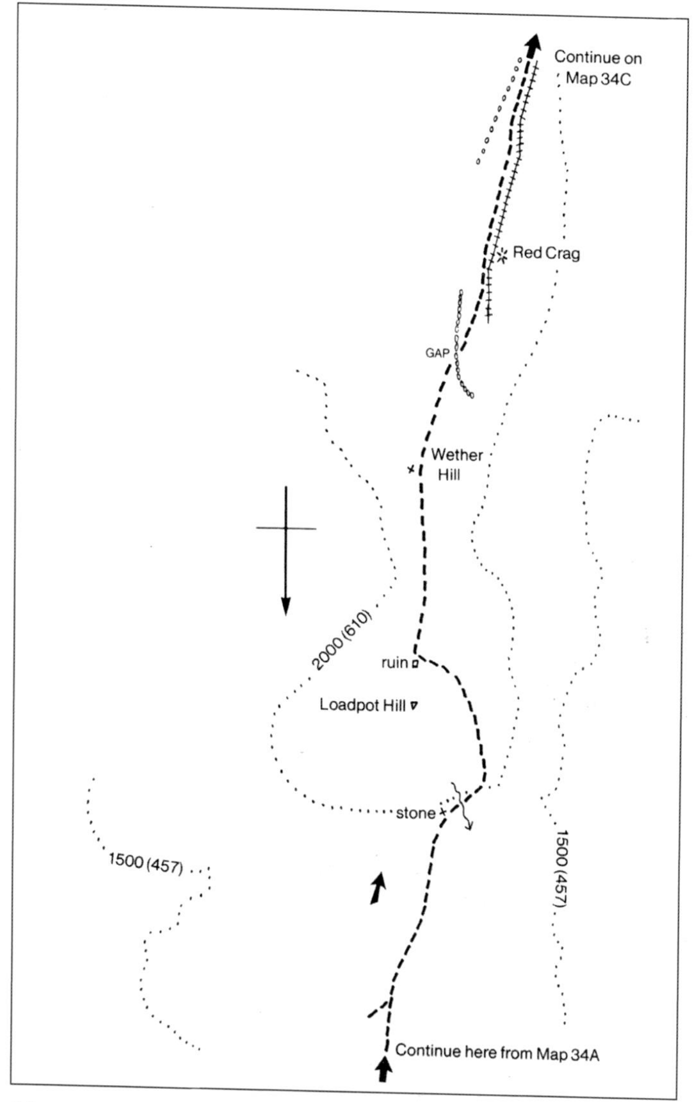

Continue on Map 34C
Red Crag
GAP
Wether Hill
2000 (610)
ruin
Loadpot Hill
stone
1500 (457)
1500 (457)
Continue here from Map 34A

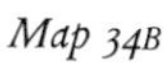
Map 34B

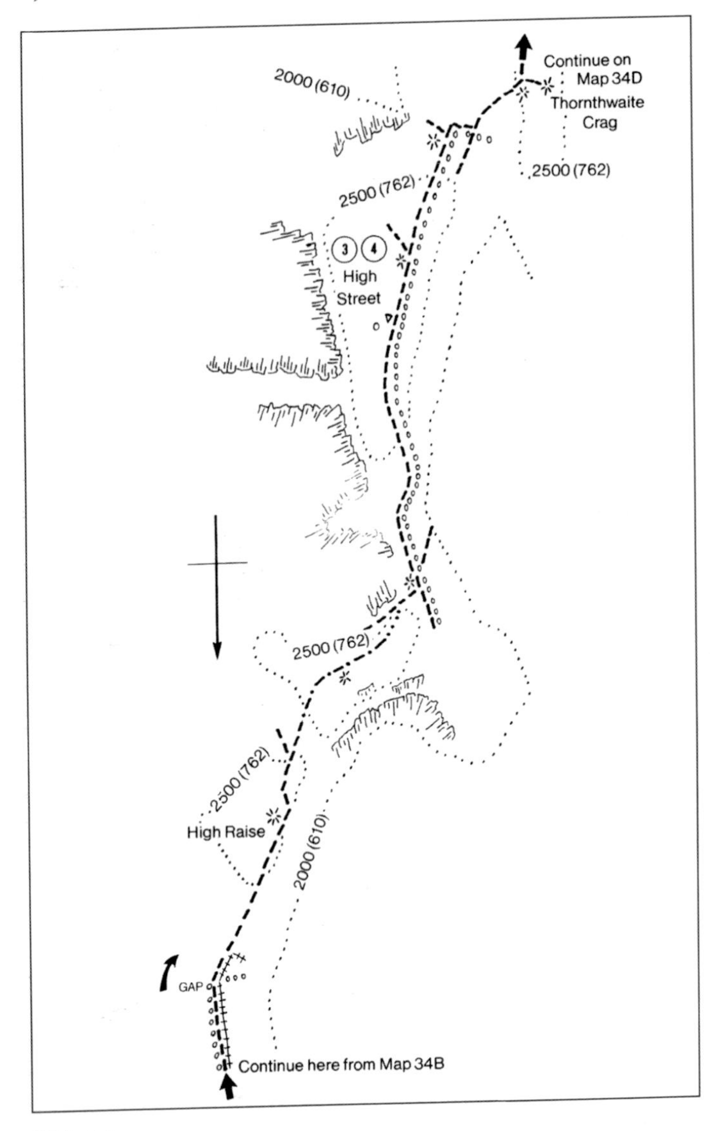
Continue on
Map 34D
Thornthwaite
Crag
2000 (610)
2500 (762)
2500 (762)
3
4
High
Street
2500 (762)
2500 (762)
High Raise
2000 (610)
GAP
Continue here from Map 34B

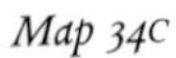
Map 34C

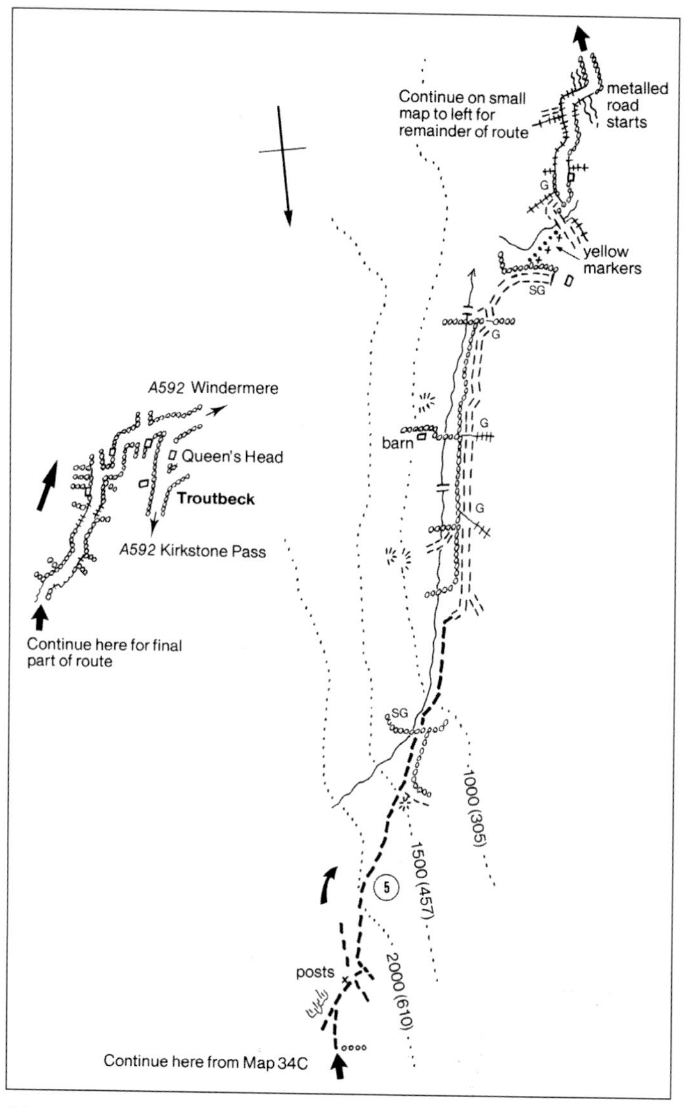
Continue on small map to left for remainder of route
metalled road starts
G
yellow markers
SG
G
G
barn
G
A592 Windermere
Queen's Head
Troutbeck
A592 Kirkstone Pass
Continue here for final part of route
SG
1000 (305)
1500 (457)
5
2000 (610)
posts
Continue here from Map 34C

Map 34D

detour). Descend down the ridge. After 600 yds (550m), shortly after several posts, take a path half R dropping down the right flank of the peak ahead, which is Froswick (see ⑤ Scots' Rake). The path drops down, with magnificent views to the R, to a wall corner. Turn L and follow the wall down to a small gate. Continue in the same direction, descending on a path to the R of a stream.

The path soon widens to a farm road, and crosses a small stream to a wall corner. Continue for 1 mile (1.6km) with a wall on your L. Where the farm road bends to the R towards a farm, go through a small gate in the wall (PFS 'Troutbeck Village') and across the field on a faint path. At the bottom join another farm road and turn L over a bridge. Follow the farm road, which later becomes metalled, for 1⅓ miles (2km) to Troutbeck.

① *The Cockpit (90–483222)*

The two concentric stone circles about 85 ft (26m) in inner diameter) lying to the south-west of Heughscar Hill are known as the Cockpit. The two circles probably formed the inner and outer facings of a stone wall that may have contained a small group of huts. Their age is uncertain.

② *Moor Divock*

At least 60 barrows and cairns in the Lake District have been shown by excavation to be of the Middle to Late Bronze Age, with a particular concentration occurring to the south-east of Pooley Bridge on Askham Fell. Some of those excavated contained urns and cremation ashes, and in one (the White Raise Barrow) there was a crouched skeleton. Bronze Age settlements were located a short distance to the north-east of these barrows, and it is likely therefore that this was a burial ground used over a long period of time. A traverse of these entails a diversion of about 2 miles (3km) there and back across the moor top from the point where the High Street Roman Road is first met (90–483227).

High Street

③ *High Street*

The long ridge running to the south-west between Ullswater and Haweswater, and reaching a maximum height of 2,717 ft (828m) at High Street, marks the line of a Roman road which connected the fort at Brougham (Brocavum) with that at Ambleside (Galava). Built in the first century AD, *it was probably based upon a much older pre-Roman road and intended for infantry and pack-horse trains rather than for wheeled vehicles. The fort at Brougham at its northern end was an important meeting point of several roads, while that at Ambleside lay on the road from the south to the port at Ravenglass. Like other roads in the upland region south of the Wall, it was used primarily for military rather than for civilian traffic. Although the line of the road has been determined for much of its length, the final reach to the south in the Troutbeck valley is still obscure. There is some evidence to suggest that the road remained in use for many centuries after the Romans withdrew.*

④ *Racecourse Hill (90–441111)*

Despite its high elevation, the flat and grassy top of High Street was until 1835 the scene of an annual Shepherds' Meet (see page 246), attended by shepherds from the surrounding dales. Although the main purpose of the meet was the exchange of stray animals, it was also regarded as a great social occasion. Horse-racing and wrestling were some of the amusements provided, and 150 years later the hilltop is still known as Racecourse Hill.

⑤ *Scots' Rake*

The final stretch of the Roman road into the Troutbeck valley down the flanks of Froswick is sometimes called Scots' Rake. The name could have originated at the time of the Scottish raids of the fourteenth century, and may therefore indicate the path down which the raiders came. In general, however, the central dales were little affected by these attacks, which were mainly directed towards the richer lowlands on the periphery.

ROUTE 35 | The Mosedale Horseshoe

The Mosedale in question is the short and quiet dale running slightly west of north from Wasdale Head, and not the Moasdale north of Cockley Bridge in the Duddon Valley. The complete traverse of the peaks forming its immediate skyline is one of the classic walks of Lakeland. Several scrambles are involved and the amount of ascent is considerable, but both can be reduced by omitting Yewbarrow; see the note at the end of the route.

Length: 12½ miles (20km) | Ascent: 4,750 ft (1,450m) | Starting and finishing point: The car-park by Overbeck Bridge on the north-west shore of Wast Water (89–168069) | Maps: Landranger 89; Explorer OL6 and OL4

ROUTE DESCRIPTION (MAPS 35A, 35B)

Leave the car-park at the far end, along a path to the R of the river. Soon pick up a fence, pass through a small gate and over a stile, and then follow the path to the R of a fence, ignoring a further stile to the L. After 650 yds (600m) cross ladder stile and follow the path half R away from the wall, taking the R fork at a junction after a short distance. This path goes to the L of the prominent rock peak blocking the ridge (Bell Rib) and to the R of a lower crag (Dropping Crag). Go up the scree between them and then up a short rock face in a gully beyond. Continue to scramble up the gully and then bear half R to the crest of the ridge above Bell Rib (the Great Door) – with a steep drop the other side down towards Wast Water. Turn L and climb the ridge above Bell Rib to the summit of Yewbarrow, marked by a cairn.

Continue across the top in the same direction, descending to a col. Cross and climb on the opposite side to the top of Stirrup Crag. With care descend the steep rocks on the far side to Dore Head. Cross, and follow the path up the opposite side, keeping to the L of the cliff edge, for 1¼ miles (2km) to the summit of Red Pike (it should be noted that this is *not* the Red Pike climbed in Route 27, which lies 3 miles (5km) to the north). The summit cairn sits right on the edge of a sheer drop down to the Moasdale valley to the east – tread carefully in mist or high winds. Beyond, continue in the same direction to the L of the cliff edge, descending to a col, then rising on the opposite side along a faint path and over boulders, to reach a wall (the path going to the R avoids the summit and should be ignored) and the summit of Scoat Fell (paradoxically the highest point is on Little Scoat Fell and not Great Scoat Fell which is 128 ft (39m) lower). The summit cairn is perched on the wall.

Turn R along the ridge. Where the wall ends, continue in the same direction, descending and then ascending to Black Crag. Continue in the same direction, descending steeply to Wind Gap (not Windy Gap which is on Great Gable). Cross, and rise on the opposite side to the cairns, shelters and OS obelisk on the summit of Pillar. This is the highest point reached on the horseshoe. Turn R and follow the path down the ridge for 1½ miles (2.5km) to Black Sail Pass. The remains of an old fence lie near or to the L of the path during the long descent. Continue rising on the path up the opposite side. Some scrambling is involved, and eventually the path follows fence posts to the main top of Kirk Fell with cairns and a shelter.

Turn L and pick up a path descending to the L of Kirkfell Tarn. Past the tarns the path bends R to the second top, and then descends to a col (Beck Head), again guided all the way by fence posts. Pass to the R of the two tarns and on the far side of the col

On the Mosedale Horseshoe

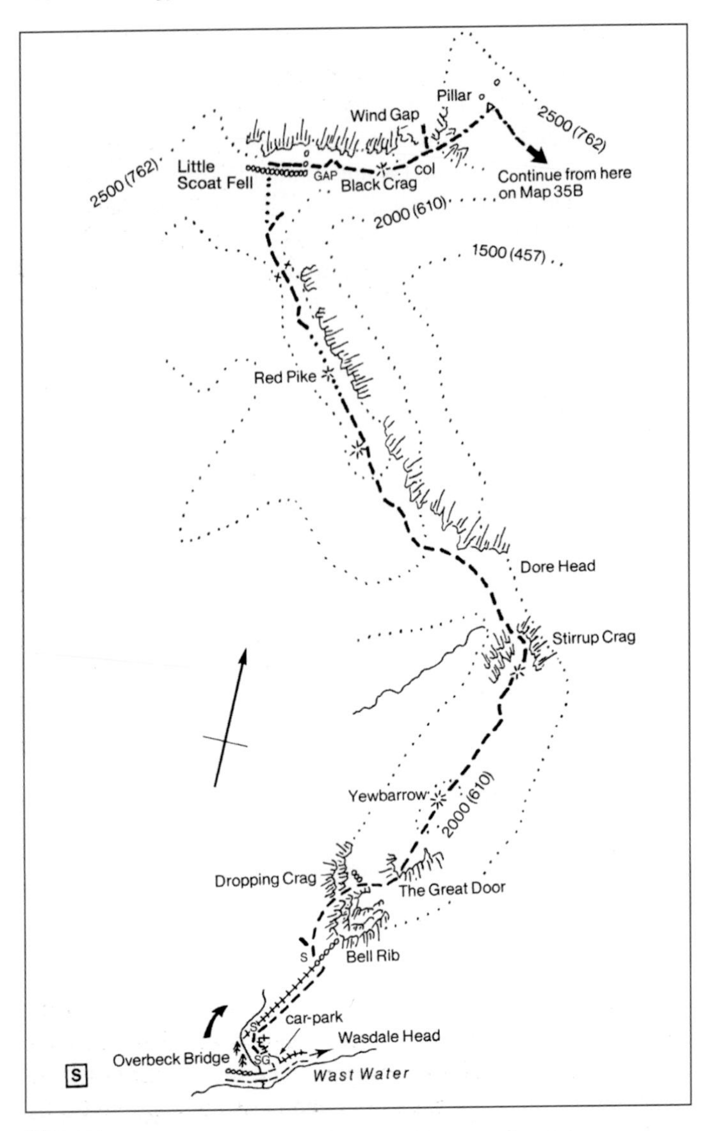
Pillar
Wind Gap
2500 (762)
Little
Scoat Fell
GAP
Black Crag
col
Continue from here
on Map 35B
2000 (610)
1500 (457)
Red Pike
Dore Head
Stirrup Crag
Yewbarrow
2000 (610)
Dropping Crag
The Great Door
S
Bell Rib
car-park
Wasdale Head
Overbeck Bridge
SG
Wast Water
S

Map 35A

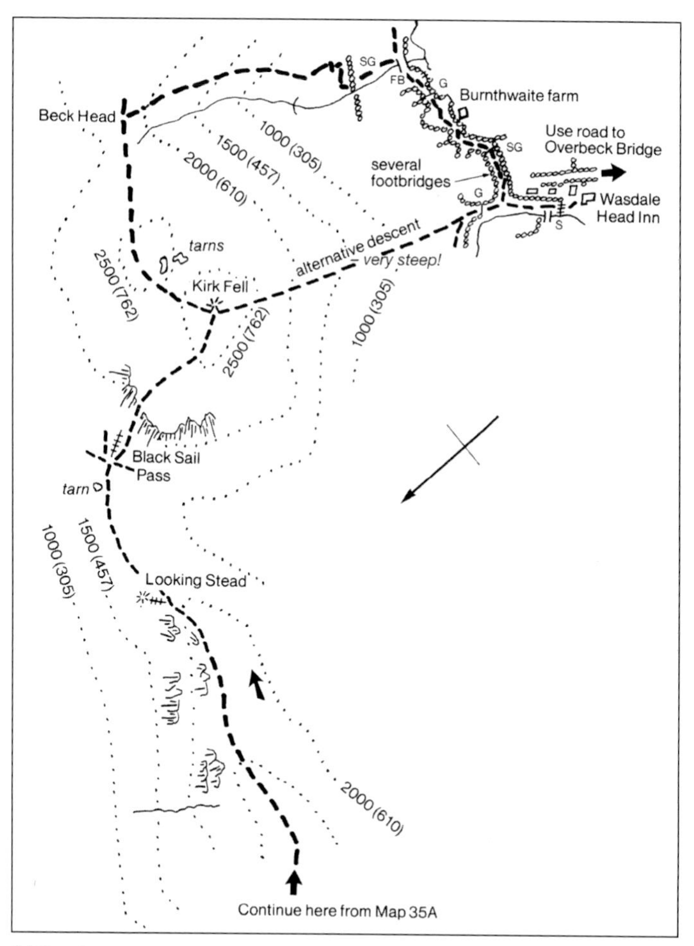

Map 35B

turn R and descend along a path across the slope to the L of the stream valley. At a rib the path turns half R and descends more steeply down to a wall. Pass through a small gate in the wall, continue down to the L of the stream and cross the long footbridge at the bottom. Keep along the lane ahead past the farm of

Down the Mosedale valley from the top of the horseshoe

Burnthwaite to the Wasdale Head Inn and the metalled road. Follow the road for 2 miles (3km) back to the car-park.

Note: The route can be much reduced by starting and finishing at the hotel at Wasdale Head, and omitting Yewbarrow. Cross the bridge by the hotel – cars can be left down the road – and turn R following the walled lane, soon passing waterfalls. After nearly 1 mile (1.6km) by the stream turn L up the steep slope by the scree to Dore Head. Turn R and continue as given above.

For features of interest at Wasdale Head see Route 28; for Pillar Rock see Route 33.

Sheep in Wasdale

ROUTE 36 | The Wasdale Head Round

Taken by itself the length of this route is within the capability of many walkers, but combined with more than 6,000 ft (1,830m) of climbing it is clearly a task for relatively few. Nor is the going easy, for much of it is over rough boulders or scree, and the ascent and descent is often very steep, especially down off Great Gable and Kirk Fell at the end of a long day. As a mountain expedition, as distinct from a peak-bagging exercise, it can undoubtedly be improved, the Corridor Route from Scafell Pike being preferable to the way over Esk Hause and the Climbers' Traverse from Sty Head to Beck Head being a vast improvement on the traverse of Great Gable. Aesthetically also, a true Wasdale Head Round should include Yewbarrow, but this would involve either a considerable

detour or a crossing of Mosedale, adding still further to the total ascent. Walkers capable of such things will no doubt be able to think these sort of alternatives up for themselves.

Length: 11 miles (18km) | Ascent: 6,250 ft (1,900m) | Starting and finishing point: National Trust car-park near Brackenclose at the head of Wast Water (89–182075) | Maps: Landranger 89; Explorer OL6

ROUTE DESCRIPTION (MAPS 28, 32B, 36A, 36B)

Follow Route 28 as far as the summit of Scafell Pike. Beyond the large cairn, follow the path which descends to the L of several shelters. This descends steeply to a col and then rises up, crossing boulders between two rocky peaks, Broad Crag and Ill Crag. Continue along the well-cairned path for about 1 mile (1.6km) to a cross track at a large cairn on a broad col (Esk Hause). Follow the cairned path to the L to drop down to a lower col, also with a cross track. Turn L and follow the clear path for nearly 1½ miles (2.5km), ignoring the R hand path over a stream at a junction, and steadily descending to the L of a tarn (Sprinkling Tarn) to the Mountain Rescue box at Sty Head.

Either continue directly across in the same direction to a well-paved path which rises directly to the summit of Great Gable; *or* go R to the far end of a tarn and then turn L up a path to the L of a stream to Windy Gap (Aaron Slack); there go L to the summit of Great Gable. The second route is slightly longer, but is more interesting.

Cross the top in a north-westerly direction to pick up cairns to a path which descends very steep and difficult scree. Keep quite close to the L edge of Gable Crag to follow a faint path down – this avoids the steepest side of scree but is still a tough descent. An alternative way down is to return to Windy Gap and turn L, traversing the flanks of Great Gable to Beck Head. This is definitely a better way for uncertain or tired walkers. Either way, at Beck Head, cross

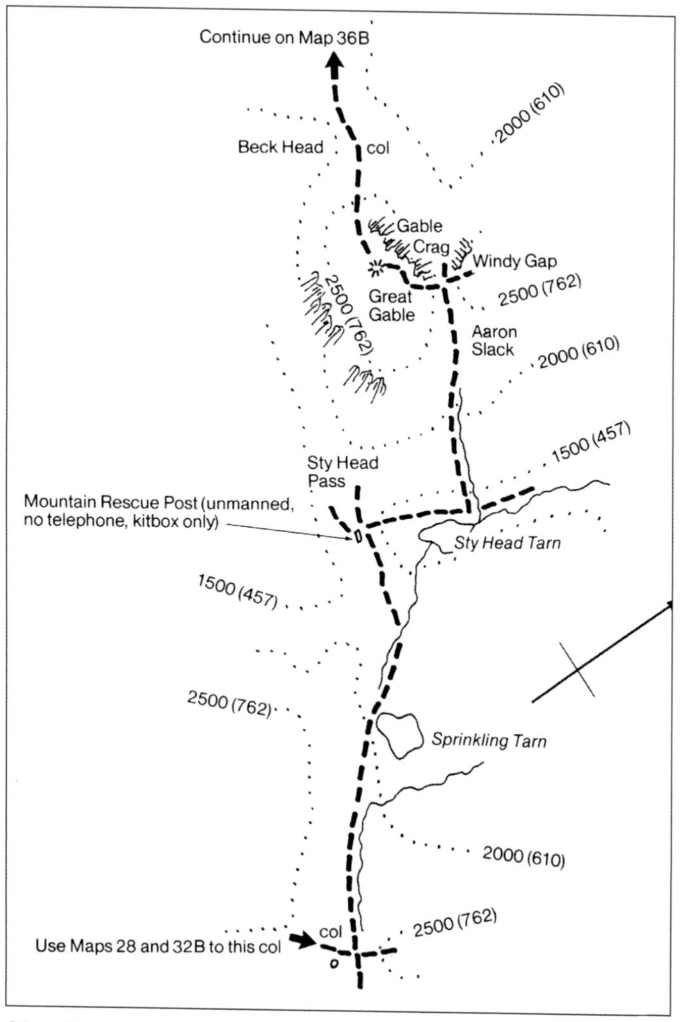
Continue on Map 36B
2000 (610)
Beck Head
col
Gable
Crag
Windy Gap
Great
Gable
2500 (762)
2500 (762)
Aaron
Slack
2000 (610)
1500 (457)
Sty Head
Pass
Mountain Rescue Post (unmanned,
no telephone, kitbox only)
Sty Head Tarn
1500 (457)
2500 (762)
Sprinkling Tarn
2000 (610)
col
2500 (762)
Use Maps 28 and 32B to this col

Map 36A

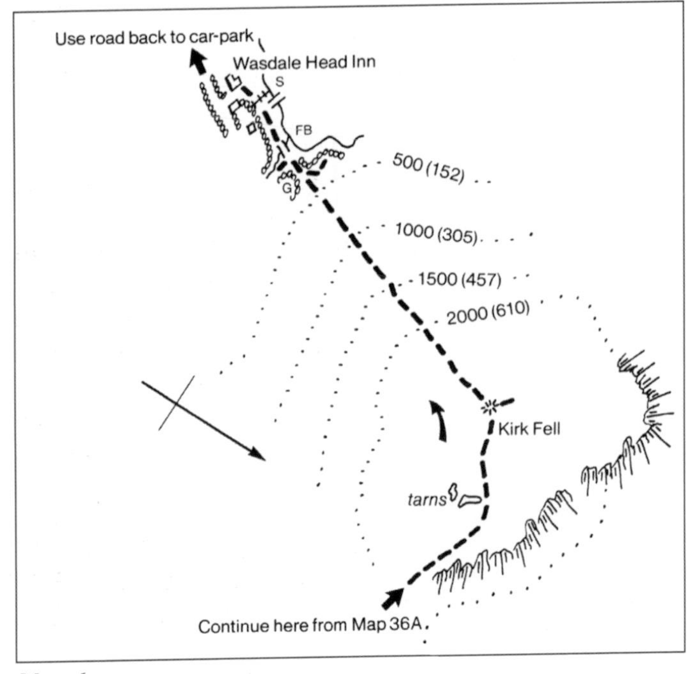

Map 36B

the col and take the path on the opposite side, marked by a line of posts, climbing to the first summit of Kirk Fell. Continue in the same direction, soon bending half L past Kirkfell Tarn (actually two tarns) to the main summit, again guided by posts.

Leave the summit in a SSW direction, aligning yourself just to the R of Wast Water, to pick up a line of cairns. Continue down steeply on a path which aims directly for the Wasdale Head Inn. The way is long, about 1 mile (1.6km), and very steep, with difficult scree at first which eventually leads to grassier slopes. At the bottom, go between walls to the stream and keep on the L bank to the hotel and a metalled road. Walk down the road back to the car-park.

ROUTE 37 | The Langdale Horseshoe

The Langdale Horseshoe, which runs along the skyline peaks of Great Langdale, is one of the finest walks in the Lake District. It is long and involves a lot of climbing, taking in the tougher parts of Routes 13, 20 and 23 combined. Note also that some paths – especially over Crinkle Crags – may be difficult to follow in hill fog. But for those with the necessary stamina, both the scenery and the walking are superb throughout. In particular, the summit of Bow Fell, at roughly the half-way point, will (if the conditions are agreeable) be long remembered as one of the finest all-round view-points in the Lake District.

Length: 13 miles (21km) | Ascent: 5,100 ft (1,550m) | Starting and finishing point: National Trust car-park by the New Dungeon Ghyll Hotel in Great Langdale (89–295064) | Maps: Landranger 89; Explorer OL6

ROUTE DESCRIPTION (MAPS 20, 37A, 23, 37B, 13)

Follow Route 20 as far as the large cairn on the Stake Pass. Continue across the col, soon passing to the L of a small tarn. Beyond the tarn the path soon bends L and goes along – and later on the R of – a broad grassy ridge, the path faint at times. After 1½ miles (2.5km) reach Angle Tarn. Cross the outflow and climb up the slope ahead, i.e, with the tarn to the L. After 300 yds (270m) take a path to the L. This curves L and climbs up to a col (see ① Ore Gap, for an explanation of the real colour of the path on the col). At a cross-path turn L along a line of cairns to the summit of Bow Fell.

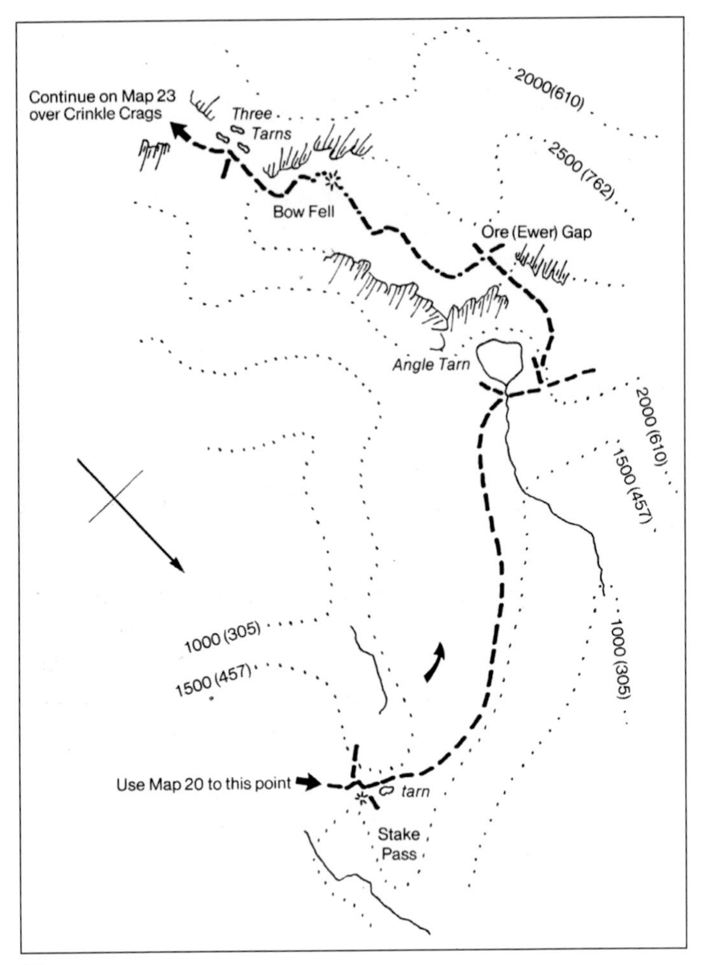

Map 37A

Cross the summit and descend over boulders in the same direction (cairns) to pick up a path. Lower the path turns to the L to avoid a line of crag. Descend to Three Tarns. From here follow Route 23 over Crinkle Crags.

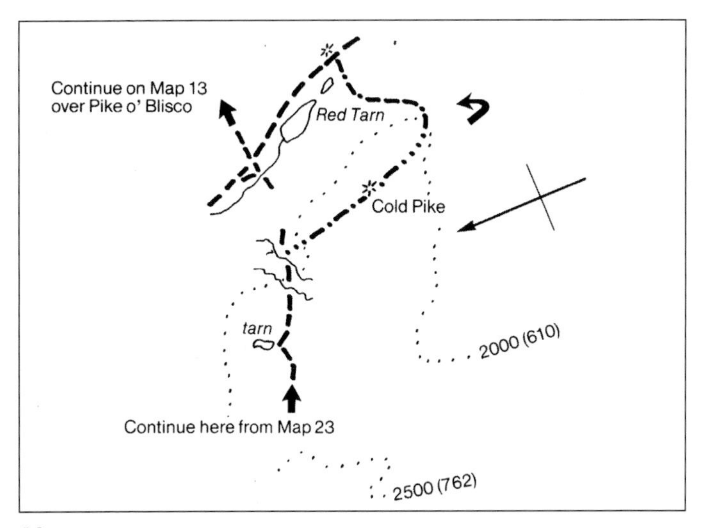

Map 37B

Beyond the last 'Crinkle', follow the path as it slowly descends across the moor. After a small tarn where it crosses two streams, leave half R towards Cold Pike. There is no path at first and then only a faint one, but the summit can be clearly seen. Make for this, then continue beyond the summit on a faint path which soon bends half L. Follow this down into, and then across, the valley to the R of Red Tarn. Again, the path is indistinct in places, but the tarn will be obvious. On the opposite side, rise up to a very clear crossing path. Turn L and pass Red Tarn to a large cairn and a crossing path.

Turn R, rising steeply to the summit of Pike o' Blisco. Turn R at the summit cairn for a few yards, and then take the path which goes down L. There are several short stretches of rock which have to be negotiated with care, but otherwise the path can be followed down to a metalled road by Redacre Gill. Turn L down the road for 1½ miles (2.5km) past the Old Dungeon Ghyll Hotel and back to the car-park.

① *Ore Gap (89–240071)*

The name of this pass may be derived from the iron ore which outcrops at this point – hence the red colour of the path. It is also possible, however, that the Gap was used in the transportation of ore from Eskdale to a bloomery in Lang Strath, and got its name from this.

Snow in the Langdale valley

ROUTE 38 | The Helvellyn Ridge

The most popular summit in the Lake District is undoubtedly that of Helvellyn, usually approached along Striding Edge, from Grisedale Tarn to the south or along one of the footpaths rising from Thirlmere. However, once away from the immediate summit area and these approach paths, the concentration of walkers falls off considerably. The northern reaches of the great ridge which runs to the south from Threlkeld to Grisedale Tarn through Helvellyn are by comparison quiet and lonely. This route, starting at Glenridding, reaches the ridge at Sticks Pass and follows it to the south to Grisedale Tarn: a real walkers' way, over wonderful whale-backed hills. The finest part of the route, however, is left to last: the return to Glenridding over Fairfield, Cofa Pike and St Sunday Crag. But be prepared for a slog: the rise to Fairfield will be found steep and hard at the end of a long day and the passage over Cofa Pike tricky too. For those tired by this stage, there is an easier escape route from the tarn, down through Grisedale.

Length: 13½ miles (22km) | Ascent: 4,750 ft (1,450m) | Starting and finishing point: The car-park at Glenridding on the A592 to the west of Ullswater (90–386170) | Maps: Landranger 90; Explorer OL5

ROUTE DESCRIPTION (MAPS 38A, 38B, 38C)

At the entrance to the car-park, i.e. by the small hut, turn L (Greenside Road) and after a few yards L again between the houses. After the Travellers Rest pub, the road bends R then L to pass some rows of cottages. Continue for about 1 mile (1.6km) to the youth hostel. The hostel and the buildings further along the valley were part of a lead mine which closed down in the early 1960s – see ① the Greenside Mine.

After the hostel turn half L over a bridge, through a gate and to the R of the Greenside Bury Silver Jubilee Hostel. By the second building (Arnold School Blackpool Outdoor Pursuits Centre), turn R (signed 'Sticks Pass'). Go up the path by fences and walls (blue arrows and signs for Sticks Pass). After several bends the path starts to run parallel to the river. Do not continue along this, but immediately take a path half R (signed 'Sticks Pass'). The path goes up the hillside away from the stream in a number of zig-zags.

Follow the path up and across the moor to a footbridge in front of some spoil heaps (ignore the path away from the heaps and make directly for them). Continue L over the spoil heaps; at the far side by a stone-lined leat turn R, and on the hillside ahead L again. The clear path runs up the R-hand side of the valley for 1 mile (1.6km), gently at first and then steeply, to a grassy col (Sticks Pass). At a cross track on the col, turn L. Rise up to the summit of Raise. During this rise a small building and tow line can be seen over to the left – see ② the Ski Hut on Raise.

From the summit go half R to pick up cairns, and later a path. Continue along the ridge on a clear path over Whiteside Bank and Lower Man (or Low Man) to the summit of Helvellyn (see ③ Helvellyn – summit monuments). Beyond the summit take the very obvious path which goes away to the R. Follow this for about 700 yds (650m) to a path fork on a col; here take the L branch, and after a few yards take the much clearer R hand path. Continue along the very clear path for nearly 2 miles (3km) around Nethermost Pike, High Crag and Dollywagon Pike, finally descending steeply to Grisedale Tarn. The path passes the tarn to a junction by a large cairn. Before turning right, continue for a few yards along the path beyond the cairn and then down the slope to the right to find a small memorial marked by a metal sign – see ④ the Brothers' Parting Stone. Take the path back half

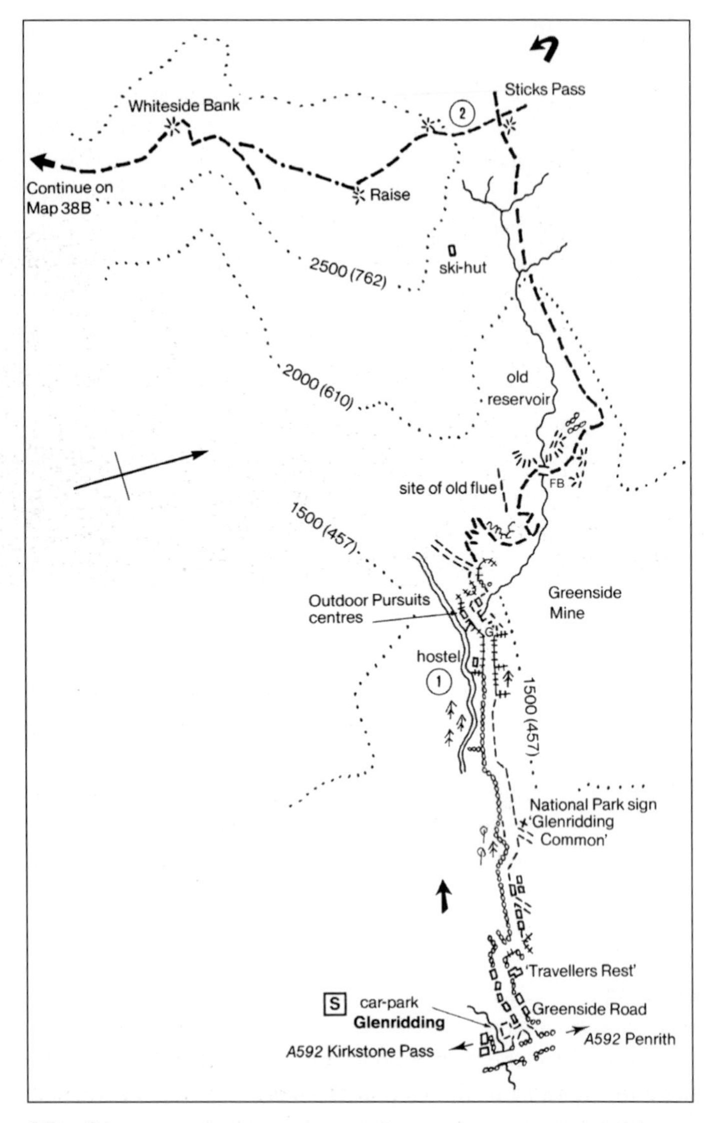
Sticks Pass
Whiteside Bank
2
Continue on
Map 38B
Raise
ski-hut
2500 (762)
2000 (610)
old
reservoir
site of old flue
FB
1500 (457)
Greenside
Mine
Outdoor Pursuits
centres
G
hostel
1
1500 (457)
National Park sign
'Glenridding
Common'
'Travellers Rest'
S
car-park
Glenridding
Greenside Road
A592 Penrith
A592 Kirkstone Pass

Map 38A

Cofa Pike and St Sunday Crag

R towards the tarn. Pass the tarn with it to your R and continue up the path to a col (Grisedale Hause). Turn L and climb steeply by a broken wall to the summit of Fairfield. Turn L at the summit and follow the cliff edge to cairns at the end of the ridge. Pick up a path and descend steeply over the small peak of Cofa Pike and down to Deepdale Hause. Climb up the obvious path ahead to the summit of St Sunday Crag.

Continue in the same direction (no path at first) to pick up a cairned path at the end of the ridge. Descend beyond on a path, which soon steepens, to a grassy col. At a path junction go along the L branch. The path descends steadily, later going down to a broken wall corner. Cross at a gap and keep to the R of the broken wall. Where it ends, keep in the same direction, contouring the slope along a path to the R of a cliff, with magnificent views

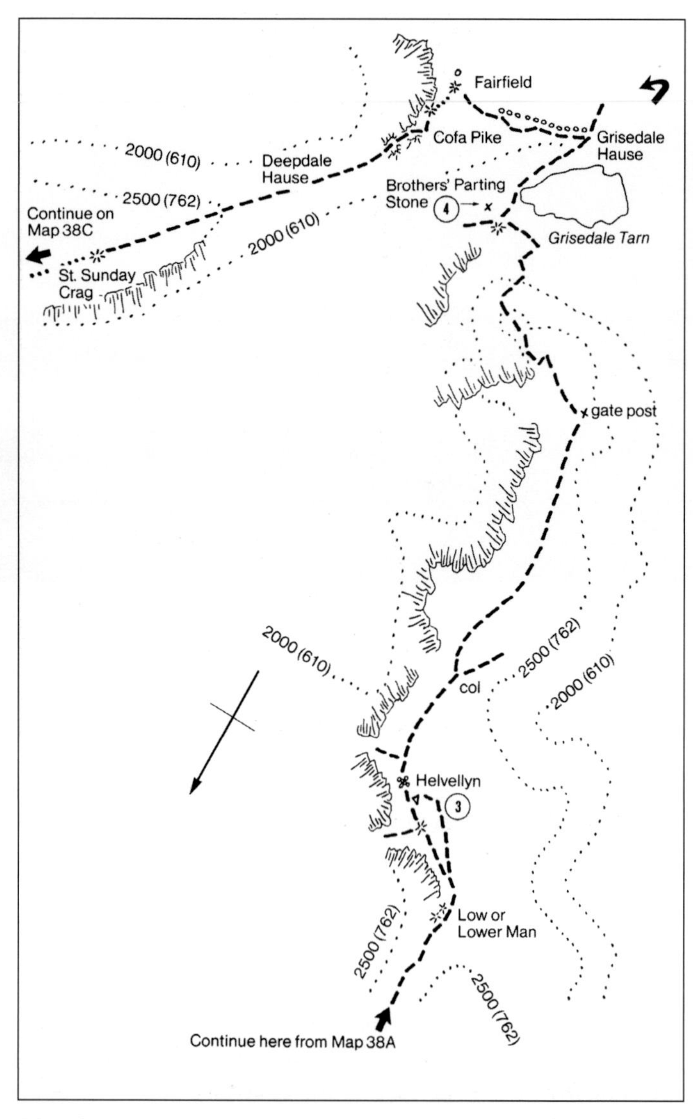
Fairfield
Cofa Pike
Grisedale Hause
2000 (610)
Deepdale Hause
2500 (762)
Brothers' Parting Stone
4
Continue on Map 38C
2000 (610)
Grisedale Tarn
St. Sunday Crag
gate post
2000 (610)
col
2500 (762)
2000 (610)
Helvellyn
3
Low or Lower Man
2500 (762)
2500 (762)
Continue here from Map 38A

Map 38B

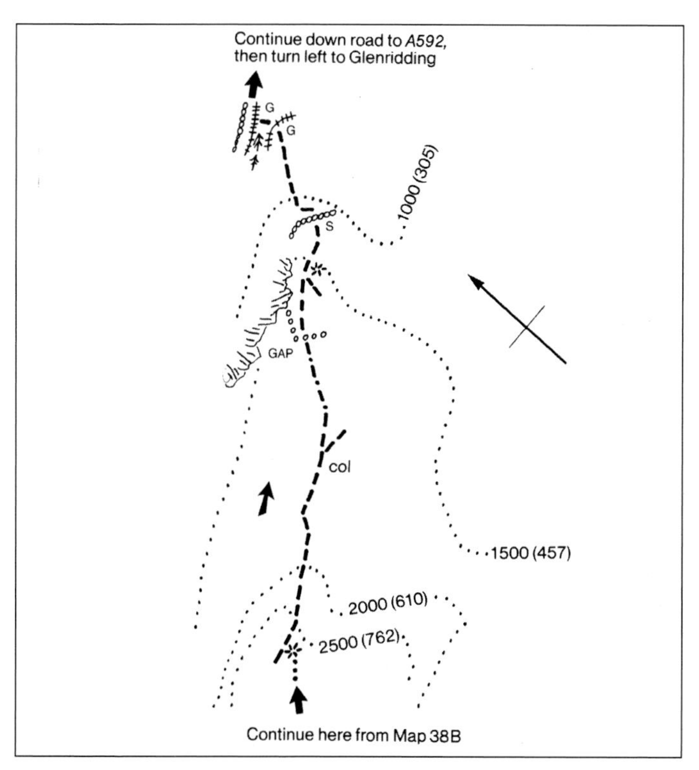

Map 38c

ahead towards Ullswater. Eventually at the end of the ridge the path descends to a stile over a wall, and beyond to a gate and stile in a fence. Turn L and follow a path to a gate and metalled road. Turn R and walk to the A592. Here turn L for Glenridding.

① *The Greenside Mine (90–365174)*

The Helvellyn Youth Hostel is housed in the former home of the manager of the Greenside lead mine, which was active from about 1790 to 1962. The original levels, i.e. horizontal tunnels into the hillside from which the ore was extracted,

were about ¾ mile (1.2km) further up the stream, the Swart Beck, which flows past the hostel and north-east of a small reservoir, Top Dam. Further levels, and later shafts, were driven lower down the valley during the nineteenth century, in an attempt to follow the course of the ore vein which runs in a north-south direction.

Before 1837 the ore was taken away for smelting, originally to near Stair and then later to the Alston area; but after the installation of equipment, crushing and smelting were carried out at the mine. From 1850 these operations were carried out around the youth hostel site, the smelt mill having a flue 1½ miles (2.4km) long in order to remove the highly toxic fumes produced by the operation. (This is passed on the rise out of the valley – see Map 38A.) Smelting consisted of heating the ore (galena or lead sulphide), first oxidizing it to lead oxide and then reducing it to lead. The yield of lead was about 80% of the ore weight, with the additional benefit of small quantities of silver.

The managers of the mine were very innovative, a factor which helped to ensure its survival until well into this century. Most of the workers at the mine – about 300 worked there in the middle of the nineteenth century – lodged locally during the week, travelling home at the weekend; but some lived in company houses built at Glenridding.

② The Ski Hut on Raise (90–346178)

The small building to the north-east of Raise is a hut of the Lake District Ski Club. Because the winds which bring the snow are generally from the north-east, this area of the Lake District receives heavy falls which tend to linger on north-facing slopes. The hut is for day use only and must not be used for overnight accommodation. More details on the club can be found online at www.ldscsnowski.co.uk.

③ Helvellyn – summit monuments

see pages 206–7

④ The Brothers' Parting Stone (90–352123)

This stone, to the north-east of Grisedale Tarn, marks the place

On Helvellyn

where William Wordsworth parted for the last time from his brother, John, who was drowned shortly afterwards. There are some lines engraved on the rock by Wordsworth – now illegible – and also now a small metal plate. Wordsworth had three brothers – Richard, John and Christopher – and one sister, Dorothy. John, younger than the poet by two years, was captain of the Earl of Abergavenny, *an East Indiaman. On 5 February 1805 the ship, on a voyage to India, was driven by a gale on to rocks near the Bill of Portland in Dorset. Although freed, she sank very rapidly with the loss of about 300 passengers and crew, one of whom was John Wordsworth. His body was found some weeks later and buried at Wyke near Weymouth. The grave is now unmarked. His death came as an immense shock to the Wordsworth family and their circle of friends. To William Wordsworth himself the effect was particularly shattering, both physically and intellectually, and has been seen by some as a major turning point in his life.*

ROUTE 39 | The Eskdale Ring

The upper reach of the Esk with its main tributary, the Lingcove Beck, is surrounded by a superb semi-circle of peaks from Sca Fell in the west to Crinkle Crags in the east. The complete traverse, starting and finishing in Eskdale to form a circular route, is known as the Eskdale Ring. The first section over Border End and Hard Knott is partly trackless, but thereafter the way can be followed along a very clear path. A careful note should be taken however of the considerable amount of ascent and descent involved – preferably before starting.

Length: 13 miles (21km) | Ascent: 5,450 ft (1,660m) | Starting and finishing point: A small parking area by the cattle-grid in Eskdale at the start of the rise to the Hard Knott Pass (89–215012) | Maps: Landranger 89; Explorer OL6

ROUTE DESCRIPTION (MAPS 39A, 39B, 39C, 39D)

Turn R in the road and, passing Hardknott Castle (see ① below), rise steeply for 1¼ miles (2km) to the large cairn on the summit of the Hard Knott Pass. Take the faint path half L which rises, soon reaching a broken wall. Beyond, keep in the same direction to the L of a stream, ignoring a stile in a fence to the L (erected following the foot and month crisis and due to be in place until 2007) and following the path to the R across marshy ground. Eventually rise to the summit of Hard Knott, marked by a cairn on a flat rock. Continue beyond in the same direction down a broad ridge along a faint, grassy path, crossing another temporary stile and then passing tarns to your R after 700 yds (640m). Lower down, about 1 mile (1.6km) from the summit, bend R to a

low grassy col. Cross the col and rise steeply up the long slope on the opposite side along an indistinct path, keeping to the R of a stream, Swinsty Gill. Above Swinsty Gill go half L to the summit ridge of Crinkle Crags. Turn L along the path over the 'Crinkles'. It is important to remember that the ridge path turns R after the highest top (see Route 23, which comes in the opposite direction). Continue down to the col of Three Tarns. Rise up steeply on the opposite side. After 300 yds (270m), above a crag the path bends L (cairns) and then R to the summit of Bow Fell. Descend on the opposite side across boulders (cairns), later bending L to a narrow col (Ore Gap). Rise up on the opposite side to Esk Pike.

Follow the path over the summit and down the ridge ahead, to a cairn on a broad col by several crossing paths. This is Esk Hause. The clear path continues ahead, bending L, over a small stream and up steps, then bending R and passing between the two small rocky peaks of Ill Crag and Broad Crag. Finally, descend to a narrow col before rising to the summit of Scafell Pike (see ② the summit of Scafell Pike: War Memorial).

From the summit, drop down to the R relative to your approach route to pick up a path, which soon bends L. About 75 yds (70m) from the bend, at a fork keep in the same direction (i.e. take the L-hand fork). Follow the path down, later crossing boulders, to the Mountain Rescue box on Mickledore. From here there are two ways up to Sca Fell – see Route 28, noting that the way via Lord's Rake is sometimes closed to walkers. If it is inaccessible ascend via Foxes Tarn. Otherwise, on the far side of the col go to the R, skirting below the crags. After 200 yds (180m) reach the foot of a wide, deep and steep ravine (Lord's Rake) on the far side of the main cliff. Climb this carefully to a small col. Descend a few feet on the far side, and then rise to a second col. Descend again and then climb up the slope ahead. At the top bend L up the slope, eventually reaching the summit of Sca Fell.

Eskdale ring

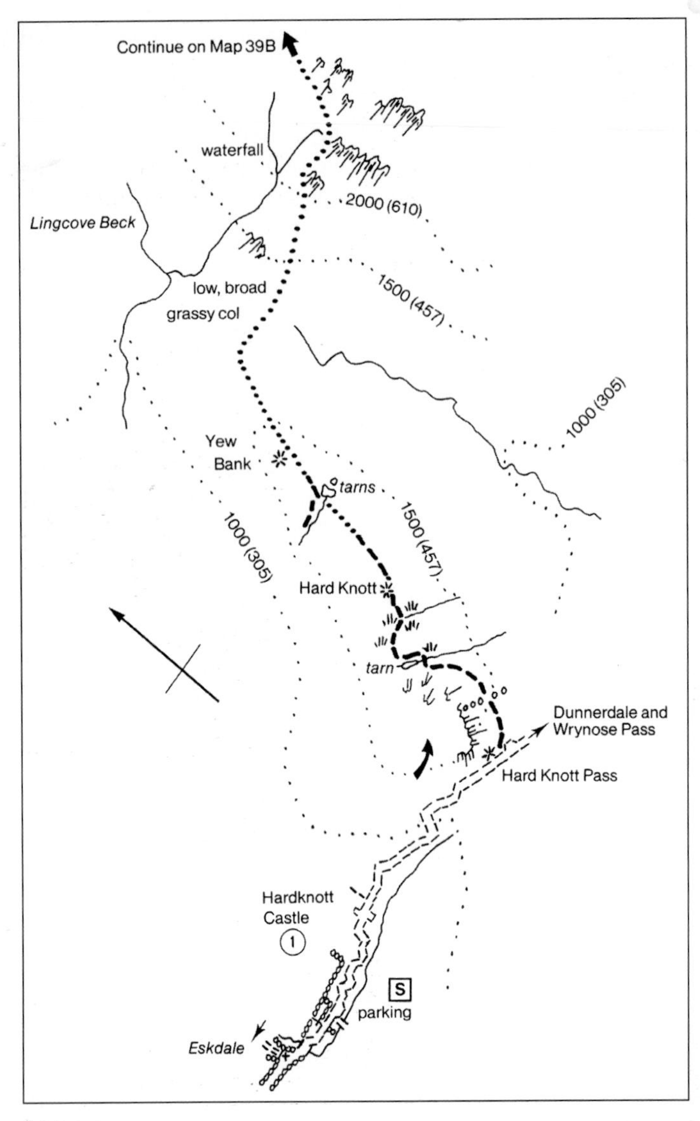
Continue on Map 39B
waterfall
2000 (610)
Lingcove Beck
1500 (457)
low, broad
grassy col
1000 (305)
Yew
Bank
tarns
1500 (457)
1000 (305)
Hard Knott
tarn
Dunnerdale and
Wrynose Pass
Hard Knott Pass
Hardknott
Castle
1
S
parking
Eskdale

Map 39A

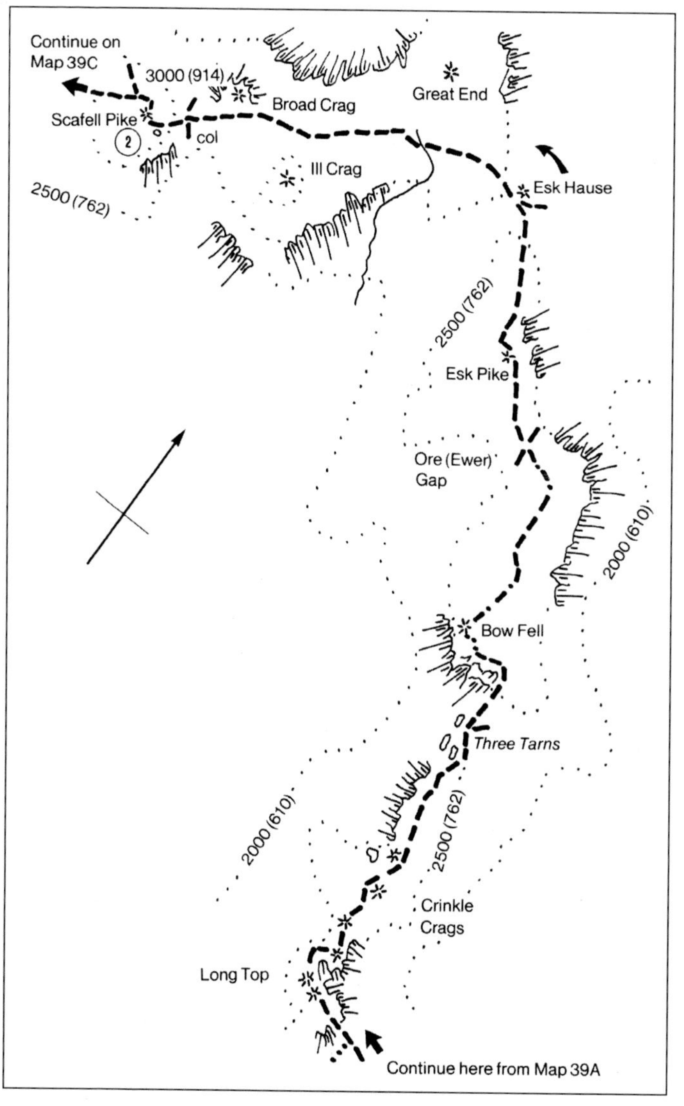
Continue on
Map 39C
3000 (914)
Broad Crag
Great End
Scafell Pike
2
col
Ill Crag
Esk Hause
2500 (762)
2500 (762)
Esk Pike
Ore (Ewer)
Gap
2000 (610)
Bow Fell
Three Tarns
2000 (610)
2500 (762)
Crinkle
Crags
Long Top
Continue here from Map 39A

Map 39B

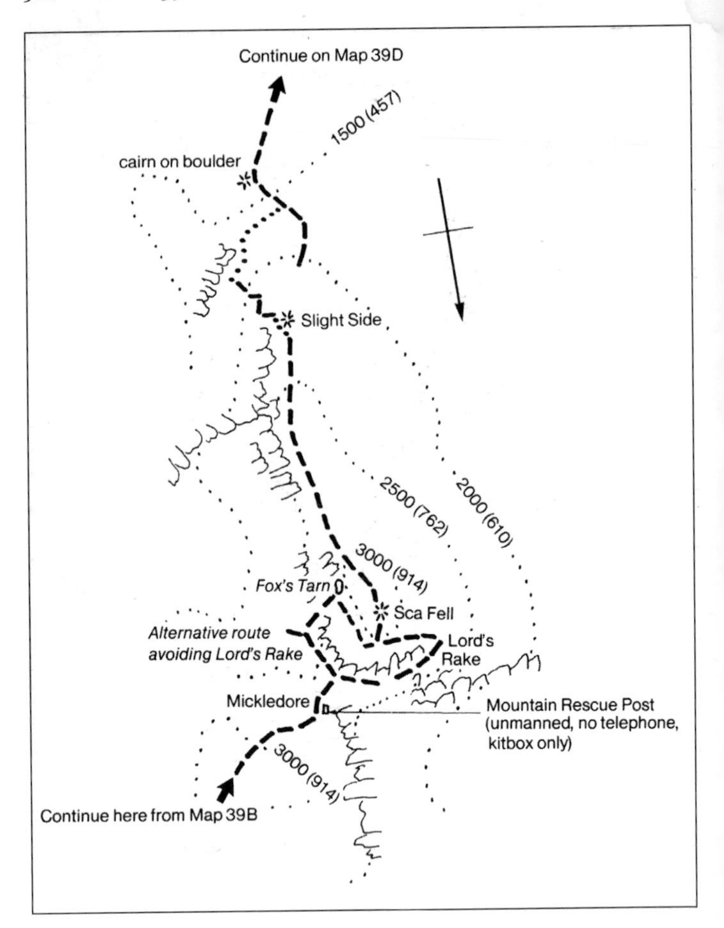

Map 39C

Leave the top approximately south-east. Descend steadily (intermittent path) keeping to the R of steeper ground (Long Green), and reaching the small rocky summit of Slight Side after 1 mile (1.6km). Pass the peak to the L. Beyond follow a line of cairns downhill. Soon go more steeply down a path to reach a

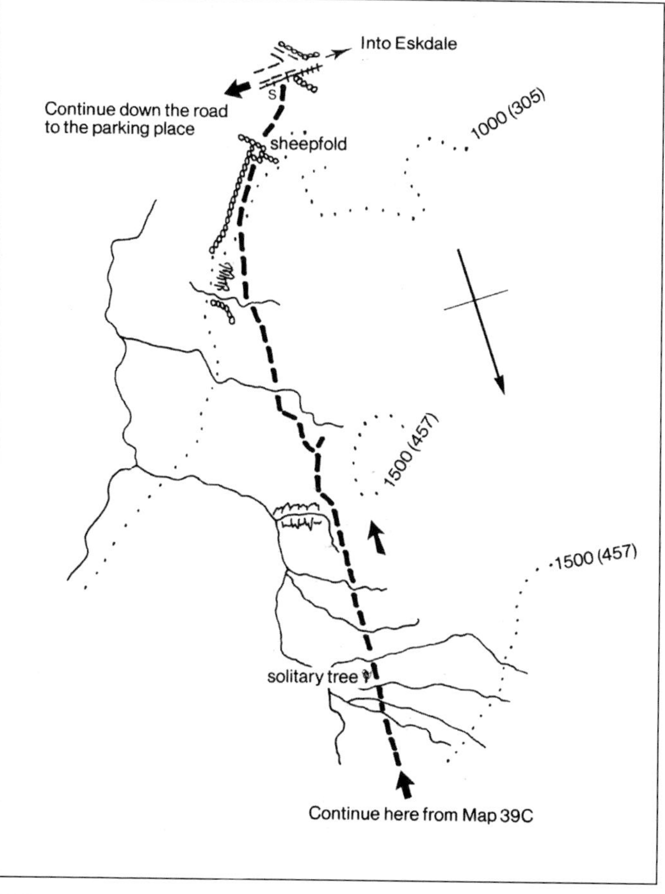

Map 39D

grassy shelf above a lower cliff. Go R along the shelf to meet a clear path after about 300 yds (270m). Turn L downhill. Lower down, cross several streams. Lower still, the path runs to the R of a flat marshy area and to the R of a ravine (Cat Crag). At a path junction 400 yds (370m) further, go L across a stream and continue

A Lakeland sheep overlooks the Eskdale valley

in the same direction to the L of a very marshy area. Later cross stream. Continue descending, eventually meeting a wall. Keep to the R of the wall, later going through a sheepfold in a corner. Continue down to metalled road. There turn L back to the parking place. If you lose your way over the marshy area, head due south and you will eventually meet the road running from west to east.

① *Hardknott Castle*

see page 145.

② *The summit of Scafell Pike: War Memorial*

see page 258.

ROUTE 40 | The Ennerdale Horseshoe

As unauthorised vehicles are not allowed in Ennerdale Forest, the approach to this route involves a two mile walk at the start and finish from the last car-park at Bowness Knott. An alternative plan, which considerably shortens the distances, is to stay at the youth hostel near High Gillerthwaite (or even at Black Sail). For very exceptional walkers the route can be extended further by: (a) walking back along the road from the car-park to Whins and then using the bridleway to near Floutern Tarn for an ascent of Great Borne: Starling Dodd can then be traversed to Red Pike; (b) continuing from Pillar over Scoat Fell and Haycock, descending to the footbridge near Gillerthwaite Farm. Even as it is, this is a full day's walking, so choose a long summer day for it. The walking is long and steep in places, but links some of the very best peaks in the Lake District.

Length: 18 miles (29km) – or 14 miles (22km) if the hostel near High Gillerthwaite is used | Ascent: 6,550 ft (2,000m) | Starting and finishing point: Forestry Commission car-park at Bowness Knott on the north shore of Ennerdale Water (89–094162) | Maps: Landranger 89; Explorer OL4

ROUTE DESCRIPTION (MAPS 40A, 27, 10, 40B, 40C)

Leave the car-park and turn L. Follow the forest road (signed 'YHA and Authorised Vehicles Only') to the L of Ennerdale Water and then past Gillerthwaite Farm and the youth hostel. At a cattle-grid 400 yds (370m) past the hostel, go L over a stile (signed 'Red Pike') and along a path up a narrow field (this is the first and only break in the forest to the L of the road throughout its entire

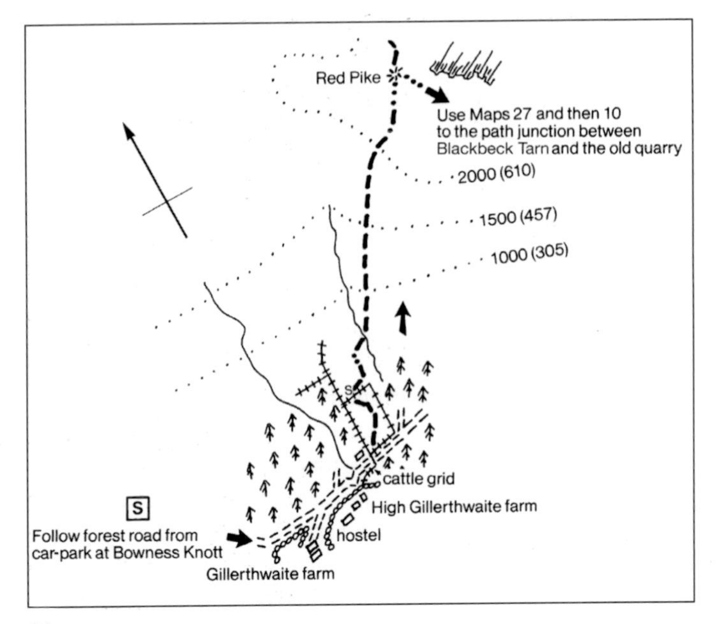

Map 40A

length). Very soon cross a stream and, at the top, cross a stile and go half R towards and past a cairn. After 200 yds (180m), the path crosses a small stream to the R and goes up the ridge, gradually leaving the stream. Follow to the summit of Red Pike.

Follow Route 27 from Red Pike to Blackbeck Tarn on Hay Stacks. Cross the tarn outflow and follow the very clear path which turns R after a few yards. After 500 yds (460m), turn R at a T-junction. Pass to the R of a crag, then a little higher cross a stile at a fence corner, picking up a path that goes to the R of a fence. Follow the path for about 1⅓ miles (2km) from Blackbeck Tarn, passing over Brandreth, to the small tarns on the col of Gillercomb Head. Continue on the path rising up to Green Gable. Descend to Windy Gap and rise steeply up on the opposite side to Great Gable. Cross the summit in a NW direction, soon

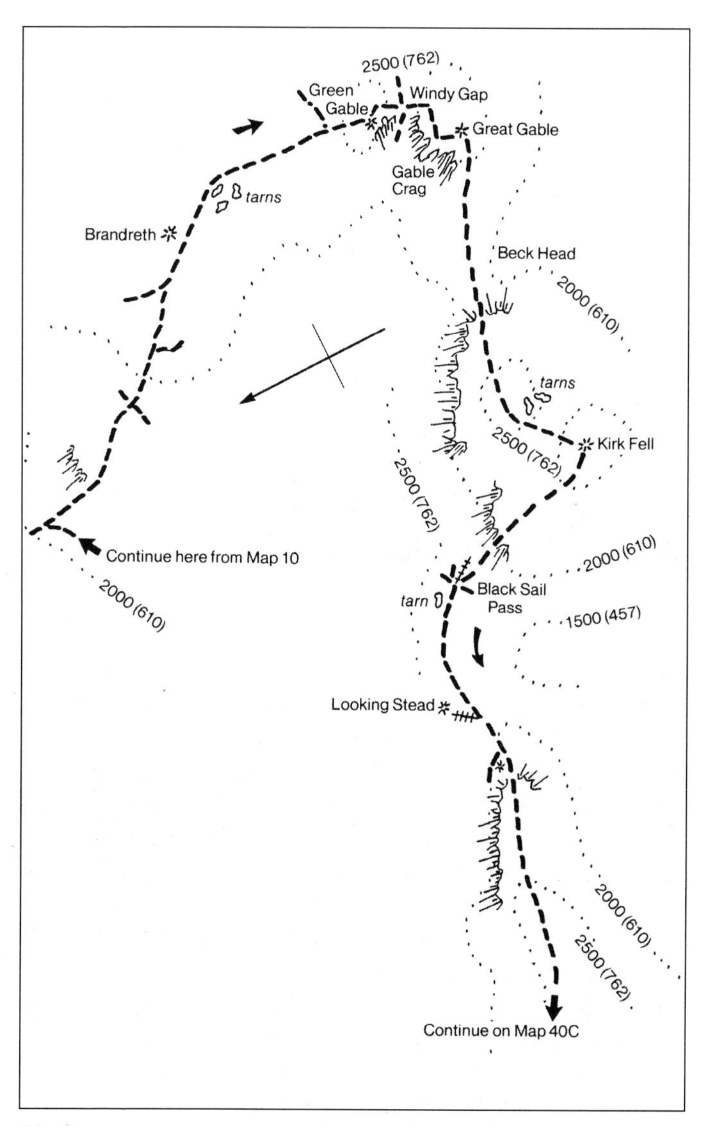
2500 (762)
Green Gable
Windy Gap
Great Gable
Gable Crag
tarns
Brandreth
Beck Head
2000 (610)
tarns
Kirk Fell
2500 (762)
2500 (762)
2000 (610)
Continue here from Map 10
2000 (610)
Black Sail Pass
tarn
1500 (457)
Looking Stead
2000 (610)
2500 (762)
Continue on Map 40C

Map 40B

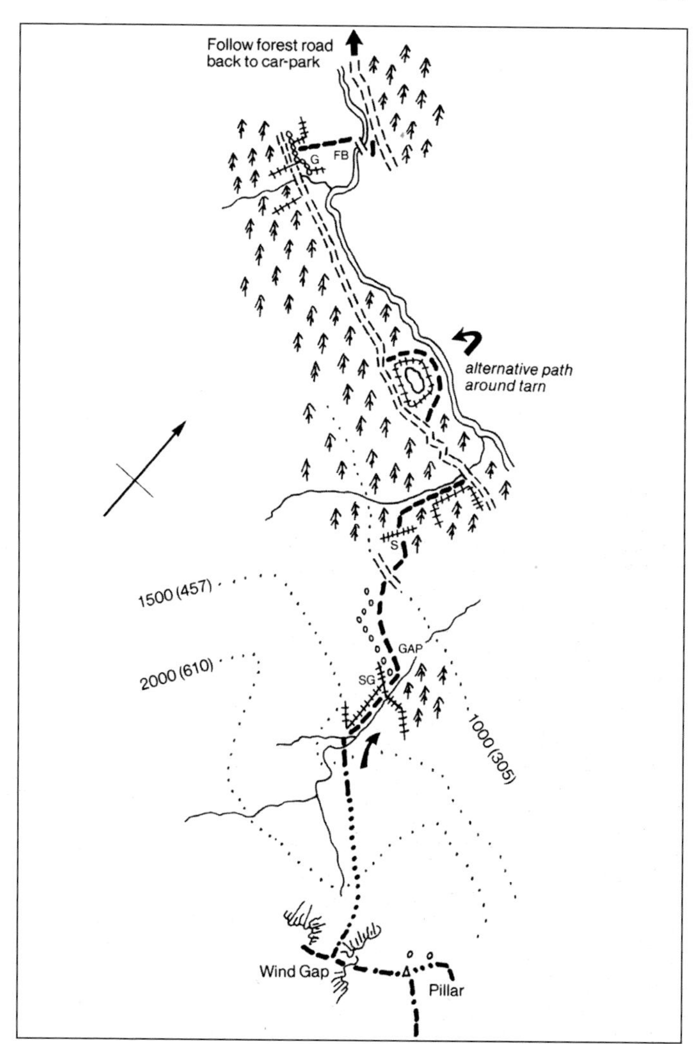

Map 40C

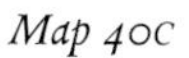

Ennerdale Water

descending steeply over scree to Beck Head. See Route 36 for notes on this steep and difficult descent.

Rise up on the far side to the first summit of Kirk Fell, guided by a line of old fence posts. Beyond, continue along the top bending half L past Kirkfell Tarn (two tarns) to the second and higher summit, again guided by posts. From the summit turn R and descend – later very steeply – to Black Sail Pass. Rise up on the far side, on a path which soon bends to the L past a tarn. Continue to climb steadily for about 1½ miles (2.5km) over Looking Stead and on to the summit of Pillar.

Turn L and cross the top, picking up a path and cairns to descend steeply to Wind Gap. Leave the Gap down to the R along a path, again steep, soon crossing a stream and going down to its R. Where the valley floor levels out, follow a line of cairns across the flat area (faint path), to cross the stream and then one of its tributaries on the far side. On the opposite, L bank at a fence corner turn R and go along a path between the fence and the stream to a small gate. Keep in the same direction by the fence to a gap. Beyond the gap, go half L to the R of a broken wall. After about 300 yds (270m) the path leaves the wall to descend to a forest road. Go L along it for a few yards, then leave half R on a path dropping down to the forest.

Follow the path down into the forest, very marshy in places, soon crossing a fence at a stile. Keep in the same direction for 300 yds (270m) to a fence corner; from there follow the fence down to a second forest road. Turn L for 1⅓ miles (2km) to a bridge. Continue for 100 yds (90m) to a gate. A short distance after the gate, turn R to cross a wall. Go half R across the large field beyond, to a footbridge on the far side. Beyond, rise up to the forest road used earlier. Turn L for 2 miles (3km) back to the car-park. If you are staying at Black Sail youth hostel, turn R and follow the forest road.

APPENDIX 1 | Other Recommended Routes

LONG-DISTANCE ROUTES

The Allerdale Ramble

Starting at Seathwaite in Borrowdale, this route runs for about 55 miles (89km) to end at Grune Point on the Solway Firth. Borrowdale, Skiddaw, the Derwent valley and a section of coastal path from Maryport are on the way. The early miles of the Ramble are marked on the OL4 sheet of the Ordnance Survey Explorer series.

The route is described in 'The Cumbria Way and Allerdale Ramble' by Jim Watson, published by Cicerone.

The Coast to Coast Walk

This is a walk of 190 miles (306km) from St Bees Head in Cumbria to Robin Hood's Bay in North Yorkshire which was devised by A. Wainwright in 1972. The route goes generally in an easterly direction to Cleator and Ennerdale Bridge, along Ennerdale valley to beyond Black Sail Hut, where it strikes over to the Honister Pass and into Borrowdale. A footpath to the south-east then leads over Greenup Edge into Easedale and to Grasmere. The way beyond – to Helvellyn and across Striding Edge to Patterdale – is the most exciting part of the entire route. After crossing the High Street ridge and following the north-west shore of Haweswater, the route leaves the Lake District National Park at the River Lowther about 1 mile (1.6km) to the west of Shap, continuing over the Yorkshire Dales and North York Moors.

This is now a very popular and well-trodden route with plenty of guidebooks for the walker. The best guide of all remains 'A Coast to Coast Walk' by A. Wainwright, published by Frances

Lincoln. A useful website for planning itineraries and finding accommodation is www.coast2coast.co.uk.

The Cumbria Way

Devised by John Trevelyan in the mid 1970s, with help from members of the Lake District branch of the Ramblers' Association, this starts at Ulverston and runs roughly north to Carlisle, a distance of 70 miles (113km), keeping mainly to the lower ground of the valleys. The route is marked on Ordnance Survey Explorer and Landranger maps. It is another popular route with plenty of guides, including 'The Cumbria Way' by John Trevelyan (Dalesman) and 'The Cumbria Way and Allerdale Ramble' by Jim Watson (Cicerone). The Ramblers' Association has some useful information on the route at www.ramblers.org.uk.

The Dales Way

This is a route of 80 miles (129km) from Ilkley, West Yorkshire to Bowness and Windermere in Cumbria. The route enters the Lake District National Park to the east of Staveley (97–485979). It follows mostly riverside paths and is well maintained by the Dales Way Association, which publishes an annual handbook for walkers. The route is marked on Explorer and Landranger maps. In addition to the annual handbook and the original guide – 'The Dales Way' by Colin Speakman (Dalesman) – several other books are now available. There are online resources at www.dalesway.org.uk and www.thedalesway.co.uk.

The Jubilee Walk

This is an 80 mile (129km) walk which was created in 1980 to celebrate 50 years of youth hostelling in Great Britain. Starting at Windermere, the route goes via the youth hostels at Patterdale, Grasmere, Borrowdale, Buttermere, Ennerdale, Eskdale, Coniston and Elterwater, to finish at Ambleside. The walk is not now mapped, but linking these hostels by foot still makes an excellent week's ramble.

Great Gable and its surrounding range

The Pennine Link

This route, first described by Geoffrey Berry in 1975, links the Pennine Way with the Lake District National Park. It starts near Horton in Ribblesdale, North Yorkshire, enters the Lake District National Park on the A6 near Bannisdale, and continues via Troutbeck, Ambleside and Grasmere to finish at Keswick, a total distance of 70 miles (113km).

A guide, 'Across Northern Hills' by Geoffrey Berry (Westmorland Gazette), is now out of print, but may be available from secondhand bookshops.

The Roman Way

A route of 48 miles (77km), almost entirely within the Park and linking the Roman forts of Brougham, Ambleside, Hardknott and Ravenglass using old Roman roads, this starts at Brougham Castle near Penrith (96–537290) and ends at Ravenglass. It is described in Geoffrey Berry's book (see above).

NATURE AND FOREST TRAILS

Unless otherwise stated, the trails are all open throughout the year, but the Information or Visitor Centres providing pamphlets may not be (see page 323 for addresses from which to obtain guides by post).

Wasdale

Nether Wasdale Nature Trail: 2½ miles (4km) and 3½ miles (5.5km). This starts at the south-west corner of Wast Water where the road reaches the shore (89–148048). The trail is circular, to Lund Bridge, Woodhow, Ashness and High Birkhow. A longer alternative adds a diversion from Lund Bridge to The Screes along the eastern shore of the lake. A guide is available from tourist information centres.

Forestry Commission

Ennerdale Forest (to the north and east of Ennerdale Water, around the River Liza)

Smithy Beck Forest Trail: 1¼ miles (2km) and 2½ miles (3.5km). This starts near Bowness Knott parking area on the north shore of Ennerdale (89–114149), reached from Croasdale or Ennerdale Bridge. Both routes combine a walk along the lakeside with a waymarked trail through the forest.

Nine Becks Walk: 9 miles (15km). From Bowness Knott parking area (see above) the route follows the north bank of Ennerdale Water before crossing the Liza and going through the forest area to the south of the river. The return is to the north of the river and along the lakeside: a superb walk into the heart of Ennerdale. There is no visitor centre at Ennerdale, but the trails are marked and details available from the Forestry Commission (www.forestry.gov.uk or tel. 01223 314546).

Grizedale Forest Park (between Coniston Water and Windermere)

Millwood Forest Trail: 1.5 miles (2.4km) of easy going. This starts at the Visitor Centre on the Hawkshead-Satterthwaite road (97–335944).

Silurian Way: 9.5 miles (15.5km). This also starts at the Visitor Centre (97–335944) between Hawkshead and Satterthwaite, and is named after the underlying rock formation. The circular route is waymarked, and runs over rough and steep ground.

Carron Crag Walk: 3 miles (5km). Again starting at the Visitor Centre (97–335944), this leads to the highest point in Grizedale Forest for fine views around.

Grizedale Tarn: 3.3 miles (5.3km). From the Visitor Centre (OL7–335944) to Grizedale's only natural tarn.

There are also three waymarked walks starting from the Visitor Centre and picnic site. Guides to the trails are available from the Visitor Centre, and the Forestry Commission website at www.forestry.gov.uk has excellent resources on all activities.

Thornthwaite Forest (to the east and west of the Derwent Valley by Bassenthwaite Lake)

Comb Fill Trail (Whinlatter Forest Trail): 1½ miles (2.5km). This circular route starts at the Whinlatter Visitor Centre (89–208245). Take the B5292 which leaves the A66 at Braithwaite about 2 miles (3km) west of Keswick. The Centre is on the north side of the road at the top of the pass and is well signposted. A map of the forest and guide to the trail are available at the Centre.

The Visitor Centre has several other trails through the forest, including short walks for children, longer orienteering courses and cycle trails. Routes are clearly marked by colour coding. There are also special events for visitors and a café. Details can be found at www.forestry.gov.uk.

Lake District National Park Information Service

Brockhole Nature Trails: Various trails, with routes for children. Guides are available at the Brockhole Visitor Centre, which is the main centre of the Lake District National Park, situated on the A591 halfway between Ambleside and Windermere (97–388010). Open mid-March to November.

Streams down to Buttermere from Red Pike

National Trust

Friars Crag Nature Walk: 2 miles (3km). This starts at the National Trust car-park at Lake Road, Keswick (90–265229), and runs southwards on the east shore of Derwent Water past Friars Crag to Broom Point, returning on a footpath by the road and through woods to Keswick. Friars Crag is the finest view-point on Derwent Water (see walk 14). A guide can be found at the nearby Information Centre.

Rothay Valley and Loughrigg: 2½ miles (4km). This starts at the Bridge House, Rydal Road, on the A591 at the north end of Ambleside. The route crosses the River Rothay to the west and circles Loughrigg Fell by Lily Tarn. More information can be had from the National Trust Centre at the Bridge House.

White Moss Common: 1½ miles (2.5km) and 2½ miles (4km). The trail begins on the A591 Ambleside to Grasmere road at White

Moss Common just beyond Rydal Water (90–349066). The walk includes woodland and open fell, with a longer optional detour along the shore of Grasmere. Guides can be had from the National Trust Centres in Ambleside or Grasmere.

United Utilities

Launchy Ghyll Forest Trail: 1 mile (1.6km). This starts on the western shore of Thirlmere opposite Hawes How Island (90–309158). There is car parking a mile up the road to the north.
Swirls Forest Trail: ¾ mile (1.2km). This starts by the car-park/picnic area on the A591, on the eastern side of Thirlmere (90-316169).

The area around Thirlmere is maintained by United Utilities, formerly the North-West Water Authority.

Miscellaneous

Belle Isle Nature Trail: 2 miles (3km). Belle Isle is the largest island on Windermere. The trail starts at the Round House on the island and runs around the shore. Windermere ferries can take you to the island.
Brantwood Nature Trail: 3½ miles (5.5km) in three sections. The trail starts at Brantwood House – the home of John Ruskin – on the shore of Coniston Water, which is open from mid-March to mid-November. A guide to the trail can be obtained from Brantwood House (97–313958).
Mirehouse Woodland and Lakeside Walk: 1½ miles (2.5km). A circular, waymarked route starting at the car-park (89–235282), 4½ miles (7km) from Keswick, on the A591 road to Carlisle. Mirehouse is open from mid-March to late October, and the house can provide details of the trail, with nature notes for children. There is a website at www.mirehouse.com.
Muncaster Castle Nature Trail: 2 miles (3km). Muncaster Castle is near Ravenglass off the A595 (96–103964) and is open all year round. It runs a 'Wild Walk' and a 'Sino-Himalayan Trail', details of which can be had from the castle. There is a website at www.muncaster.co.uk.

WALKS FOR DISABLED AND HANDICAPPED PEOPLE

The choice of a walk for people in these categories must depend upon the nature and severity of their handicap and also upon the amount of help available. The Lake District National Park has produced an excellent guide for those with limited mobility: 'Miles Without Stiles' lists 21 routes across the park with maps, all tested using wheelchairs. It is available online at www.lake-district.gov.uk. The guide is based on 'Countryside Access for People with Limited Mobility', a print guide available for purchase from information centres.

The Grizedale and Whinlatter Visitor Centres of the Forestry Commission have details of 'easy access' facilities and trails. Details can be found online at www.forestry.gov.uk, or by calling Grizedale on 01229 860010 or Whinlatter on 01768 778469. The Lake District National Park Visitor Centre at Brockhole– www.lake-district.gov.uk or 01539 446601 – has good wheelchair access and details of suitable trails, as should most visitor and information centres around the Park.

The Calvert Trust Adventure Centre, Little Crosthwaite, Under Skiddaw, Keswick, Cumbria. This offers an excellent range of activities, including walks, to people of all disabilities. More details can be found at www.calvert-trust.org.uk or tel/minicom 017687 72255.

ORIENTEERING

Several orienteering trails are situated in Thornthwaite Forest. Map packs are on sale at the Whinlatter Visitor Centre (see above for directions). It is open all year round.

APPENDIX 2 | Addresses of Useful Organizations

Camping and Caravanning Club
Greenfields House, Westwood Way, Coventry CV4 8JH
Tel. 02476 694995

Council for National Parks
246 Lavender Hill, London SW11 1LJ
Tel. 020 7924 4077, www.cnp.org.uk

Countryside Agency
John Dower House, Crescent Place, Cheltenham GL50 3RA
Tel. 01242 521381, www.countryside.gov.uk

Cumbria Tourist Board
Tel. 01539 444444, www.cumbria-the-lake-district.co.uk

Cumbria Wildlife Trust
Plumgarths, Crook Road, Kendal, Cumbria LA8 8LX
Tel. 01539 816300, www.wildlifetrust.org.uk/cumbria

The Dalesman Publishing Company
Stable Courtyard, Broughton, Skipton BD23 3AZ

English Tourist Board
Tel. 020 8846 9000, www.visitengland.com

Forestry Commission
Silvan House, 231 Corstorphine Road, Edinburgh, Scotland EH12 7AT
Tel. 0131 334 0303, www.forestry.gov.uk
Local office: Grizedale, Ambleside, Cumbria LA22 0Q1
Tel. 01229 860373

Friends of the Lake District
Murley Moss, Oxenholme Road, Kendal, Cumbria LA9 7SS
Tel. 01539 720788, www.fld.org.uk

Lake District National Park Authority
Murley Moss, Oxenholme Road, Kendal, Cumbria LA9 7RL
Tel. 01539 724555, www.lake-district.gov.uk
Information Centres:
Ambleside (01539 432729)
Bowness Bay (01539 442895)
Coniston (01539 441533)
Keswick (01768 772645)
Pooley Bridge (01768 486530)
Borrowdale (01768 777294)
Hawkshead (01539 436525)
Grasmere (01539 435245)
Ullswater (01768 482414)

Long Distance Walkers Association: www.ldwa.org.uk

National Trust
36 Queen Anne's Gate, London SW1H 9AS
Tel. 08706 095380, www.nationaltrust.org.uk
Local office: The Hollens, Grasmere, Ambleside, Cumbria LA22 9QZ
Tel. 08706 095391

Ordnance Survey
Customer Service Centre, Ramsey Road, Southampton SO16 4GU
Tel 09456 050505, www.ordnancesurvey.co.uk

Ramblers' Association
2nd Floor, Camelford House, 87–90 Albert Embankment, London SE1 7TW
Tel. 020 7339 8500, www.ramblers.org.uk. There are several local groups in the area around the National Park. Details can be found on the website.

Youth Hostels Association (England and Wales)
Trevelyan House, Matlock, Derbyshire DE4 3YH
Tel. 08707 708868, www.yha.org.uk

APPENDIX 3 | Glossary

Arête: a very narrow rocky ridge formed when the side walls of adjoining cirques have almost met, e.g. Striding Edge, Sharp Edge.

Beck: a stream

Bottom: a broad and fairly level area lower down a valley, e.g. Wrynose Bottom.

Boulder Slope: a mountain slope covered with large boulders, which have usually fallen from a higher cliff.

Buttress: a prominent rock-face often flanked by gullies.

Cairn: a small heap of stones marking a mountain summit or part of a route.

Col: a dip in a ridge between two mountain peaks, usually offering an easy way from one valley to the next. Examples are Black Sail Pass, Scarth Gap, Hause, Gap and Saddle in the Lake District.

Cove: A large depression in a mountain side caused by glacial erosion during the Ice Age. Usually they have a steep – often precipitous – back wall and they often contain a small (but, in many cases, deep) tarn. Also known as a cirque, cwm (Wales), corrie or coire (Scotland). Good examples of cirques are those containing Red Tarn (Helvellyn) and Blea Water (High Street). But not Black Combe, which is a hill.

Crag: cliff

Dale: a large valley in the Lake District or Pennines.

Edge: a narrow mountain ridge; in extreme cases this becomes an arête, e.g. Whiteless Edge.

Exposure: a term used in climbing to indicate that there is a considerable drop below the climber which, because of the nature of the route, is very apparent. Only occasionally applied to walks, but Sharp Edge on Blencathra, for example, may be said to have some exposure.

Fell: a term used – either in a specific name or generally – in the Lake District and northern Pennines for a mountain or shoulder of moorland, e.g. Kirk Fell.

Force: waterfall, e.g. Aira Force.

Gill, Ghyll: a ravine with a stream, e.g. Piers Gill. Also often used as the name of the stream in the ravine. 'Gill' is the original Norse word; 'Ghyll' is an eighteenth century corruption.

Grain: a small tributary stream, meeting another at a fork.

Gully: a wide and steep cleft down a cliff-face.

Holme: an island, e.g. Maiden Holme and Crow Holme on Windermere.

How: a small hill.

Knott: a rocky hill.

Moss: a fairly level, usually marshy, area.

Pass: a relatively easy passage, with high ground on each flank, from one valley to the next, e.g. Hard Knott, Wrynose, Kirkstone Passes.

Pike: a mountain peak with a sharp, well-defined appearance.

Pinnacle: a large rock face whose sharp-pointed summit is separated from the main fell, e.g. Scafell Pinnacle. (Also Needle, e.g. Napes Needle; and Rock, e.g. Pillar Rock.)

Rake: derived from the Old Norse word 'reik' used for a hillside path up which animals were driven to their summer pasture, e.g. Scots' Rake, Lord's Rake, Jack's Rake.

Ridge: used in several slightly different ways. A narrow buttress of rock, e.g. Eagle's Nest Ridge, Arrowhead Ridge on Great Gable; or a spur of a mountain, e.g. Hall's Fell Ridge on Blencathra; or a long, narrow and substantially horizontal fell-top, perhaps with several summits and cols, e.g. the Red Pike ridge.

Scramble: a climb up fairly broken rock requiring the use of hands for balance purposes, but not difficult enough to justify the use of a rope.

Scree Slope: a slope covered with a layer of small rock fragments, produced by the weathering of higher cliffs.

Tarn: a small lake in the hills, e.g. Blea Tarn.

Traverse: a movement across a rock-face or fellside without any loss of, or gain in, height.

Water, Mere: lake, e.g. Derwent Water, Windermere.

Index

Illustrations are indicated by italics